THE
SCINDIA
LEGACY

THE SCINDIA LEGACY

FROM RANOJI TO JYOTIRADITYA

ABHILASH KHANDEKAR

RUPA

First published by
Rupa Publications India Pvt. Ltd 2022
7/16, Ansari Road, Daryaganj
New Delhi 110002

Sales Centres:

Allahabad Bengaluru Chennai
Hyderabad Jaipur Kathmandu
Kolkata Mumbai

ISBN: 978-93-5520-279-6

First impression 2022

10 9 8 7 6 5 4 3 2 1

The moral right of the author has been asserted.

Printed at Sanat Printers, India

In loving memory of the late Professor Suresh Mishra,
an acclaimed historian, who provided me with his rare
insight into the writing of history.

Contents

Author's Note

Last year, when the country was slowly limping back from the first lockdown, post the COVID-19 assault on India and the world, I got a surprise call from one of the top editors of Rupa Publications asking me if I would be available for writing a book they had in mind.

Having lost a couple of dear friends just a few weeks ago to the deadly virus, I was not in the right frame of mind to quickly respond to the offer. The lockdown period and the spectre of the virus spreading aggressively again was already looming large in mid-2020, making me slightly worried and indolent. Perhaps this was the case with many of us then. We were trapped in the vortex of extremely uncertain times and creative thinking had taken a back seat, at least for me.

Hence, when the second call came, and they spoke about the theme of the book, I was a bit stupefied. 'We want a book authored by you on the Scindia family of Gwalior,' the caller said and proceeded to set a deadline. I would have preferred to have been engaged in writing a book on the environment or wildlife—subjects I have been more keenly involved in for the past two decades or more, though politics remains my 'first love'.

Given the fact that I knew at least three generations of the Gwalior royal family relatively well, it should have made my task easier and I should have gleefully jumped at the proposal. However, when the subject matter was discussed in detail, it made me a little nervous. For two reasons: first, I had never looked at the Scindias as a potential material for a book—even after Jyotiraditya Scindia had left the Congress dramatically to join the Bharatiya Janata Party (BJP) in March 2020, and second, I have never been a history student, much less a writer on topics related to vast aspects of ancient or modern history, not to speak of the medieval part. One is more adept at handling politics and social issues a little better than history, or so I thought. Historical books are a tricky business indeed, and I have realized it much more severely due to my current book.

As I go down the memory lane—early 1983 at the Rajgarh Kothi, Indore, to be precise—I vividly recall my first meeting with Gwalior's 'prince charming', Madhavrao Scindia. He had instantly greeted me in chaste Marathi, something that had floored me completely, I must confess. He had become the president of the Madhya Pradesh Cricket Association (MPCA), for the first time, a few weeks ago and I, as a green-horn sports journalist with the *Free Press Journal* (FPJ), met with him to explore the possibility of doing an exclusive and detailed interview with him at a later day. Madhavrao, then 38, was a three-term old Member of Parliament (MP), at that point on a Congress ticket.

However, his compelling aura was just too profound for a person who had never met a Maharaja, let alone the shining star of a 21-gun salute royal state. He did not fit my (ill-conceived) idea of a typical 'Maharaja'. Madhavrao was exceptionally suave, down to earth and very regal in his handling of a newcomer like me. His witty and comforting conversation style brought us closer in the first meeting itself. This tie thickened and blossomed into mutual respect for one another until his untimely and shocking death in 2001.

Rajmata Vijaya Raje Scindia was kind of a 'godwoman' when I met her in the late '80s, courtesy of Sumitra Mahajan, then a young and promising BJP leader who later became the Lok Sabha Speaker. It was my first meeting with the Rajmata and I found her quite dignified, polite and respectable. She had come for Mahajan's first Lok Sabha poll campaign from Indore, in which Mahajan defeated a powerful Congress leader and Union Minister of national stature, P.C. Sethi. Her persona was likened to a spiritual leader, rather than a hard-core politician. Though she was already into the rough and tumble of politics for over two decades, having had the 'distinction' of pulling down her own party's government in 1967 and being shot into national fame as a politician of a different hue, when I met her first, she was a much-mellowed lady.

Elderly and drawn away from materialistic attractions (she would always be seen draped in a white saree), the Rajmata evoked an instantaneous respect from those who met her. The general public and political leaders such as Kushabhau Thakre, former chief ministers Sunder Lal Patwa and Kailash Chandra Joshi and others like Kailash Sarang, Lakhiram Agarwal, Vikram Verma and the lot, held her in high esteem, which she deserved anyway. The BJP of those days, I must mention, was much different than what we see today.

The influence of the Rashtriya Swayamsevak Sangh (RSS) and the Jana Sangh—the simplicity, respect for values, probity in public life and so on—was evident. The BJP was genuinely a 'party with a difference.' But no longer!

There appeared a semblance of values and ideological commitment among the leaders, who detested ostentatiousness. I had the opportunity to have interacted with most of them very closely.

Rajmata's close aide and senior journalist, Rajendra Sharma, has shared with me a plethora of stories about the simplicity of Vijaya Raje, easily the richest politician of the day and about her empathy for the downtrodden, some of which have found mention in the book.

Writing a book on such an esteemed family was not an easy job at first, and the more research I did, the more readings were required, as the period the book has covered spans over three eventful centuries. For instance, very little reliable material or references on the Scindia dynasty's founder Ranoji Shinde are available. Then, the available books by some of the British authors and others give you a different picture or present an entirely different perspective. Checking and cross-checking facts, family ties of the generations of yore and dates were thus a daunting task. And yet, one cannot really cover everything one would have liked to because of time and space constraints.

While writing this introduction, I must admit that it has been a very challenging assignment and took much more time than I initially thought it would. But I must confess that I hugely benefitted from several very old books that I had never bothered to even flip through before despite them being in my personal library for decades. I have inherited them from my grandfather, the late C.G. Khandekar, who was a high-ranking official in the Holkar state of Indore more than a hundred years ago.

Another tough task was to join the missing dots of 'Operation Lotus' (in chapter 10), which brought down the 15-month-old Congress government led by Kamal Nath in Madhya Pradesh, making history of sorts. Jyotiraditya Scindia, the grandson of the Rajmata, staged a coup in 2020 exactly on the lines of what she had done five decades ago. Did he take out a leaf from her old book, about 20 years after her demise? Well, we are given to believe that both did whatever they did to protect the *asmita* (goodwill or prestige) of the glorious Gwalior dynasty. The chapter that deals with this will give the reader a much better idea of everything that happened and how the secretive 'Operation Lotus' was carried out in Delhi and Bhopal. Scindia was a front runner in the race to become the chief minister in 2018, but the coterie around Sonia

Gandhi, the INC supremo, had reportedly stopped him in his tracks and instead made an old warhorse, Kamal Nath, the chief minister. Incidentally, this came at a time when Narendra Modi was picking up younger leaders one after another to install as chief ministers in BJP's newly-pocketed states. Be it in Maharashtra (Devendra Fadnavis), Tripura (Biplab Kumar Deb), Assam (Sarbananda Sonowal) or Uttarakhand (Rawat and Pushkar Singh Dhami), the BJP had hoisted new faces and created a second line of leadership. The political warrior of the Congress felt wronged by the Gandhis but waited for the right time to strike. Was his decision to leave the Congress and join BJP ill-timed or futuristic? Only time will tell since there is nothing permanent in politics!

Writing *The Scindia Legacy: From Ranoji to Jyotiraditya*, has truly been a new and surreal experience for me, mainly because the narrative has been set in entirely different periods. My earlier book, a story woven around the developmental aspects of a 'BIMARU state' like Madhya Pradesh with a particular focus on Shivraj Singh Chouhan, is about seven years old. Much water has flown down the Narmada River in these years and political dynamics have undergone huge changes. Shivraj Singh, a towering BJP leader with mass appeal, is a much more seasoned and shrewd politician now than he was a decade ago. Shrewd he has always been, but under the Modi regime he has learnt new skills in the game of individual survival, if not governance.

The Scindia Legacy: From Ranoji to Jyotiraditya traces the valours of successive Scindia headmen, but it also, in its different chapters, records the ups and downs of the dynasty over several decades, while noting the politics of successive generations played out since the Independence. If the family feud among the Scindias over property and other issues has been the darker side in recent years, the untimely and heart-rending crash which claimed Madhavrao's life has been the most brutal jolt to the Scindias ever. A most promising Congress leader's life was cut short abruptly by the controller of our destiny. Could he have become the prime minister, but for the air crash? Readers will find its answer in Chapter 7.

Many thinkers wonder if the future is nothing but history reinvented. The recent political developments with Jyotiraditya at the centre have proved that history is being reinvented.

Writing this book provided me with an opportunity to dive deep into historical facts, analyse them to the best of my abilities and put them in a modern perspective while blending the story with contemporary politics. The events in the book do not reflect merely on Madhya Pradesh state politics but also national politics, in some way or the other.

I am confident you will enjoy reading the book that throws new light on the globally famous Scindias.

Abhilash Khandekar
November 2021
Bhopal

Foreword
Scindia: India's Bridge to Its Past

Ranoji Scindia could not have imagined that when he looked after Balaji Vishwanath's belongings during the Peshwa's meeting with his sovereign, he would be the founder of India's longest-running political dynasty. In the early 1720s, an ordinary heir of the Patils of the village Kanherkhed near Satara, Ranoji, steered his family's rise into India's future. Ranoji rose in the Peshwa's service due to his military service and a strong sense of loyalty to the family of the Maratha prime minister. He fought shoulder to shoulder with Baji Rao Peshwa over the two decades that the Maratha power grew from western India to the bank of the Yamuna and Chambal. Eventually, he was awarded one-third of the saranjam of Malwa. A saranjam is a grant of land (initially non-hereditary) for maintenance of troops or for military service. After Baji Rao's death in 1740, his samadhi at Raverkhedi was built by Ranoji Scindia.

Ranoji passed away in 1745, and the torch was passed on to Jayappa Rao, who led the Maratha power into the doab. Along with Malhar Rao Holkar, Jayappa signed the famous *ahadnama* of 1752, promising to 'protect' the Mughal throne from all enemies. In exchange, several Mughal provinces (Agra and Ajmer) were given to the Marathas, plus a substantial sum of money. Tragically, Jayappa lost his life during a campaign at Nagaur in 1755 when he was set upon by assassins. His brother Dattaji Rao took over and led the Scindias to victory in many a battle. Eventually, Dattaji laid down his life defending Delhi at Burari in January 1760 against the overwhelming invading force of Ahmad Shah Abdali and his Indian ally Najib Khan.

At Panipat in 1761, the Scindias sustained another body blow. Tukoji and Jankoji Scindia were killed in battle while Mahadji, Ranoji's only surviving son, returned injured and lame in one leg. He was rescued by a water carrier named Rana Khan, and Mahadji bestowed many honours and high posts on his saviour. However, for a few years after Panipat, the Scindia house was eclipsed. There was more than one claimant for taking over the reins of the family, and it was only in 1768 that Madhav Rao Peshwa appointed Mahadji as the chief of his clan. Over the next three decades, Mahadji repaid the Peshwa's trust in ample measure.

Mahadji, with his sagacity, statesmanship and abilities as an astute general, held the Maratha power together after the death of Madhav Rao Peshwa and Malharji Holkar. As the sword arm of the Peshwai in the north, Mahadji was largely autonomous in the field, although he had to contend with Nana Fadnavis's diplomatic skills that helped keep the Maratha flock under the authority of the Peshwa at Pune. Mahadji was instrumental in extending Maratha sway over Delhi from 1770 onwards. He escorted the phantom king Shah Alam II to Delhi and sacked the fort of Pathargarh that belonged to Najib Khan, thereby avenging the killing of his brother Dattaji and nephew Jankoji. Indeed, Najib Khan's dynasty met its end in 1788 at the hands of Mahadji when he hunted down and killed Najib's grandson Ghulam Qadir. Ghulam Qadir had taken over the Red Fort and blinded Shah Alam in one of the most gruesome scenes of eighteenth-century India.

Mahadji was thereafter supreme in north India, and he returned to Pune after visiting the Muslim saint Mansur Shah. Here, in the remaining months of his life, he tried to tutor the young Peshwa on the nuances of administration, seeking to bring him out of the shadow of his powerful regent Nana Fadnavis. His death at Pune in 1794 marked the end of an era.

The five battles of 1803 against the English in the Second Anglo-Maratha War ended the power of the Scindias. The nineteenth century saw the British control the actions of the Gwalior Maharajas—as they came to be called—with an iron hand. In 1818, Daulat Rao was prevented from providing direct aid to Baji Rao Peshwa II in the Third Anglo-Maratha War. In 1858, the Scindia garrison at Gwalior joined the Rani of Jhansi while the Maharaja left for Agra. The advice to leave Gwalior was rendered to Jayajirao by his regent and advisor Dinkar Rao, and after the war of 1857–58, Gwalior was restored by the British to the Scindias. Indeed, the Scindia family survived after 1858 due to the advice given by this loyal advisor of the family.

The early twentieth century saw the Maharajas build schools, provide citizens amenities and begin a proper administration in the Shindeshahi* territory, which earned the family tremendous goodwill of the people. The respect the family earned during this period is what has sustained them to this day.

As the longest running dynasty in Indian politics, from the 1730s to the present, the Scindias have remained relevant in central India. With six able sons, the legacy has been forwarded. The Scindias, in many ways, are India's bridge to its past.

Dr Uday S. Kulkarni
Historian and Author

---

*The empire of Shindes (Scindias)

1

Scindia Dynasty in Pre-Independence India

The Scindia princely dynasty of Gwalior, in Madhya Pradesh, is among the very few major royal houses of India that is not only continuing to survive today, despite severe setbacks, but also has a sizeable influence on people and politics. The rich history of the famous and powerful family from its very beginning (the early eighteenth century) is much more gripping and eventful than perhaps most other royal families of India for more reasons than one. The series of inheritance or naming of a successor was anything but routine and smooth in this family, be it of its founder Ranoji or his successors, such as Jayajirao who ruled from 1843 to 1886. And yet, the family has earned a glorious name and a lasting reputation for itself, political criticism notwithstanding.

The Gwalior family, with its roots in Maharashtra's Satara district, has had an unparalleled history spanning almost 300 years (since the family is still around and remains influential in 2021–22, it is almost three centuries from 1731 onwards) braving political upheavals, untimely deaths, intense power struggles, bitter issues about legal heirship, deaths on the battle field, unending wars and, of course, some peace. If one goes by the primogeniture theory followed historically by most of the erstwhile Indian royal families and add a contemporary political perspective to that, Jyotiraditya Scindia, a Member of Rajya Sabha (India's Upper House of Parliament) and, lately, a popular BJP leader, remains the sole titular head of the illustrious and erstwhile rich royal family. They once ruled a substantially vast portion of land in what is now known as the central Indian state of Madhya Pradesh. Gwalior has always remained the seat of power for the Scindias, though Ujjain (spelt as Oojein in British times by celebrated authors such as Sir John Malcolm, a former major general in India) was the initial capital when Ranoji (Ranojee) Shinde founded the dynasty, rather unwittingly. Surely, he was unaware of the fame and big name the family would come to be associated with in the successive decades. After Ranoji, Ujjain's importance in Shindeshahi continued up to Daulat Rao Scindia (1779–1827). The city, close to Indore, now the commercial capital of Madhya Pradesh, is one of the most ancient cities of India having found mention in the sacred Hindu texts, the Puranas, and has also been mentioned by some Greek authors.

The dramatic series of events that unfolded about three centuries ago and which catapulted an ordinary and poor but brave young man as the king of the Scindia (Shinde) empire may outshine—hands down—any popular, modern-day Bollywood script. Driven by poverty, a footwear carrier with a fairly modest background, and therefore placed lowly in the societal hierarchy, reaches the dazzling heights as the headman of the widespread Maratha kingdom and later gets permanently embedded in its rich historical legacy, is an incredible story from whichever angle you look at it, even in the modern times. It is not an ordinary rags-to-riches story that is so often heard in the corporate world. It is much beyond that, and real!

Ranoji, however, does not get much importance in the

history of Scindias for unknown reasons. He was the trusted man of the Peshwas who had, after many confabulations within the Peshwa royal family of Satara, chosen him to control the politically sensitive Malwa region of central India when Peshwa Bajirao had decided to expand the Maratha confederacy beyond the Deccan (south of the Narmada region) and come to the central Indian plains.

As per the royal practice of yore, followed rather mandatorily during the pre-Independence days in India, Jyotiraditya Scindia, the 50-year-old debonair politician, is (still) reverentially addressed as 'Maharaj' in the Gwalior-Chambal belt. He is a direct descendant of Ranoji Shinde, the founder of the Scindia dynasty (1731–1947). Most writers and historians appear to be silent about Ranoji's birth year. Captain C.E. Luard (superintendent of Gazetteer of Central India), the author of *Gwalior State Gazetteer*, categorically wrote in 1908 that 'The date of Ranoji's birth is unknown.'[1]

On 2 February 1731, the Peshwa Bajirao, a young man from the royal family of Satara, had formally presented the seal of office, thereby entrusting the affairs of the Malwa region to the Scindia—historical documents and other writings use various spellings of Scindia such as Sindia, Sindhia, etc., which are clearly the corrupted versions of Shinde, a common family name among Kunbis and Marathas as well as some lower-caste communities in Maharashtra. Sushil Kumar Shinde, former Union home minister (from 2012 to 2014), for instance, belongs to the 'Dhor' caste, which is among the lowest castes in Maharashtra.[2]

Along with the Scindias, the Holkars of Indore were also given the seals of office by the Peshwa. The duo, Malhar Rao Holkar (1693–1766) and Ranoji were approximately coeval of their times.[3] Though the seals of office were actually given in 1731, there is also a reference in the authenticated *Gwalior Gazetteer* of 1908 that the Peshwa had also authorized the

Scindias, the Holkars and the Paurs (Dewas) to collect *chauths* (some portion of levy collected against total revenue collection which ranged from 25 per cent to 35 per cent). That was in 1726, five years before the seals of authority were officially handed to them. What significance did these five years bear on the Scindias, the Holkars and the Paurs? Were these years a part of their training by the Peshwas or were they being secretly tested to prove their unflinching loyalty? Not much light is thrown on the period between 1726 and 1731 for one to get clarity of various important events that may have taken place during that time. But there is a brief mention in some documents that Malhar Rao Holkar got his first parcel of lands north of the Narmada (Nerbudda) in 1728—three years before power was formally vested in him by the Peshwas. He first received 12 districts and then, in 1731, along with a letter of administration from Peshwa, 70 additional districts were granted. Apparently, the letter was about administering the Maratha (read Peshwa) interests in the Malwa region.

India has been ruled by a large number of royal families— Hindu and Muslim—for centuries and from the north to the south of this vast ancient country, there has been no dearth of the notable and noble rajas, maharajas and nawabs. The list of these royal families include, among many other well-known dynasties, the famous ancient Mauryan empire of the Magadha kingdom that existed around 320–21 BC. Indian history is replete with umpteen legends, fascinating fables, palace politics, generosity of the royal rulers, their expansive approach of governance, love for the arts and architecture, collection of precious gems and jewels, about their unique statecraft, taxation systems, finicky personal habits, religious shrines that they built for people, extramarital affairs of the kings, multiple marriages to produce a male heir, stories around beautiful queens, battle stories of the maharajas and rajas, size of their armies, army of elephants they kept and trained, forests they created and the hunting parties they would host and so on.

In the pre-British era, we see Muslim monarchs, Rajput rajas and Maratha maharajas dominating the literary landscape of this historically-rich nation. However, the Scindia aristocracy, quite strikingly, dots the physical landscape too. Gwalior state was the largest in the Central India Agency with an area of 25,041 sq. miles—equivalent to any small European nation. Maharaja Fatehsinghrao Gaekwad of Baroda describes the state of Gwalior as being 'shaped like an arrow aimed up across central India towards Delhi and stopping just short of its target.'[4]

In the democratic set-up of today's India, the erstwhile Gwalior rulers stand out for one more strong reason. Many of the notable Scindia family members, from Rajmata Vijaya Raje—who played both roles effectively, first as a living maharani and then as a part of the vibrant Indian democracy as an MP—to the late Madhavrao Scindia, to the former Rajasthan chief minister Vasundhara Raje, her son Dushyant Singh, also an MP, Yashodhara Raje, presently a senior minister in Shivraj Singh Chouhan's BJP Government, to finally the latest scion Jyotiraditya, all have taken to the democratic life like a fish to water. Just the way they and their able royal ancestors had served their subjects over the centuries, the present generation is equally keen and engaged in public welfare. With personal family trusts as well as through government funding, the younger generation is actively involved in the running of educational institutes or the building of hospitals, roads, dams and so on, both in Madhya Pradesh and Rajasthan.

The Marathas enjoyed a place of pride in Asian history not merely because they were the ones who fought against the Muslims—who came from Afghanistan—and then the British, but also due to the influence the all-powerful, all-pervasive Maratha confederacy had over 'Hindustan' in the early nineteenth century. Noted historian and author of many well-known history books, Prof (Dr) Suresh Mishra, says that the major turning point in Maratha history was the ambitious and well thought-out plan of the Peshwa (prime minister) to move out of his comfort zone and enter central India. 'If that had not happened, the Holkar, Scindia and Pawar (Puars of Dewas) dynasties would not have born at all to eventually build up such powerful royal states and resultantly, entire course of history that we know of today, would have been completely different,' he affirmed.[5]

Curiously enough, the Marathas were neither called Rajputs nor Thakurs. They did belong to the warrior class or the larger clan of the Kshtriyas, as per the quaint/archaic Hindu Varna Vyavastha (class or caste categories) which included Brahmins, Vaishyas and Shudras, in that order of primacy. Many societies in India still firmly believe in this caste system and have embraced the same, mainly the two upper classes. So, the Kshatriyas fell in between Bramhins and Vaishyas, which indicates they were up there in the social and occupational hierarchy, at number two. Of them, the Scindias are one of the 96 *kulas* or clans in which all pure Marathas are divided.[6]

It is important to mention that as per the ancient scriptures, the Hindu caste system (slightly complex and not a single system) is called the vedic caste division. In that 'varna' has religio-mythological origins which believed in separation of population into ranked and hereditary groups. Thus, the four main castes or varnas, according to a theory, sprang into being from the creator God's body: from the mouth came the Brahmins, from the arms came the Kshatriyas, from the thighs, the Vaishyas and the Sudras came from the feet of God. Another theory, defining the same four classes, was based on *jaatis* explaining occupation. Thus the highest ranking caste was of the Bramhins (priests or teachers), then came the Kshatriya, closer to the first category but were rulers and warriors; Vaishyas came third in that order and were engaged in farming and trading activities while the last and lowest stood the Sudras, who were involved in menial jobs of slavery or doing unclean jobs of disposing dead animals and cleaning up streets and other such works depending on the prevalent social conditions. Once upon a time, the Shudras were commonly called the untouchables; today they are known as the Scheduled Caste. Kautilya's magnum opus *Arthashastra* (AD second century), a much more authoritative treatise on society, politics and statecraft of ancient India, also deals with this caste system in greater detail, stating that the three Vedas have defined the four varnas very well.[7] In the latter day literature, famous author Khushwant Singh attributes the varna system to philosopher Manu (circa 600 BC), the author of Dharma Shastra (Book of Sacred Law), who was a great apologist of the caste system and had explained that Brahmin is the Lord of all castes. The word for caste is varna, meaning colour![8]

Thus the Marathas, being Kshatriyas, were entrusted with the responsibility of securing their states, protecting their people, keeping armies and maintaining their fiefdoms across large tracts of lands, engaging in wars (to claim new territories and expand their kingdom) and using diplomatic tactics or by aggressions, mostly both! Needless to say, keeping people's welfare was always on the top of their agenda. One of the Maharajas from the Gwalior aristocracy is quoted as having said: '...A ruler should not wait for his people to agitate for more power, but should hand over as they become capable of using it.'[9] Accordingly, Majlis-i-Aam and Majlis-i-Kanoon (later Praja Sabha and Samant Sabha) were set up as two representing bodies many years ago to incorporate the common people into the administration of Gwalior and decision-making process.

PALACE TO PARLIAMENT: SMOOTH SAILING

It is not just the erstwhile royal dynasties that were generally and genuinely held in awe by people; their successors too are still revered and addressed locally as Maharajas and Rajas across a country that had already embraced a democratic way of governance seven decades ago. These decorative titles became almost irrelevant about the same time when the Maharajas were gearing up to merge their properties and powers with the Indian state as desired and executed by Sardar Vallabhbhai Patel, Union minister of state for Home, in 1947. Some did it willingly, others reluctantly. However, there was another section of rulers who were eager to go with Pakistan, the newly created Muslim nation, if they had their way! The massive integration process of 554 Indian states (while this number varies from author to author, at the time of integration these many small and big states were merged into the Indian dominion) undertaken by the Government of India had physically and psychologically unsettled most of the former kings and vassals as they had to forswear a number of things they may have never imagined or liked to do.

In fact, some of the Muslim dynasties, such as Hyderabad, Junagadh and Bhopal did contemplate going with the newly-created Pakistan, instead of staying with the Indian dominion, by refusing to sign the Instrument of Accession.

*In September 1948, the Government of India was forced to send army troops into Hyderabad to control the law and order situation there due to the fierce opposition of the ruling Nizam family to join India, months after other regions of the country had an Indian government ruling over them. Upon the surrender of the Nizam in four days of 'Operation Polo',** a

---

*Instrument of Accession: a legal document introduced under the Government of India Act, 1935, and enforced for the first time in 1947. The document gave the rulers of the princely states under British India a choice to join either of the new dominions of India or Pakistan created after the Partition of British India.
**Operation Polo: the code name given to the military action of the Indian Army which was sent to the princely state Hyderabad to contain the unrest following its annexation to India and its integration into the Indian dominion.

THE SCINDIA LEGACY • 9

military government was installed there. Such was the scenario when princely India was slipping into the oblivion. Many other ex-rulers too had tried to extract their pound of flesh from the newly elected Nehru Government by showing stubbornness before finally falling in line.[10]

That mammoth exercise took five long years, thanks to the vexed legal and egoistic personal issues involved, to amicably integrate many willing states into India by diffusing the surcharged political atmosphere in the last few years leading up to India's ultimate freedom with the lapsing of the British paramountcy. Unprecedented tension had built up in many states because the rulers there did not want to sign on the dotted line, as was proposed by 'Iron Man' Sardar Patel and the last British Governor General Lord Mountbatten, to pave the way for a united India bound by a single Constitution. As V.P. Menon, the civil servant who worked tirelessly with Patel in the Herculean task writes,

> the first announcement of accession was made by the Dewan of Gwalior M.A. Srinivasan, on behalf of the Maharaja Sir Jiwajirao Scindia of Gwalior. The latter (Scindia) had been of great help during the negotiations and had undoubtedly exercised a healthy influence on several rulers.[11]

That goes to show, among many other gestures, the Scindia family's unflinching statesmanship.

Meanwhile, a situation had arisen then wherein the kings and queens and Nawabs and Begums found themselves having been left high and dry, sans the trappings of powers and unlimited sovereign freedom enjoyed thus far; they were now being ruled over by a set of newly elected representatives who came from the lot of 'commoners' to become the MPs, MLAs or ministers and chief ministers with new-found powers and responsibilities at their command. Ultimately, the advent of democracy was the undoing of princely India.

It is pertinent to see what the Britishers thought of the Indian ruling class then: Maharaja Bhupinder Singh of Patiala (ruling period 1900–38), in a *Sunday Express* (London) article of 1928 queried British public opinion, which held that the Indian princes 'have nothing else to do except live in luxury and spend money with a shovel.'

It was indeed tough for most of the ex-maharajas to breathe comfortably in a new environment filled with fresh air of freedom even as the jubilant mood had swept the masses who had just started happily experiencing the long-awaited independence. But the maharajas' position was a little different. They had to reconcile a great deal with the new political set-up. For all the maharajas, maharanis and their families, it was quite an onerous task to manage their vast properties and maintain old lavish standards of living while still looking after their own people and palaces, albeit, sans the old power and pelf. It was also an emotional shock of giving away many of their beloved properties. Rajmata Gayatri Devi of Jaipur, in her memoir, recalls the shock when she learnt, in 1958, that her home, the beautiful Rambagh Palace, was being turned into a hotel. Many smaller royalties actually petered out in the next few years for want of adequate income sources, although their privy purses were discontinued much later, in 1971, by Prime Minister Indira Gandhi through the 26th Amendment to the Constitution.

A few of the erstwhile maharajas, on their part, were more enterprising than others and took the bull by the horn. They joined politics! Banking upon their old popularity among the new but free electorate, they took the plunge having clearly seen the writing on the wall. Most of them succeeded in the new 'profession'. And the tradition continues even today. The flight from the palace to the parliament was rather smooth and rewarding!

The Scindias were among the leading lights who tried

their luck with politics and persisted with it, clocking a high success rate generation after generation in Madhya Pradesh and neighbouring Rajasthan. Others included: former prime minister V.P. Singh who was connected with a much smaller kingdom of Manda in Uttar Pradesh, the former Punjab chief minister Captain Amarinder Singh who hails from the royal house of Patiala, Dr Karan Singh from Jammu and Kashmir, K.P. Singh Deo from Dhenkanal in Odisha, Nawab Mansoor Ali Khan of Pataudi (a tiny, former princely state) who was only once an Indian cricket captain and unsuccessfully fought a Lok Sabha poll from Bhopal on a Congress ticket, and a few others from Rajasthan (three-time MP from Swatantra Party, Gayatri Devi of Jaipur in 1962, 1967 and 1971 and Jodhpur's Hanwant Singh Rathore in 1952). While some joined politics immediately after the first general elections, others joined a little later. Maharashtra, Odisha, Uttar Pradesh and Gujarat too sent a few erstwhile Maharajas to the Parliament, including the present descendant of the great Shivaji Maharaj—Udayanraje Bhosale of Satara. Ranjitsinh Pratapsinh Gaekwad, belonging to the famous Baroda family, won twice as an MP, to name just a few.[12] An elaborate, year-wise list of former kings and queens who donned the hat of a full-time politician would be quite long and perhaps out of place here.

Coming back to the Scindia family, it can be easily surmised that Gwalior always held a supreme position among other ruling Rajas or small Jagirdars. Not just because they were among the elite club of the highly prestigious five states enjoying the rare privilege and honour of a 21-gun salute in India (others included nizams of Hyderabad, maharajas of Jammu and Kashmir, maharajas of Mysore and the Gaekwads [Gaekwar or Gaikwad] of Baroda), but also because despite serious familial challenges, such as an issue-less maharaja, multiple marriages as per the customs in fashion then, adoptions of sons to perpetuate and secure the raj-gharana or carrying royal rule into the next generation, etc., they continued to remain formidable. The first few generations of the Scindias, it is said, either had only daughters or had no issues at all. For example, Mahadji Scindia (1730–1794), the shining star of the dynasty who ruled for 34 long years, was, somehow, very unlucky. He married as many as nine women (queens), as the legend goes, but none could produce a male child for him. If Scindias are known for diplomacy, valour and sustained victories that consolidated their empire, the leader who must get the credit for keeping the dynasty's flag flying high is Mahadji.

RANOJI SCINDIA: THE FOUNDER

The founder of the Scindia dynasty, Ranoji Scindia, was not a born prince; he was born in a humble family of *shiledars*,* and grew up to be an honest and hardworking man. It was his modesty and loyalty that provided him with the rarest of the rare honour of becoming the head man of the Scindia house that was built over the next few years. Some ascribe his astronomical reach to the top as sheer good luck, if nothing else. Although little amount of literature is available about his heroic deeds as a soldier, it is said that the second Peshwa, Bajirao I (1700–1740), also known as Bajirao Ballal, was so impressed with his unquestionable loyalty and dedication that he promoted him, first as a bodyguard and later as the Maratha general in Malwa, Central India. About the Peshwa, suffice it to say: the descendants of Shivaji Raje Bhosale (1627–80) in the second generation reigned only as pageant kings of Satara, and the real sovereignty was passed to their Bramhin minister or Peshwa, Balaji Vishwanath, who founded the Peshwa dynasty seated at Poona (now Pune). Poona was the nerve centre of

---

*Shiledar was a term used for a soldier's position in India's Maratha Empire, particularly during the reign of Shivaji.

the Maratha Confederacy which included Marathi-speaking chieftains of Gwalior and Ujjain (Scindia), Indore (Holkar), Dhar and Dewas (Paur/ Pawar), Baroda (Gaekwad), Nagpur (Bhosale) and Jhansi (Newalkar). Their combined possession of India was formidable and massive for many years.

About Ranoji Shinde, Sir John Malcolm had this to say:

> The family of Sindia [sic] are Sudras of the tribe of Koombee (also Kunbi), or cultivators. Ranojee Sindia, the first who became as soldier, had succeeded to his hereditary office of headman, or Potail [Patil], of Kumerkerrah [Kannerkhera] in the district of Wye [in Satara, Maharashtra] before he was taken into the service of Paishwah Ballajee Bishwanath, after whose death he continued in that of his son Bajerow Bullal. The humble employment of Ranojee was to carry the Paishwah's slippers; but being near the person of the chief minister of an empire in any capacity, is deemed an honour in India.[13]

Though Balaji Peshwa died in 1720, his inexperienced son Bajirao, in his 20s, spotted the intelligence, the leadership abilities of Ranoji as a soldier and above all his loyalty to Peshwas and decided to send him to Central India or what was then famously known as the Malwa province. Ranoji was driven by poverty to become a personal attendant of the Peshwa, according to C.E. Luard who obliquely quotes Sir Malcolm. Bajirao was the first eminent Maratha chief to set foot in Malwa territory (the famous Amjhera battle near Indore is mentioned in some of the old writings, indicating the arrival of the Marathas). Malwa was eventually given to Malhar Rao Holkar of Indore (southern portion) and the remaining portion (northern) to Ranoji Scindia. Ranoji Scindia and Malhar Rao Holkar were the equal flagbearers of the Peshwa empire outside the old Maharashtra state.

Ranoji married Meenah Baee of his own tribe, who gave

him three sons—Jayappaji, Duttaji and Jotiba; the eldest two became distinguished commanders. Further, as Malcolm adds, 'He (Ranojee) also had two sons by a Rajpoot woman, a native of Malwa, Tukajee and Madhajee Scindia [Mahadji Scindia], and the latter of whom became the head of family.'[14]

Jankoji, the son of Jayappaji, was anointed as the head of the family on the death of Ranoji in 1745 at Shujalpoor (also known as Shujalpur, a municipality in today's Shajapur district in Madhya Pradesh, located some 95 kilometres northwest of Bhopal) where his small cenotaph is still seen standing, though not in great condition. People, however, go there for darshan of a temple.

Ranoji's three descendants were eliminated in quick succession. Jayappa (who ruled from 1745–59), referred to as Jeypah, as per Malcolm, was assassinated and a year later his brother Dattaji was killed in a battle against Najeeb-ud-Daula in 1760. Tragedies were riding piggyback on the Scindia rulers, as it seemed then. Jayappa's son Jankoji led the Scindia army into Panipat in (now located in the state of Haryana in northern India; the small region has witnessed three bloody wars) the battle against Ahmad Shah Abdali, the invader from Afghanistan. The Maratha forces lost the battle badly and Jankoji was taken prisoner and executed.

Ranoji was certainly a powerful and notable personage from 1726 to 1745 and proved to be a leading soldier of great gallantry in campaigns against Delhi (1736), against the Nizam (1738) and against the Portuguese at Bassein (1739).[15]

THE ASCENT OF MAHADJI

Any history or family stories involving erstwhile maharajas make for a delightful reading, as one can expect to come across unexpected twists and turns. The rise of Mahadji Shinde, also known as Shrinath Madhavji, was, indeed, considered a major turning point in the history of the Scindias. A great statesman, Mahadji Shinde left an indelible mark on contemporary history chiefly because of his valour and war strategies, despite a physical ailment that he suffered during the Third Battle of Panipat that the Marathas had lost terribly. There are many interesting accounts of this battle and how the combined might of the Maratha confederacy had to face the ignominy of losing the most important battle of their times (Panipat), completely changed the course of history.

Historians, at times, are seen divided over various issues and incidences and the way they look at them and analyse them with their own understanding and perception. Many British historians wrote different accounts at different times reflecting their ostensible bias towards Indian kings and rulers. Some mentions are found in old records using words such as Hindu writers and Muslim writers. Sir Malcolm's observation is thus worth quoting here:

> From the commencement of the reign of Aurangzebe [sic], the Mahomedan writers cease to be so minute in their details, as they are at former and most prosperous period of the Moghul Empire. The theme was not inviting, and their hostile feelings towards the Mahrattas have made them general and unfaithful narrators of the success of that people.[16]

But Mahadji Scindia is one of the few honourable exceptions about whose extraordinary accomplishments and valour most historians (Hindu, Muslim and British) have sung paeans at all times. Almost all scholars of Indian history are unanimous in acknowledging the fact that he was a brave soldier who provided the Scindia dynasty a solid and permanent place in history. P.E. Roberts (1921) gives an accurate description of Mahadji and of the political events in the later half of the eighteenth century in these words:

The greatest Maratha chieftain, in personal ability and in extent of his dominions, was Mahadji Sindhia, who since 1784, controlled Hindustan from the Sutlaj to Agra, held valuable territories in Malwa and the Deccan and possessed a fine army disciplined and recruited by De Boigne, a brilliant Savoyard soldier of fortune. In 1771 Mahadji captured Delhi, the Mughal capital and that was the high point of Maratha Confederacy. The environs of Delhi for nearly 100 miles all around became Mahadji's personal fief. It is true that Sindhia for a time suffered vicissitudes of fortune. He was defeated by a Rajput coalition in 1786, and in 1788 he temporarily lost his hold on Delhi, when a savage Rohilla chief imprisoned and blinded Shah Alam, the miserable blind old man of eighty-three. But by 1792 he (Mahadaji) had recovered his position, had rescued and restored the emperor, and again stood forth...[17]

The Battle of Panipat, led by Sadashiv Rao Bhau, a cousin of Peshwa—not known to be a shrewd war strategist—proved disastrous for the Marathas. During this battle (in January 1761), known to be the blackest chapter in Indian history, Ahmad Shah Abdali, the cruel Afghan ruler, almost crushed the Maratha army, half of which was untrained. With regards to how many people were butchered on the field, the numbers vary, but it can be safely said that thousands of Marathas were killed within a few hours.

It was in this battle that the Afghans attacked Mahadji, with his right leg amputated by battle-axe. His enemy, content with inflicting the wound and stripping him of some ornaments and his (Deckny) mare, left him to his ill fate. Luckily, he was spotted on the field by a water-carrier, of the name Rana Khan, who was among the fugitives: this unknown man Khan, placing him upon his bullock, carried him towards the far away Deccan. The bleeding Mahadji almost got a second life, thanks to Khan, who was appropriately rewarded later. The survivors of the battle had fled from Panipat to the Deccan, and for a period the nation seemed stunned with the effects of that dreadful carnage in which thousands of Marathas lost lives. In the battle of Panipat, the Scindia family was nearly wiped out, except Mahadji, a deeply religious person, but one who was rendered permanently disabled. He became a Subedar* in 1764 and died in Pune on 12 February1794.[18]

MAHADJI SCINDIA AND GENERAL BOIGNE: AN UNLIKELY ALLIANCE

However, until his death, Mahadji did not get bogged down by the grievous injury; rather, he utilized the adverse situation to his advantage upon reaching the Peshwa camp. After partly recuperating from that deep wound, he planned a number of new strategies. To establish his supremacy over Northern Hindustan, he took full advantage of the system of neutrality pursued by the British government. He was assisted by Benoît de Boigne (1751–1830)—also known as General Count de Boigne—the genius French commander who had made a name and fortune in India with the Marathas. It will not be an exaggeration to say that while the 'Treaty of Salbai' gave Scindia a free hand in establishing an independent principality, it was the army raised and maintained at a high state of efficiency by de Boigne that had enabled him to surpass all his rivals in the acquisition of territory and consolidation of power. Although Mahadji did not trust de Boigne fully when he met him for the first time, a reintroduction, through a common person, in 1780 or so assuaged his doubts and changed his fortunes forever.

The story of de Boigne joining the Scindia army and empowering it with skills and strategy-making needs to be

---

*Subedar is a rank of junior commissioned officer

recounted here, in brief, to provide a sense to my readers of those hard yet interesting war times, when there were no advanced tools of communication at anyone's disposal. But for the Frenchman, Mahadji would not have been what he became in the later years—the most powerful head in the Maratha regime since Shivaji Bhosale I (famously known as Chhatrapati Shivaji). The Holkars too had a French officer but he did not attain fame was comparable to de Boigne.

Son of a hide merchant, de Boigne seemed to have an itchy foot. He left his native country and obtained an Ensign's commission in the famous Irish Brigade. He passed several years in Flanders only to resign in 1774 and join Admiral Orloff, the Russian commander in the Greek Archipelago. In this campaign, he was taken prisoner by the Turks. Ultimately, his peregrinations helped him make his way to St Petersburg. He got employment and commanded an escort sent with Lord Percy, a son of Duke of Northumberland who was touring in the Greek Archipelago. Later on, becoming dazzled by a description of India, he determined to proceed there overland via Tartary and Kashmir, a hazardous journey in those days. However, his attempts failed, and in 1777 he sailed for Madras where he joined the 6th Madras Infantry as an ensign. After resigning in 1782, he went to Calcutta (now Kolkata) and was warmly received by Warren Hastings.

He then went to Lucknow, and via Agra, to Delhi. At that time, Scindia was besieging Gohad. Scindia's Resident, James Anderson, hosted de Boigne. But Scindia did not trust him at once so the French soldier tried to join his opponent, the Rana of Gohad, against the Maratha chief. So confident was he about his capabilities and strength. But the Rana was too parsimonious and refused him a job. He then approached the Jaipur Maharaja and joined him for some time. All this time, Mahadji was keeping a close track of his movements. One day de Boigne was approached by James Anderson on behalf of Scindia and was recruited. He was given a monthly pay of ₹1,000 and was entrusted with the task of raising two battalions of 850 men each.[19] Thus began the greatest connection between a military strategist and a Maratha king which lasted for 10 years—from 1784 to 1794—until the death of Scindia, and in the process it scripted a golden page in Maratha history.

The two battalions which were raised by de Boigne were headed each by a gallant Scotsman, John Hessing and another by Fremont, a Frenchman. In 1789, de Boigne quit his job but was recalled the very next year with enhanced responsibilities thrust upon him by Scindia. The task at hand included raising 10 battalions of infantry with a suitable train of cavalry and artillery; the whole lot was to be disciplined in English style and officered by Europeans. The results were soon to be witnessed by all and sundry. Battles of Patan and Merta in 1790 proved the mettle of these troops. By the end of that year, the entire North India was literally at Mahadji's feet. Buoyed by the successes, Scindia decided to augment his regulars by raising two more brigades in 1791 and 1793. Scindia's force was thus armed with 800 cavalry, three battering guns, 10 howitzers, two mortars and 36 fieldpieces attached to it. Scindia had more than 15,000 horses at one time, an indicator of how advance the King was in war preparation and planning.

Mahadji had earlier put Boigne on the job, kind of a test—of winning Bundelkhand where, in his first action as commander, he won over the Fort Kalinjhar in October 1783.

With his confidence in Boigne escalating as the days went by, Mahadji took him along to watch his possessions in northern India. As Boigne went about taking an active role as Mahadji's military commander, the latter knew he could remain, with absolute confidence, in the Deccan, directing his affairs at the Peshwa's court—a position no other Maratha chief could command.[20]

Three years after Mahadji's untimely death, de Boigne reached London carrying with him a fortune of £400,000 after 19 years of service, and huge fame. He had introduced path-breaking changes during his tenure that revolutionized the warfare tactics of the day and are remembered till date.

A mutual trust created between an Ujjain-born Maratha royal king and a French-born military master brain was never belied!

THE FURTHER ASCENT OF MAHADJI SCINDIA

Praising Mahadji, Sir Malcolm underlined his personality succinctly:

> The nominal slave, but the rigid master of Shah Alam, Emperor of Delhi; the pretended friend but the designing rival of the House of Holkar...the oppressor of Rajput princes ....and the proclaimed soldier but the actual plunderer of the family of Peshwa.

On assuming control of the government, Mahadji busied himself with consolidating his power and enlarging his sphere of influence. Imbibing in himself the qualities of the general and of the statesman, he formed his armies on the western models and engaged the best military talent he could find. An example of the French commander is already mentioned above.

From 1775 to 1782, Mahadji Scindia continued to engage in a power struggle against the British East India Company. During this period, however, he lost the fort of Gwalior, hitherto considered impregnable, and Ujjain. As he gracefully accepted his defeat, Mahadji also began to see the advantages of forming an alliance with the British. Thus came into existence the 'Treaty of Salbai', signed between Warren Hastings and Mahadji Scindia in May 1782. This Treaty was signed after long negotiations to settle the outcome of the First Anglo-Maratha war (1775–1782).

Peace finally prevailed between the two thereafter, at least for 20 years.

The war which started in 1775 was an extended one but the Marathas, led by Mahadji, had an upper hand all through over the British (or the East India Company). The Battle of Wadgaon fought in January 1779 was part of the bigger on-going war which Mahadaji's army had also decisively won defeating the British forces. Mahadaji's luck was favouring him all the way. Between 1775 and 1782, Mahadji was unchallenged in North India. When the Salbai (Gwalior district) Treaty was signed, halting the war for over 20 years, it gave Mahadji time to expand his territory in North India before his sudden death in 1794 at Poona at the age of 64.

However, there are historians (Vinayak Ramdas Kathrdekar, author of *DaulatRao Shinde*, a Hindi book) who believe that this treaty gave Britishers an upper hand and the Marathas were on the losers' side—though not all records say so. This could be because the 15 or more conditions of the treaty severely restricted Mahadji's, and in turn, the Maratha regime's powers in more than one manner. Through this treaty, Warren Hastings, the Governor General, skilfully concluded a separate peace agreement with Scindia and diplomatically detached Raja of Berar (Nagpur) from the Maratha Confederacy. He restored all territory west of Jumna (now Yamuna River) to Scindia and the status quo before the war was re-established at Bombay (now Mumbai).[21] The Salbai Treaty also helped Mahadji establish his independent principality, which was possible only due to the strength of his army trained by de Boigne.

DAULAT RAO SCINDIA (1779–1827): A TARGET OF INTERNAL POLITICS

Daulat Rao, Mahadji's brother's grandson, had no chance of accession to the *rajgaddi* (throne), but since Mahadji was issueless, he had Daulat's name in mind as his heir, and he had expressed it over and over again to his family members as he was affectionately attached to Daulat's father Anand Rao. Daulat Rao, though destined to be the head of the family, as later events revealed, could not be crowned until 10 April 1794, two months after Mahadji's demise at Wanwadi, Pune, on 14 February 1794. The prince was still in his teens then. His succession turned hugely controversial as it did not go well with Mahadji's widows, including Laxmibai, who all ganged up and eventually fought a war against a young Daulat Rao to foil 'his' bid to be the head of the family. This was palace politics at its worst. They wanted another prince to head the dynasty but did not succeed. Daulat Rao went on to rule for 33 long years and, naturally, his tenure witnessed many historically significant events that find mention all over Maratha history.

Shifting of Ujjain as capital of the Scindias from Malwa to Lashkar (Gwalior) was Daulat Rao's decision. In 1810, he bid adieu to Ujjain and built the Gorkhi Palace in Gwalior as his residence. He also encouraged his principal sardars to build their own mansions and thus the city of Lashkar was founded. According to Ajay Agnihotri, author of *Gwalior: Art, History and Culture*, many of those buildings and palaces are still seen in Gwalior city today, where Lashkar is a well-populated locality.[22]

The Second and Third Anglo-Maratha wars were fought during his time. The Marathas were divided at the time and were thus defeated. Their strong bastions fell one after the other, thus resulting in the breaking of the Maratha Confederacy. Daulat Rao Scindia was humiliated at the hands of Arthur Wellesley—the Duke of Wellington who had earlier defeated Napolean—at Laswari. Scindia was forced to sign 'Treaty of Surji-Anjangaon' against his wishes, whereby he conceded Ganges-Jumna Doab, the northern areas of Agra and Delhi and so on. In the south, the Ajanta was given to the British. The Mughal Emperor, Shah

Alam II, who was under the Scindias' protection, now passed under the Britishers. This way, writes Agnihotri, the sovereignty and independence won by Mahadaji, was surrendered.

Another treaty that Daulat Rao signed was just before the Third Anglo-Maratha war broke out in 1817. It was at his newly set up capital Gwalior. Daulat Rao tactically remained a mute spectator in the third war. The Peshwas had to face the ignominy of losing the battle and the British pensioned them off to Bithoor, near Kanpur.

A cursory glance at India's recent history may give an impression that the princely states were jointly or single-handedly fighting the alien power all the time, but the truth is that, on many occasions, they were fighting among themselves too. An interesting piece of history tells us that the Maratha kings had some kind of predatory feelings among themselves which resulted in creating fissures in their unity against the Company's dominance. There was a time in during the early nineteenth century when both Daulat Rao and Jaswant (Yeshwant) Rao Holkar contested for the control of Peshwa Baji Rao II's government. In 1802, the Holkar forces defeated Scindia and the Peshwa with the result that Baji Rao II fled from Poona to Bassein (now Vasai) and appealed to the British government for their assistance. This was the time internal politics of the Maratha confederacy was in complete turmoil. It is said that the death of old statesman Nana Fadnavis (1742–1800)—some also called him the Maratha Machiavelli—removed the last force which could have an effect of moderation on individual princes among the Marathas.

L.F. Rushbrook Williams, former foreign minister of the Patiala royal state, in his book observes:

but the Marathas and the British represented two distinct and diverse theories of government, which by their very nature could hardly co-exist in adjacent areas. Company's main endeavour was to secure the substitute of order for anarchy throughout India. Lord Wellesley (Governor General) realised that if peace were to be established, the Marathas must agree to live under a more settled form of government.[23]

On 31 December 1802, the Treaty of Bassein was thus finalized by which the Peshwa agreed to enter into a subsidiary alliance with the British and Baji Rao was restored to Poona by the British. Here again, Daulat Rao refused (also Berar's Bhosale) to accept the position and the Indore Maharaja remained aloof. In the following year (1803), war broke out in three areas–territories occupied by Scindia and Holkar as well as the Deccan territories. It was in the Deccan, just a few years ago, that the Marathas had defeated the Nizam in the Battle of Kharda to become the supreme rulers. The Company officer who led the hostilities in north India was General Gerard Lake. He captured Aligarh from the Scindia troops and routed the pick of the Gwalior Army near Delhi. With this victory, the two keys of Hindustan—Delhi and Agra, passed into the hands of the Company. Towards the end of 1803, Daulat Rao accepted a subsidiary alliance of the usual kind and surrendered a considerable portion of his territory. Again, the next year, Scindia and Holkar as well as the Raja of Berar admitted British Residents to their courts. Scindia went a step further; early in 1804, he entered into a defensive alliance with the Company.

While Daulat Rao could not match his predecessor in warfare tactics and strategy making, he was known to promote arts in his own manner. He invited classical dancers to his court and with that came Hindustani classical music. Thus was born the famous Gwalior music gharana,* which continues to

*(in South Asia) any of the various specialist schools or methods of classical music or dance.

flourish even today. Not many in music circles today know the fact that the founder of the famous gharana was Daulat Rao Scindia who thus joined the ranks of royal patrons of the arts such as Maharajas of Jaipur, Baroda, Travancore or Indore who had managed to keep alive the Indian arts and music during the 150 years of British rule in India. Needless to say, he was not a singer himself but was a true connoisseur of arts and music. Some writers have termed him to be a dilettante and a person given to sensual pleasures.

JANKOJI RAO SCINDIA II (1827–1843)

Daulat Rao's successor Jankaji or Jankoji (also referred to as Jankuji) was an adopted son. After Daulat Rao's death without an issue, he was sworn in as the Maharaja of Gwalior, in 1827. For about 10 years, the Council of Regency governed the Scindia state on behalf of a minor Maharaja until 1836 from the day of his installation. He died rather early, in 1843, and thus could rule for about six years only. Baijabai, the widow of Daulat Rao and daughter of Sarje Rao Ghatge, was a strong-willed person who liked to dominate people and situations and was ambitious.[24] She is said to have deliberately not promoted education and training of young Jankoji. But she did not succeed in usurping power and had to leave Gwalior, and his supporters ran the administration de facto, defying all the palace intrigues. When he too died sans any offspring, there again rose a problem of finding an able legal heir to the Gwalior throne.

JAYAJIRAO SCINDIA (1834–1886)

If the ruler had passed away without naming any successor, the Company officers, with the help of British officers, could have annexed the Gwalior state. This pre-empted Tarabai, the widow of Jankoji Rao Scindia II, then aged just 13 years, to adopt a son when her husband was on his deathbed—as were the traditional practices of those times. The story of how the adoption took shape is pretty hilarious.

A trusted nobleman, Sambhaji Rao Angre, was immediately sent out in search of an eligible candidate. He chanced upon a group of kids playing marbles and pebbles in a nearby ground of the palace. The unmindful boy, busy as he was in his little game, was surprised when he was approached by Angre who was instantly impressed with his ability to 'shoot' accurately. Taking this as a good omen, he was picked up by Angre and the pandits hurried through the adoption ceremony while Jankoji was breathing his last. Eight-year-old Bhagirath Shinde, thus became Jayajirao Scindia, the eighth Maharaja of Gwalior who ruled from 1843 to1886.

During the First War of Independence in 1857, Jayajirao was nurturing some kind of sympathies for the British, mainly due to his inexperience in diplomacy and administration. Whether this was tactical or a natural limitation is not well recorded in the history books written by various scholars. One Dinkar Rao Rajwade, an intellectual Bramhin, was appointed as his Diwan. He was credited with introducing many administrative reforms; he introduced a competent administration system in the State. He was brought in when the Scindias lost two wars with the British in quick succession—one in Maharajpur (Maharajpore) and the second in Panihar (Punniar), both in 1843. Rajwade not only strengthened the army, but also introduced a proper revenue collection system and justice delivery system. He set up a number of courts in 1862, including a Supreme Court (Mehkama Appeal Khasokhas). The public works department and education departments were started under Michale Filose, who was a unique combination of being the architect and also an army Colonel.

Coming back to Jayajirao Scindia, what is perhaps well known is that his own army revolted against him, leading him to leave Gwalior for Agra. The then Governor General, Lord Cunningham, wrote and gave a fair warning to Scindia that if he revolted, he would have to leave Gwalior with his bag and baggage. Tatya Tope, Lakshmi Bai and Nana Saheb were also looking out for Scindia's support. The Maratha court was anti-British and their army wanted to fight with them. Dinkar Rao Rajwade and the British Resident refrained him from going against the British. But Scindia had ordered a surprise attack against Tatya Tope. It was in this battle that Lakshmi Bai (Newalkar) met with her martyrdom at Gwalior and became an amar (immortal) personality in chapters of India's rich history. People still respect her profoundly, all over, not just in central India.

Jayajirao had to leave the imposing fort of Gwalior on 17 June 1858 which the British conquered forthwith. However, it was restored to Scindia in 1886, just before his death. He died a rich man, leaving behind treasury which was much bigger and valuable than that of Alladin! Gold was in tonnes in Gwalior, not to speak of other precious stones and diamonds and pearls and stones.

Some of the beautiful monuments of Gwalior that stand today, with a sense of pride, were built by him. These include, among others, the magnificent and sprawling Jai Vilas Palace, the Moti Mahal, the Usha Kiran Palace and similar other stylish buildings. He died at the Jai Vilas Palace, the present abode of Jyotiraditya Scindia.

MADHAVRAO SCINDIA II (1876–1925)

When the young prince was being prepped to wear the mantle of the Maharaja, after his father Jayajirao's death, Madhav Rao was just 10 years old. As was the rule, the Regency Council was formed for the third time in a century, to act as his guardian until he came of age to ascend the throne.

It was also a period which saw rapid progress in the state. The modern postal system, telegraph, telephone and railways network were introduced. It was also the time when the Indian freedom movement was gaining momentum and the Morley-Minto Reforms of 1909 were introduced, apparently to appease Indians. Gwalior was undoubtedly a forward-looking state. The first municipal council came into being in Lashkar during Madhav Rao's regime. Municipal governance had begun in earnest. Madhav Rao was pro-people and a democracy-loving Maharaj.

Madhav Rao Scindia had quietly introduced a constitutional system of governance in his state by forming representative bodies. Ajay Agnihotri, in his well-illustrated coffee table book on Gwalior's history, writes that the Maharaja constituted Majlis-i-Kanoon in 1912 and Majilis-i-Aam in 1920.

Jyotiraditya, the present scion of the family, in an interview with the author, put it so:

> The Scindias were always forward-looking rulers. My forefathers thought of municipal governance very early; they laid their own rail lines from Gwalior to Sheopur, to Bhind, to Shivpuri and even upto Mandsaur-Neemuch, not to mention, road networks and building schools and dispensaries. Jiwajirao and Madhavrao and rulers before them pushed for modernity for the sake of the people of Gwalior State.

In a detailed article, Gwalior's senior journalist Rakesh Achal has written about the state's beautiful narrow gauge railway line which was started from Jai Vilas by Madhavrao Scindia II for his travel up to Shivpuri and which would go to the places mentioned above. The train was later dedicated to the public who began using it. About 5000 villagers used to travel and benefit from these trains. King George V and Queen Mary had also travelled in the train in 1911. Achal has said that

Gwalior's unique heritage, the narrow gauge train, needs to be protected for the posterity. Until 1950, the narrowest line of the country belonged to the Scindia family and afterwards it was taken over by the Indian Railways. 'If protected by all means, it could boost present-day Gwalior city's tourism potential', says the writer.[25]

It was unfortunate that Madhav Rao II passed away in France on the way to England in June 1925, but he had already planned for irrigation facilities and agricultural reforms for the populace of his state of Gwalior. The Tighara dam and Harsi are gifts of his reign. Credit of modernizing Gwalior goes to him too as he worked hard for creating efficient systems of administration in the early twentieth century.

How much advanced and modern were the Scindias can be gauged from the following excerpts of the Gwalior State Darbar Policy[26] document about education:

> Inasmuch as the prosperity of the State and the well being of its people are dependent on the Education and upbringing of the Ruler, it is of extreme necessity that the child (minor Prince), as soon as he is able to move about, should be kept in such a wholesome and healthy atmosphere that he may from very beginning tread the proper path. By wholesome atmosphere I mean that the manners and conduct of the people in attendance on the Prince should be such as to benefit him.

It further states:

> Whatever the age of the child, he should be sent out for an airing daily and as long as he is not able to stand up and move about, he should be sent for an hour or two in the open air in a perambulator. When he is strong enough to move about, he should be taken to a well-shaded place where he could play in the open air. The place provided

for this purpose should be covered with soft dust or sand to allow of his playing barefooted.

Another point of the policy states:

The children should be sent regularly to a Regiment which has the reputation of having good discipline and efficient training so that an idea of discipline and obedience to order should be instilled in their mind. It is not necessary that for the purposes of this training any difference should be made between a male and a female child, both should be equally subjected to this course. For subjecting the children to this course, it is not meant that they should undergo a regular course of training at this tender age, but objective is that they should remain under an atmosphere of discipline...

JIWAJIRAO SCINDIA (1916–1961)

As was the case of Madhav Rao II, who was a minor at the time of his succession, Jiwajirao too, was merely nine years old and thus the Regency Council was required to come into play, as was the practice then, to support a minor maharaja. He was finally given the powers of administration when he turned 20. Like his father, he too followed up with constitutional reforms; he introduced a new constitution in 1939 and two sabhas—Praja Sabha and Samant Sabha—similar to the present day Lower House and Upper House of the Indian Parliament. The perspectives, however, changed when World War II broke out in 1939. Reforms were put on the hold as resources were turned to the British and Allied powers. After the war was over, the two 'houses or chambers' were reconstituted as Praja Sabha and Rajya Sabha in 1946. Ajay Agnihotri writes in his book that 'Gwalior was one of the first states that signed the

Instrument of Accession. Thus in 1947 ended the story that had begun in 1728 at Amjhera.'[27]

Jiwajirao had a very lengthy official title, which was rather uncommon. It read: Lieutenant General, Mukhtar-ul-Mulkraj, Azim-ul-Iqtidar, Rafi-us-Shan, Wala Shikoh, Mohra-Sham-i-Dauran, Umdat-ul-Umra, Maharaja dhiraj, Alijah, Hisam-us-Sultanat, His Highness Sir George Jiwajirao Scindia Bahadur, Srinath Mansur-i-Zaman-fidwi-Hazarat-i-Mali-Muazzam-i-Rafiud-Darjat-i-Inglisia G.C.I.E., G.C.I.S.[28]

Jiwajirao, the father of India's former railway minister Madhavrao Scindia (1945– 2001) and husband of Vijaya Raje Scindia, is considered, technically, the last Maharaja of the Scindia dynasty. This was because by the time he died (in 1961), all the independent royal states, including Gwalior, were systematically and legally merged into the Indian dominion after India gained independence in 1947. The honorific titles, privy purses, etc., were, however, removed much later and, in that way, Madhavrao Scindia was considered the last titular 'maharaja' of the Gwalior princely state.

As far as princely states are concerned, the 550 plus in number and which covered two-fifths of India's land mass, with one-third of population of India, a new history began to be written after 1947. The prefix, so far non-existent, was permanently stuck before the glorious names of all the Maharajas—erstwhile!

2

India's Tryst after Independence

India's tryst with destiny actually began much before 1947.
While many parts of the world were witnessing and suffering
from the horrible impacts of World War II that had ended in
August–September 1945—India, despite being under the British
rule then, had remained largely safe and unaffected. It was also
precisely during this time that India's domestic fight for freedom
against the British was in its penultimate phase. The Quit
India Movement led by Mahatma Gandhi had become hugely
successful, overwhelming the British to the extent that they
failed to retaliate. The new dawn of democracy, disseminating
energetic signals, was on the horizon for people to see and feel.
But it was only in August 1947 that the triumphant culmination
of the long drawn and violent struggle for independence against
the foreign rule finally happened. An independent India was
born on 15 August 1947 but not without the deep scars on
its body of a bloody bifurcation. In the early 50s, a toddling
democracy, promising to grow into the world's largest one
in a few decades to come, India began to stand up firmly, if
slowly, having discarded the colonial crutches it had been used
to walking with for decades.

The end of the British Raj heralded the inevitable end of princely India and also caused the advent of people's rule in its true sense. Though democracy had come to stay here in 1947 and Pandit Jawaharlal Nehru (1889–1964) had become the first elected prime minister of India, the old aura of influential feudatories, rajas, royal vassals (thakurs, jagirdars, talukdars and thanedars) and the maharajas did not fade away at once. The unique raja-praja (king-subject) relationship lingered on even as the Indian tricolour, signifying the newly acquired pride of a sovereign republic, began unfurling all across India. Underlining the unique structure of the system, a British author who studied princely states closely wrote,[1]

> While successive dynasties of kings and kingdoms came and went, the institution of Hindu kingship itself remained constant for many years, providing an autocratic, paternalistic but primarily benevolent authority under which a range of Indian cultures flowered throughout Indian subcontinent.

With the achievement of the freedom, the entire social and political order began to change in India. Rudyard Kipling, the famous Indian-born British author, once significantly observed: 'Providence created the Maharajas to offer mankind a spectacle.' Those who have seen the royal splendour and the heydays of Indian maharajas fondly recall all the beautiful dimensions of the spectacle even today but have been truly disheartened by the fact that the Indian Raj is far behind them.

SPECTACLE ENDS, DEMOCRACY BEGINS

The spectacle that Kipling referred to began disappearing into the pages of history over the next few years with the government taking a series of actions towards establishing democratic foundations. First, in 1947, the new ruling order came with the promulgation of the Indian Independence Act 1947 (the British Parliament Act simultaneously created India and Pakistan as two separate nations) and, then in 1970–71, Nehru's daughter Indira Gandhi delivered a blow by ending privy-purses system of the erstwhile princes. For the former rulers who had gradually started to taste the 'not-so-sweet' fruits of democracy, the stoppage of the political pension was kind of a final nail in the coffin. The erstwhile Maharajas thus got two jolts in the first 25 years of free India and then they were consigned to history, forever. Most royal heads of different independent states were naturally very angry with the ruling Congress party under Nehru. Clearly, time was not kind to them, nor was the new government.

And while many ex-rulers were helpless in the face of this blow dealt by Indira Gandhi, there were some who eventually ventured into politics, sustaining themselves in the changing political environment. These included Gayatri Devi of Jaipur and Vijaya Raje of Gwalior, to name just a few.

But before we delve into the Scindia family's foray into politics, albeit forcibly, it would be interesting to know what did the renowned Rajmata Gayatri Devi, easily the most beautiful and richest woman of her times with a global fan following, feel about the times then. 'For all of us, the Swatantra Party and Rajaji's intelligent realism seemed like an island of sanity in the turbulent political sea around us,' she wrote in her memoir, providing readers a sense of those tumultuous times when they had no one to look up to other than Rajaji.[2] Incidentally, she was approached twice by the Congress to stand in the elections on their ticket but she turned down the offer in favour of Rajaji's party, thus signalling her apparent dislike for the Congress. Truly, various accounts of the first two decades of independent India, when amalgamation of states into Indian Union was taking place and the times soon after that, paint a vivid picture of the turbulent times, both for the rulers and the ruled, given their age-old bondings.

A large number of former Maharajas or Maharanis, upset as they were with the Congress, as also due to the creation of a Muslim nation, were regularly exchanging ideas with each other about planning their future and how to retain their hold on to their properties, people, palaces and power—the last one was, of course, rapidly slipping like sand from a tightly held fist. They would often meet either in Delhi or in some other location of their choice. The Chamber of Princes which was formed in 1921 provided a forum to the princely rulers of the time to discuss issues pertaining to their privileges and rights. This platform helped them discuss and debate their own problems as also their relationship with the British, and in later years, briefly with Congress leaders. The standing committee of the Chamber, with Jiwajirao Scindia as its important member, met for the last time in July 1947 in New Delhi, before formally winding up. An informal union of ex-rulers was also formed at the behest of the Baroda Maharaja after Independence but it was short-lived.

The partition of India that led to a mass displacement of people as well as the killing of an estimated one million people in riots in northern India had completely shaken the maharajas. The political and social upheaval triggered by the Hindu-Muslim riots over the blood-letting Partition was too horrible to witness for the peace-loving practitioners of regal lifestyles. Not that they or their forefathers had not seen or heard of wars and that they hadn't been party to causing casualties, however, this mass killing on the basis of religion was shocking and unheard of.

It was against this backdrop that the first general election was held in 1952 in which a few erstwhile royal family members had contested. On the basis of their experiences and success in the next successive elections, the number of ex-royals seeking to enter the political arena grew substantially, representing both, the Indian National Congress (INC) and the opposition parties. Rajmata Vijaya Raje Scindia fought her first election in 1957 under much duress from the Congress leadership; something she was utterly unwilling to do but had been cornered by the top brass of the Congress party in Delhi. Her husband had then just put down the office of the Rajpramukh* of the Madhya Bharat state that had been created after the merging of the two major princely states of Indore and Gwalior. Madhya Bharat later became Madhya Pradesh (in November 1956), with Ravi Shankar Shukla as its chief minister. It was Rajmata's first Lok Sabha election after Madhya Pradesh was born. She was a political novice and stood for the election against her own wishes. One can imagine her state of mind while undertaking whirlwind campaigning in the rural and dusty heartland as a debutant politician. Obviously, as the maharani of India's richest state, she could ill-afford inviting the wrath of the government in Delhi. She eventually joined the BJP via the Jana Sangh.

Nine years after Independence, the Congress had strengthened its hold in what had once been British-ruled India. In a way, the Congress was a natural successor of the Raj. Only in princely domains, such as Gwalior, did it encounter challenges, initially, in spreading its tentacles deeper, much to the anguish of its leadership. The Scindia subjects of these areas did not take to the new Congress rule easily simply because it had actually replaced that of their own maharaja's. People realized, due to various reasons, that democracy and Congress rule were not necessarily analogous. Of the several political parties that mushroomed after Independence, the Akhil Bharatiya Hindu Mahasabha (ABHM) seemed to have a special appeal to the educated middle class and the farming community. It had made considerable headway in the Hindu belt.

---

*Rajpramukhs were the appointed governors of certain Indian provinces and states.

In the erstwhile Gwalior state territory, the Hindu Mahasabha won the first general election of 1952, both in Guna and Gwalior, with consummate ease. The Congress was defeated in both places and also in the by-election held the same year in Gwalior. This rang alarm bells for the Congress party in Delhi. Congress was dismayed and distressed by the setback.

◆

'George' Jiwajirao Scindia, known for his extraordinary love for horse racing, was Gwalior's ruling maharaja at the time of Independence. How did a Hindu raja get an English name like George? Researcher Charles Allen has this to say: 'The continuing support of the British Royal Family was also ensured when Madhav Rao asked George V and Queen Mary to be God-parents to his two children, whom he named 'George' Jiwajirao and 'Mary' Kamalaraje.'[3]

George V, the king of the United Kingdom and the emperor of India, had paid a special visit to Gwalior with his wife Queen Mary, as state guests for enjoying the famed shikar (hunt) in the verdant jungles of the state. Inside what is now the Madhav National Park, a castle was built for his overnight stay as part of the elaborate arrangements for the shooting of the tiger. The imposing castle is still standing erect after over a century, though in a state of neglect. The relationship between Madhav Rao Scindia II and George V was quite friendly as can be seen from the meticulous planning done by Madhav Rao for the royal visit and the huge expenses incurred for his grand reception and stay in 1911.

Jiwajirao would spend hours and days together in Bombay and Poona where he had his well-bred horses not just dominating but winning races every Derby season on both the courses, especially the Royal Western India Turf Club, Mahalaxmi. In the Pune's sprawling Manjri Stud Farm of the Scindias (shown physically to this author personally by Madhavrao Scindia, then India's tourism and civil aviation minister). There were 200 thoroughbred horses during the heydays of the popular Maratha chieftain from Gwalior. Much later—sometime in the '80s, about 20 years after the demise of Jiwajirao—it was sold off to Pallonji Mistry, as neither Rajmata Scindia nor Madhavrao, both full-time politicians, had much time to spend on the racecourses.

Jiwajirao's hands were also full with his own administrative affairs of a sprawling state, travel and his new love for flying. He had bought a private plane, a war-surplus Dakota and then three smaller planes, including a Tiger Moth for training. Jiwajirao soon became a trained pilot but never went solo flying.

Thus, he did not appear to have much time or interest in active politics, which was emerging as a new and attractive profession, in Independent India.

Christophe Jaffrelot, the French political scientist, wrote:

Scindia dynasty was, in 1947, at the helm of one of the largest princely states of northern India and it controlled— thanks to its own power and prestige and network of former *jagirdar*—nearly a one fifth of the assembly constituencies. In 1952, 'the Palace', the name under which the Scindias are known in Gwalior, discreetly supported the Hindu Mahasabha which emerged as the main rival to the Congress in Madhya Bharat. Nehru realised that it would pose a serious threat to his party. He, therefore, requested the Maharaja, Jiwajirao to side with Congress just before the elections of 1957. The Maharajah declined the invitation but the Maharani, Vijaya Raje Scindia, was persuaded to contest the elections under the Congress banner and she won with a large margin against the Hindu Mahasabha candidate. The Mahasabha lost ground throughout Madhya Bharat whereas Congress established a dominance which remained unchallenged till 1967 when 'the Palace' left the ruling party and once again sided with the Hindu nationalist opposition.[4]

More details of this important political development are there in the following pages, but it was important to know how a foreign author of eminence saw this significant political development from his eyes.

Well, Jiwajirao's predecessors and successors did indulge in serious politics but Jiwajirao was an exception. Of course, after the integration of the princely states into the newly created Indian republic, Jiwajirao's political status and clout went up as he was made the Rajpramukh of the amalgamated states of Gwalior, Indore and other smaller ones, known as Madhya Bharat. But it was a titular administrative post not a political appointment per se. Gwalior and Indore were made the capitals for six months each. Scindia was little above the elected chief ministers in hierarchy. Liladhar Joshi, from Shujalpur, of the Gwalior state, was the first chief minister of Madhya Bharat. The state was born on 28 May 1948 after merging as many as 24 princely states of the Central Indian Agency. Maharaja of Indore (Yeshwant Rao Holkar) was made the Uprajpramukh. The other state that came into being, in this region, at the same time was Vindhya Pradesh, merging 35 princely states of Bundelkhand and Baghelkhand political agencies of central India and the Khaniyadhana state of the Gwalior residency. Maharaj Martand Singh of Rewa was made the Rajpramukh there.[5]

Madhya Bharat (it was also called the United State of Gwalior, Indore and Malwa) later became present-day Madhya Pradesh in November 1956 as part of the states reorganization exercise, largely done on linguistic basis, across India. The post of Rajpramukh was abolished when the constitutionally elected chief minister was appointed in Madhya Pradesh.

As far as Jiwajirao was concerned, he was a popular and social Maharaja but with a low-profile image. In the Gwalior of those days, the Hindu Mahasabha and later the Ram Rajya Parishad were quite active. Madhya Bharat was a citadel of right-wingers. The rulers were naturally seen to be inclined towards the right wing, something an intelligent Nehru sensed early. As the new prime minister and the Congress leader of international fame, Nehru would not have risked the party's fortunes in the initial period of the country's joyous freedom mood and the associated celebrations. The Congress, having fought the freedom struggle from the front, was naturally credited with winning freedom for the countrymen. In the eyes of the people, it was *the* party which took the British head on and then drove them out of the country. There was just no formidable opposition to Congress which won 364 seats out of 489 in the first and crucial general election of 1952. Incidentally, it spanned over four full months for the first elections to be completed—from 25 October 1951 to 21 February 1952—something unthinkable in today's times of electronic voting machines (EVMs) and other information technology advancements.[6]

The first election in Independent India in 1951–52 was otherwise a smooth affair barring results from the Gwalior region. They spoiled the 'party' of the Congress government in New Delhi. From the Gwalior seat for the first ever parliamentary polls, the Akhil Bharatiya Hindu Mahasabha fielded its general secretary Vishnu Ghanshyam Deshpande who was from Vidarbha and not a local person. Yet, he was such a popular leader that he not only contested from Gwalior, but also fought simultaneously from Guna, the adjoining Lok Sabha seat and won both the seats with consummate ease defeating the Congress candidates. He retained Guna where he defeated Gopi Krishna Vijayvargiya, former chief minister of Madhya Bharat, and a native of Guna, bagging 40.70 per cent (56,518)

votes; in Gwalior, he performed better by securing 45.49 per
cent votes (65,695) against Vaidehi Charan Parashar. Both the
rival candidates belonged to the Congress. In the resultant by-
poll that happened in Gwalior in 1952, following Deshpande's
renouncement of Gwalior over Guna, the Hindu Mahasabha
again registered a facile win. The candidate was Narayan
Bhaskar Khare, its all-India president and an acerbic and
influential public speaker who was also a great Nehru-baiter.
Khare's famous quote about Nehru would invariably creep into
political narratives of the '50s. '[Jawaharlal was] English by
education, Muslim by culture and Hindu by accident.'[7]

Congress was defeated twice in the same year in the Gwalior
belt of Scindia influence, setting off an alarm bell for the
country's most popular political party. Incidentally, of the four
seats the ABHM had won in 1952 in the first parliamentary
polls of the independent country, two were from Guna and
Gwalior—both Scindia's pocket boroughs.

The outcome of the Gwalior-Guna polls may have surely
created the impression in the mind of Nehru that the Gwalior
ruler Jiwajirao was lending his tacit support to the Hindu
Mahasabha and not to the Congress party. It was not an
outrightly wrong perception to be formed by the Congress
leaders—considering the impressive victories of the Mahasabha's
two candidates in three elections—and by the French scholar
Christophe Jaffrelot.

A little more interesting description of Prime Minister
Nehru's visit (28 May 1948) to Gwalior would be in place
here in providing an insight into what he thought of the
maharajas and how their mutual relations were! He had come
to capital Gwalior to inaugurate the Madhya Bharat state of
which Jiwajirao Scindia was made the Rajpramukh, in line
with Scindia's stature and clout at that time. He was the most
important maharaja of Central India and Rajputana having a
hugely spread-out geographical territory (25,041 square miles)

under his control. Was Gwalior not, after all, one of the few 21-gun salute states of the British times and also the wealthiest one?

'He [Nehru] was displeased that the public of Gwalior had not lived up to his expectations of them,' Vijaya Raje Scindia wrote about this important political event in her autobiography.[8]

'My husband rose to introduce him at a public meeting in the heart of town, he was greeted with wild cheering. But when Nehru began his speech, the applause was noticeably muted.' Her husband later told her (Rajmata) how upset Nehru had looked and that he had made no secret of his displeasure, rebuking his Gwalior audience with these words:

> Times have changed, and everyone, everywhere else, has come to realise how they have changed. Everyone, everywhere else knows that I hold in my hand the key to all cities—all but this perverse city, Gwalior. Here people are still mired in the values of the past.

The crowd's applause, upon hearing his speech and the dig he took at them openly, was even much less enthusiastic. 'My husband,' further wrote Vijaya Raje, 'embarrassed as if it was somehow his fault, saw to it that it never happened again. Whenever Nehru came to give speeches, he always sent along a hundred or so of his own men among the audience to act as cheerleaders.' While Nehru visited the sprawling Scindia palace as the prime minister during the oath-taking ceremony of the new state's chief, Jiwajirao and Nehru struck a relationship, but it never rested on a solid foundation. 'Neither readily took to the other, and each bristled with suspicion about other's efforts to be amiable,' wrote Jiwajirao's wife.

What perception Nehru carried back home from Gwalior, after the lukewarm response from the innocent and untutored people, if not actually from the 'palace' is anybody's guess. However, the series of events that unfolded later made it abundantly clear about what he thought about the Scindia family and the real popularity in their former territory which influenced as many as eight parliamentary seats and 60 assembly seats. The 1952 election outcome had firmed up his opinion about the perceptible dislike of the people for him or more precisely for the Congress and the extreme attachment and respect for Jiwajirao which he had seen with his own eyes a few years ago.

The seeds of suspicion had been sown in Nehru's mind over the years, but the Maharaja of Gwalior was completely unmindful of what was simmering in New Delhi's political circles, as he neither had any interest in politics nor the right set of friends at the right places to guide him in the games politicians play.

Since Jiwajirao was busy indulging his horse-racing hobby in Bombay, the political pulse was left to be felt by Vijaya Raje, the most admired maharani of the dynasty. She gauged it rather well, like a seasoned politician, though she was not one at that time.

'I knew that the mildest expression of disapproval from an ex-ruling prince was looked upon as blasphemy; for one of them to join the opposition would be something in the nature of high treason,'[9] as is written in her biography giving clear hints of things that were expected to come the powerful family's way, especially after the 1952 Lok Sabha poll results.

There is a fleeting mention in her book of how the maharaja of Baroda, Pratap Sinh (Gaekwad) was summarily deprived of his privy purse and privileges for the 'sin' of merely attempting to form a union of ex-rulers. She was perhaps anticipating something on those lines if the Scindias were to support an opposition party, which they had not done so far.

That the Congress had never fancied Jiwajirao was well known in local political circles. But the circumstances that forced the Gwalior Maharani into politics are just unthinkable in today's times of advanced telecommunication technologies when you can connect with anyone across the globe in a matter of seconds, not even minutes. The mighty Maharani of Gwalior, however, could not connect, via a trunk call or a lightening call, with her husband in Bombay for a whole day when she desperately needed to consult with him on an urgent political matter. That was in 1956, sometime close to the election. Telecommunication technology had not come of age yet. A combination of an 'abortive telephone call' and 'tissue of rumours' forced 'an anxious wife' to jump into politics. She writes:

> Spurred on by the friends who shared my apprehensions of the punitive action that the Government might resort to against my husband, I decided to go to New Delhi before it was too late and to explain to the Prime Minister, Pandit Nehru, whose patience was proverbially thin, that the rumours of my husband's involvement with the Mahasabha were entirely baseless. Not that I ever found Mr Nehru anything but urbane, charming and even helpful.[10]

There was a very crucial and high-level political dialogue to decide the future of the Scindias in a way, between a man of none other than the stature of prime minister himself and a very influential and wealthy maharani, albeit a political novice. It was during this conversation that Nehru convinced (or rather forced) the Rajmata to contest the election as a Congress candidate. It went something like this:

> Vijaya Raje: Panditji, my husband is not against the Congress.
>
> Nehru: Well, if he is not against us, then let him show that he is with us.

Vijaya Raje: But Panditji, he simply hates politics! He
will never be a candidate for any party! That is precisely
what I have come here to explain to you!

Nehru: Well, in that case you stand as our candidate (he
told her glibly). Go and see Shastriji; Indu, will take you
to them. They oversee party tickets.[11]

A completely shaken Maharani Scindia had nothing left to
offer. She was demoralized and alone in the Congress office.
She was then quickly asked to go with Indira Gandhi and meet
Panditji and Shastriji. Apparently, Nehru was not keen on taking
the brief conversation any further. His order was final. When
Vijaya Raje protested that she did not want the ticket, she
was largely ignored by Nehru and was instead straight taken
to Home Minister Govind Ballabh Pant (1955–1961) and his
junior colleague in the cabinet, Lal Bahadur Shastri. The more
she tried to convince the veteran Congress leaders, the more
convinced they were that just the right candidate was sitting
in front of them who would take on the formidable Hindu
Mahasabha. For Pant and Shastri, the suggestion from Nehru
was like a command that they had to follow. The wealthy
Maharani had been cornered!

Luckily, Vijaya Raje could finally speak with her husband
over the phone from Delhi and narrated what the Congress
leadership was up to in New Delhi. An equally shocked Jiwajirao
decided to fly back to Gwalior and asked his wife to rush
back too.

In the end, the couple decided, after weighing all the options,
that it would not be prudent for Vijaya Raje to refuse the
Congress ticket offered to her for it would look like an open
defiance of the very people she had tried to placate, though
unsuccessfully. Jiwajirao was still distrustful of the Congress
leadership and so he forced Sambhaji Angre, a member of the
Hindu Mahasabha and his close friend and relative, to join the

Congress to give company and support to his wife.

It is very interesting to note that a maharani who was a reluctant political entrant to the Congress and the one who wanted to make it just a formality, went on to become first, the right-wing party Jana Sangh's founder and then the BJP's founding member in 1980 and a vice president for a long term, creating a place for herself in the national politics alongside Atal Bihari Vajpayee and Lal Krishna (L.K.) Advani.

She first agreed to stand for the 1957 Lok Sabha election from Guna on Congress's ticket and defeated the ABHM candidate V.G. Deshpande by over 60,000 votes. Then in 1962, she changed her constituency to Gwalior to again come out with flying colours. She routed Manik Chandra of the Jana Sangh by 148,820 votes, giving the Congress a solid foothold in the region.

There is also an absorbing story about the 1962 elections.

Jiwajirao had suddenly passed away, after a brief illness, in July 1961 at the age of 45 in Bombay's Samudra Mahal residence of the Scindias. Due to acute diabetic conditions he had lost one eye and was generally bedridden and a bit depressed. Expert doctors from London had been summoned but to no avail. Upon hearing of his passing away at such a young age, people made a beeline at Samudra Mahal in Bombay. His only son Madhavrao, barely 16 then, was at his bedside when his father breathed his last. His body was then taken to Gwalior by special plane for cremation. Hundreds and thousands of people, sobbing uncontrollably, thronged the airport and the pilot faced great difficulty in landing as grieving population had spilled on to the tarmac.

His funeral procession attracted huge crowds from Gwalior and areas around, reflecting his popularity well after 14 years of Independence and when royal rulers had already slipped into history. But clearly, Gwalior's equation with its 'ruler' had not changed much.

Vijaya Raje had become a widow after only 20 years of marriage. She had four daughters and a son to look after besides huge properties and legal issues linked to that. As was the prevailing practise then, she got the status and honorific title of rajmata of Gwalior. Her entire life changed. A young and inexperienced Madhavrao was anointed as the new maharaja of Gwalior after his father's death in 1961. Until he came of age, it was his mother, Rajmata Vijaya Raje, on whose shoulders rested the running of the affairs of the Gwalior state.

The untimely death of her husband demoralized her a great deal. For some time, naturally, she slipped into her shell. It also resulted in her, a religious person to the core of her heart, being detached from God and stopping her daily pooja, other rituals and the good time she used to spend in her palace temple enjoying every bit. 'My gods had played me false,' she wrote many years later. She gave up colourful sarees and instead opted to wear white sarees, something she continued until she passed away in January 2001. She had also given up on eating mangoes which Jiwajirao used to love so much and would regularly savour despite his diabetic problem. She had also vowed not to go out of her palace for a year.

It was during the long mourning period, however, that she started getting feelers to get prepared for the impending general elections of February 1962 for which again, due to an entirely personal reason, nay tragedy, she was not at all keen to contest. One day, Chief Minister Kailash Nath Katju, an emissary of Nehru, visited her with a message from the prime minister that she should contest and that she would not have to campaign. 'If needed Pandit Nehru himself would come to Gwalior to campaign on her behalf. What she was required to do was merely fill in her nomination papers,' assured the chief minister.[12] This did the trick perhaps. She could not turn down the offer to change the seat from Guna to Gwalior.

Those who had thronged the funeral of her husband and had showered rose petals on him, also showered votes on her just a few months later. Vijaya Raje was elected for the second time in a row. She was the only woman candidate to have won twice consecutively in Madhya Pradesh.

Old timers of the area recall that she did not have to do much of campaigning in her first ever election of Guna, and the next one in Gwalior, although the Guna opponent was a popular leader of the Mahasabha and the sitting MP.

Her big wins added a new chapter to the already luminous Scindia family's political history. Her entry into politics was the main turning point that scripted this family's political journey for next many years.

◆

END OF THE PRIVY PURSES

The abolishment of the privy purses as per Article 363A, the 26th Amendment Act, 1971 of the Constitution, ran contrary to the promise Sardar Patel had made to the princes (at the time of their states' merger with the Indian Union). As a result, they were not very sure if it would actually happen. Patel had made a speech at the Constituent Assembly supporting the rulers and the provision of privy purses and its logic thereof. Also, as late as February 1947, Nehru had assured the Negotiating Committee of the Chamber of Princes that neither the monarchical form of government, nor the integrity of the states, would be touched. Sardar had repeated this guarantee a few months later in his statement on 5 July.[13] The logic was simple: in exchange for signing the instrument of accession and merging their states and identity forever, they needed to be compensated decently. The later-day premier Indira Gandhi would not bother herself with Patel's political 'promise' given many years ago to bring the princely states around.

The sudden move from a shrewd politician caught them off-guard, though it was not without a solid political reason. Indira Gandhi, then a very powerful prime minister, unlike many of her successors in the post, was unhappy with the princely families. The reason? Some of them had fought a parliamentary election in 1967 under the banner of the Swatantra Party and had won handsomely. Gwalior's Rajmata Vijaya Raje Scindia and Jaipur's gorgeous Gayatri Devi were among those who had defeated the Congress candidates with huge margins in the same year. Both were highly critical of Indira Gandhi and were also later jailed during the Emergency between 1975 and 1977.

According to Arvind Datar, eminent lawyer and constitutional matters commentator, 'the renewed attempt to abolish privy purses was perhaps prompted by several rulers who joined the Swatantra Party of Rajaji (ex-Governor General C. Rajagopalachari) and defeated the Congress candidates in the 1967 elections.'[14] A bill to amend the Constitution (Article 366 (22) and abolish the privy purses as recognized under the aforesaid article, was hurriedly brought in as a consequence and passed in the Lok Sabha (motion carried by 336 votes to 115) when most of the Opposition, including the Jana Sangh, had voted against the Bill. While it got passed in the Lower House, it was defeated in the Rajya Sabha (Upper House) on 5 September 1970. It was a huge ignominy for the government and the prime minister, as her original design got defeated, unexpectedly.

A presidential order was thus inevitable as the government, which was hell-bent on discontinuing the benefits to the erstwhile rajas and maharajas had to save face after its shock defeat in the Upper House. A few hours thereafter, using provisions of Article 366 (22), the president signed the historic but controversial order.

Interestingly, there are two versions available about Nehru's approach towards continuing the privy purses or otherwise. General impression has been that it was Indira Gandhi who was against it. So, it won't be out of place to make a cursory reference to the long correspondence which continued well into 1955 between Prime Minister Nehru and Jaipur's Sawai Man Singh II (1912–1970), popularly known as Jai. Nehru had observed in a letter to him: 'How long can we justify to our people the payment of large sums of money from the public funds to the Princes, many of whom discharge no functions at all.'[15] The letter is quoted in acclaimed author John Zubrzycki's recent book *The House of Jaipur*. Jai had sent a firm rejoinder to Nehru.

Providing a slightly different perception on this whole issue, Sagarika Ghosh, noted journalist and author, has this to say:

> After bank nationalization, Indira Gandhi's government moved to discontinue special privileges for India's hereditary princes by abolishing privy purses, or payments that hereditary princes received from government, through a Constitution amendment bill brought before Parliament in September 1970. What could be a more striking example of the battle against elite privileges than a battle against feudal Maharajas with their inherited riches, a move that brought over 6 million dollars to the exchequer? She would say: What irritated people most was not the privy purses but the rest of it, the fact that princes didn't pay water and electricity rates. The poor man had to pay but the prince did not...these privileges were an irritant to the common man.[16]

On the night of 28 December 1970, that 'spectacle' Kipling was referring to was brought abruptly and clumsily to an end as the President of Republic India (V.V. Giri) was roused from his bed to sign an ordinance de-recognising the Princely Order.[17]

The presidential order was not only quickly challenged in the Supreme Court, by H. H. Maharajadhiraja Madhavrao Jiwajirao Scindia Bahadur (notice the title which was readily accepted and officially mentioned in the verdict in 1970 as it is by the Supreme Court of India), Scindia secured a stay order against it from the Constitution Bench headed by the Chief Justice, M. Hidayatullah, on 15 December 1970. The Supreme Court ruled that the de-recognition was unconstitutional. But ultimately, the maharajas of small and big royal houses lost the case, perhaps the first of its kind legal battle challenging the order of the president himself. Within nine days of the humiliating verdict by the apex court, Indira Gandhi met President Giri and called for fresh elections which she won emphatically riding on the now-famous socio-economic slogan (suggested by P.N. Haksar, her most powerful principal secretary) of 'Garibi Hatao' (eradicate poverty) in the year 1971. After her grand return to power (she won two-thirds majority with 352 seats) she made many constitutional amendments that politically suited her most, notwithstanding all round criticism.

On 18 March 1971, Indira Gandhi was again sworn in as the prime minister, the first time had been in 1966. As the radiant prime minister reflected in the glory of huge victory, Congress (R) radicals were more than convinced that it was her socialist agenda—bank nationalization, abolishing privy purses and to top it all, the catchy 'Garibi Hatao' slogan that reversed the losses of 1967. Clearly, she was on the top of the world.

'He [Mr Giri] set the pattern of "rubber-stamp President" for at least two of his successors,' wrote Vijaya Raje in her autobiography without concealing her anguish against Indira Gandhi who had made Giri, then the vice president, her own personal candidate in the just-concluded presidential elections, brushing aside the official candidate of the Congress party, Dr Neelam Sanjeeva Reddy. Giri, an independent candidate supported by Indira Gandhi, won and Reddy, the official candidate, lost.

Nehru and Indira and their party, the Congress, were not much in favour of the royal rulers as was seen from the above-mentioned instances. But Sardar Patel and Morarji Desai, two Congress stalwarts of Nehru's time, were supportive of the princes, as is seen in various documents, as and when issues relating to princely states came up before the two. The first instance was the integration of states into the Indian Union which was in a way unavoidable if democracy had to be ushered in after achieving independence. Second was about abolishing privy purses (a pensionary provision) given to the former royal rulers as constitutional guarantee under Articles 291 and 362 for merging their power and states with the new Indian dominion. Patel was said to be in favour of continuing the privy purses, though when they were discontinued, he was not around.

The issue was finally settled once Indira Gandhi bounced back in 1971 with a bigger majority. She was a different prime minister now. Princes, their problems or their privy purses did not matter to her at all what with her newly acquired global image, confidence and much enhanced power!

3

The Political Turmoil

M uch before the controversy of the privy purses had erupted and there appeared to be a clash of titans at the national level, with Prime Minister Indira Gandhi on one side and on the other, most of the princes, led by the Gwalior house (mother and son). In 1970–71, Vijaya Raje's disillusionment with Congress had started creeping in slowly. The noting of her mental reaction—never expressed in public— to Nehru's speech in Parliament post the crushing defeat of India at the hands of China in 1962, is an adequate indication to know what was going in her mind. It goes like this: Nehru admitted in Parliament, 'We have been living in a world of our own making.' Scindia felt as if it 'was like a General blaming his officers and men for a defeat he had led his army into.'[1]

Imagine what and how an important sitting Congress MP was thinking about an otherwise admirable Prime Minister Nehru and his 'mishandling' of the Indo-China War which ended in late November 1962.

So, the die was cast but she was clearly not aware of the future political upheavals that would offer her, on a platter, an opportunity to divorce the Congress and be a leader in her own right. A series of events happened in the next few years, unplanned as they were, which showed that she was suffocating within her own party, the party she had been absolutely reluctant to join just about a decade ago.

As a two-time MP from two different constituencies, and having won handsomely, she was naturally an emerging star for the Congress party in the mid-'60s. Her second consecutive victory, in 1962, now from Gwalior, was with a margin of over 140,000 votes, clearly establishing her as a popular leader across the state, although it was more of her personal charisma than an influence of the Congress party that had mesmerized the electorate. It is believed that Ramsingh Bhai Verma (once an MP from Indore) boasted in his campaign of Nehru's remark that 'There are two Congress leaders who could win from any constituency. They are the maharani of Gwalior and Ram Singh Verma.'[2]

The Congress had won a lesser number of seats (361) in the third general elections of independent India. The Congress's vote share too had dipped across the country from 47.8 per cent in 1957 to 44.7 per cent in 1962 due to various local and national factors.[3] Several new and smaller parties were successful in making their presence felt, about the same time, on the national political canvas. The Swatantra Party and the right-wing Jana Sangh, headed by Dr Shyama Prasad Mukherjee, were among the prominent ones trying to eat into the Congress share of the large electoral cake. A bright and popular leader like Rajmata Scindia should have ideally been looked after well by the party leadership who had wooed her first and then forced the Gwalior chieftain to join their ranks.

Did the Congress make a mistake then of not keeping its promising leaders in its fold and kept repeating it in one way or the other even after 50 years down the line? For the Rajmata, it was sheer destiny that had willed something else for her as is explained in the events that unfolded one after the other.

Curiously enough, she was not at all keen on entering politics in the first place and then she was uneasy to join and contest on the Congress ticket. On both occasions, however, she had to swallow her pride, given the circumstances she had been trapped in. But she went ahead confidently and bit the bullet bravely. Perhaps, the path was preordained to make a peace-loving Maharani a hardened politician who would eventually go to a party she was meant to be in, *dil se*!

The mid-'60s were the days of political turmoil in Madhya Pradesh and in India. The Indo-Pak War came close on the heels of the Indo-China War which had just got over, but many issues remained to be resolved. Prime Minister Lal Bahadur Shastri had to visit Russia on the invitation of Prime Minister Alexei Kosygin where he was to meet President Ayub Khan of Pakistan for further talks in January 1966. A global communist leader was working out a truce formula between two non-communist nations. On 10 January, the famous Tashkent Declaration (peace agreement) was signed between India and Pakistan.

The same night, within few hours of inking the historic deal, Shastri passed away in a rather shocking manner—as per many accounts, under 'mysterious' conditions at Tashkent. Indian media was full of stories of all sorts about how he had died. Veteran journalist and author Kuldip Nayyar had extensively written about it and a movie *The Tashkent Files* has also recently been made on the so-called mystery surrounding Shastri's death. However, the then home secretary of India, L.P. Singh, an ex-ICS officer of the 1935 batch (later to be governor of Assam) and an upright bureaucrat who had accompanied the Shastri entourage, has written in his beautiful little book the *Portrait of Lal Bahadur Shastri* that 'the PM had suffered heart attack and he died a natural death and in view of his medical history (of heart ailment), there was nothing exceptional or mysterious.'[4]

Suddenly, a pall of gloom enveloped India, as she was just

recovering from the death of Nehru. In 1964, Nehru had passed away at the age of 75, having had pyelonephritis (a kidney affliction) and in 1966, a much younger Shastri, 62, followed him, mainly due to a persistent heart disease. Congress lost its two stalwarts and well-known freedom fighters in two years! But politics being such a self-seeking and ruthless profession, it does not tremble a bit by such shocks or saddening events that may easily jolt an individual. A multitude of pressures immediately clashed and coalesced in full public view in Delhi.

No sooner had the tragic news arrived in India around 5.00 p.m., hectic lobbying began in Delhi to look for his successor. Since the prime minister's position can't be kept vacant, Gulzarilal Nanda, the then home minister, was sworn in as acting prime minister at 3.15 a.m. by the president, S. Radhakrishnan. 'Outwardly politics were suspended the day Shastri died. Behind the scenes, however, certain moves were set afoot, thoughts were spoken, and events occurred, which all indicated that self-restraint was incomplete in the pursuit of power. Cynics observed that the struggle for succession began as early as 6 a.m. on that day, Tuesday, the 11th, and there is evidence to support this view.'[5]

Elsewhere in Delhi, late-night political parleys for the election of the new prime minister had started taking place in right earnest, much before Shastri's body had arrived in New Delhi from Tashkent. When the body arrived at Palam Airport and was subsequently being taken to his residence, Nanda reportedly took chief minister of Madhya Pradesh, Dr Dwarka Prasad Mishra (1901–1988), at the former's residence seeking his support for the top job. He had no time to shed even crocodile tears for the departed prime minister. Indira Gandhi too was politicking in her own way seeking support either with Congress president K. Kamaraj or through others.

Mishra, who finds repeated mentions in Brecher's book, *Succession in India: A Study in Decision-Making*, as someone very important in national politics, was first in the Morarji camp and then solidly with Indira Gandhi. As a front runner, she was being challenged by Morarji Desai who was much senior to her. Eventually, elections were held, and Indira Gandhi became the prime minister on 24 January 1966. The 'Goongi Gudiya' (dumb doll), defeated a more seasoned aspirant, Morarji Bhai (1896–1995), hands down. She secured 355 votes for herself in a direct contest, leaving 169 for the veteran Gandhian leader from Mumbai. The secret ballot helped her in some way. Her overwhelming victory created fissures in the Congress party at the national level and in the states too and in the next two years, the party got officially split. But that is a separate story.

Mishra, a strong-willed, literary-minded veteran, always found himself mired in one controversy or the other, owing to his uncompromising working style and apparent arrogance, albeit his honest intentions. Though he was a state player, he had tremendous clout in Delhi, a reason why it was necessary to write about the role he had played in national politics in 1966 in what was called the 'second succession' at a time when the Syndicate* was active and the 'Kamaraj Plan' was the flavour of Indian politics.

Dr Mishra, an outspoken politician and former home minister in Central Provinces (CP) and Berar government at Nagpur, was known to have been against Jawaharlal Nehru and closely aligned with Sardar Patel (he had left Congress in the early '50s due to differences with Nehru). The Jabalpur politician became closer to his daughter when she became the prime minister. When he became chief minister in September 1963, Nehru was the prime minister and when he demitted office in 1967, Indira Gandhi had stepped into her father's shoes comfortably, following Shastri's untimely demise. Mishra,

---

*An unofficial group of very influential leaders of the Congress led by party president K. Kamaraj.

a canny politician, successfully served with three prime ministers and thus was an experienced leader who was witness to many significant events of the '60s and had a role to play as is mentioned above. Many believe his political wilderness of 12 years had come to an end due to the intervention of Indira Gandhi and only then could he become the chief minister.[6]

In fact, he became one of Indira's closest advisors and a well-known strategist of her team on whom she used to bank upon heavily, initially. Significantly, when Shastri died in Russia, it was Indira Gandhi herself, then a minister in Shastri's cabinet, who woke Mishra up in the wee hours in Bhopal to not just inform him of the sad demise of the PM but also to summon him to Delhi immediately.[7] This particular fact once again underscores his political stature of the time.

But that proximity with the three prime ministers and being a heavyweight in the Delhi circles did not really help him in many matters of his own in his state of Madhya Pradesh. During his eventful tenure of four years, severe drought wreaked havoc, student agitation flared up all over the state and a well-known tribal raja Pravir Chandra Bhanj Deo from Bastar was killed inside his palace in an indiscriminate police firing, sending shock waves among the club of former princes. Mishra, incidentally, known to be an opponent of the feudal leaders, was squarely blamed for physically eliminating the Raja in 1966, lest he emerged as a political star, if not a direct threat to the throne. The charge was never proven. Political observers have written that Mishra was a master of the Machiavellian manner of treating opponents.

'JALLIANWALA BAGH' IN BASTAR

Bastar is a beautiful place in Central India and was ruled by a tribal Royal family for many decades. Now situated in a far southern corner of the tiny Chhattisgarh state that was carved

out from Madhya Pradesh in November 2000, it is surrounded
by hills and hillocks and dense forests where tribal traditions are
kept alive by the local people despite modern-world challenges.
It has been a backward area for decades. Known as part of the
erstwhile and very vast Dandakaranya region, it got converted
into a safe and secure den for Naxalites for over 40 years now,
thanks to the topography of the sprawling area and the abject
failure of the successive policy makers in bringing development
to the region. They also failed to contain the Maoists before
they became a nuisance for the local population and killed
hundreds of innocent citizens and police personnel.

The iconic Bastar district, however, has always fascinated
painters, craftsmen, writers, foreign tourists, jungle lovers,
authors and other creative people over the decades despite
its remoteness and lack of infrastructure. Most of them were
appreciative of the way the local people lead their life, away
from the public gaze, and although they have limited natural
resources, they are a happy lot. Verrier Elwin (1902–1964), a
celebrated British-born Indian anthropologist and ethnologist,
is among the early researchers who did extensive studies of the
Bastar tribes and their socio-cultural traditions and heritage.
He was of the firm opinion, after spending over two decades
among them, that the Bastar tribals were waging a battle for
existence and that they should be saved from 'the deadly shafts
of exploitation, interference and repression that civilisation so
constantly launches...if the Muria [tribe] continue as they are
today, happy, free and innocent, I shall be content.'[8]

It is this tribe and its rights that the slain Maharaja was
trying to protect.

A RIGHTEOUS RAJA'S FIGHT FOR THE TRIBES

Pravir Chandra Bhanj Deo, (1929–1966) was the twentieth
and last maharaja of the Bastar state—among the largest in

Chhattisgarh region with an area of 13,026 sq. miles.[9] Known
to be a popular king, he always championed the cause of the
poor and illiterate tribes of the Bastar 'state.' He was the last
king of the Kakatiya dynasty—which merged with the Indian
Dominion on 1 January 1948—and, like many other ex-princes,
entered politics, joining the Congress with great hopes. His
hopes of uplifting the tribes were, unfortunately, dashed by
none other than the ruling Congress in the undivided Madhya
Pradesh.

Deo became an MLA in 1957 from Jagdalpur constituency
of Bastar on a Congress ticket. He provided his subjects, or
people, the political leadership required to fight corruption in
land allotment and other livelihood issues of the backward
area and thus became hugely popular. While he was fighting
to get justice for the tribes, the then Congress government in
the state took him as a political adversary. Sensing no scope
of a future for himself and the tribes in the Congress's scheme
of things, he formed his own outfit and fielded 10 independent
candidates in the 1962 Assembly elections and won nine seats
from Bastar.[10] This probably widened the gap further between
him and the state Congress leadership to an irreparable extent.

Support for him among the Bastar tribes was swelling; he
was truly a very popular raja among the indigenous groups.
People would worship the young raja like a god, much to
the chagrin of other prominent politicians and also some
bureaucrats who were close to the chief minister. He was seen
as a thorn in the flesh of the Congress. According to journalist
N. Rajan, the Congress government penalised Bhanj Deo for
his wayward political loyalty by appointing a 'court of wards'
to manage his property. Pravir Chandra was therefore in a
combative mood since 1961 when he had been arrested while
returning from Delhi on 11 February. His younger brother
was announced to be the next maharaja. He was also eager to
free his property from octopus-like grip of the court of wards!

Deo's anger was directed towards the unresponsive government. Eventually, his property was released on 30 July 1963.

Between 1961 and 1966, several episodes occurred which further proved how strained his relationship with the local administration was, but the tribes always stood by him. He had personally met and had complained to the Union home minister Govind Ballabh Pant in 1961 about issues being faced by the tribal community in Bastar. Once when he was returning from Delhi in 1966 (some allege it was after meeting Prime Minister Indira Gandhi and complaining about the state meddling in his family affairs, but that has not been confirmed. He did try to meet Home Minister Gulzarilal Nanda who refused to meet him), the Raja was driven to despair, it was said.[11] And what he was planning remained with him as he was soon killed thereafter in a gruesome police firing that took place inside his palace. An IPS officer, V.N. Singh, was the head of the local police force whereas 'Maharaj' Virbhadra Singh, divisional commissioner, Raipur, was a scion of the Dungarpur royal family.

As many as 11 indigenous people were also killed on the spot on that ill-fated day. Apparently, these people had gathered at the palace to have a 'darshan' of their debonair and well-behaved Maharaja, who had been cooped up inside the palace for long. The police did not allow the restive mob an entry into the palace premises but as the pressure mounted and the number of people shouting slogans ballooned, they opened indiscriminate fire after an arrow hit a police constable who died on the spot. The melee that ensued witnessed one of the most brutal killings in Madhya Pradesh, in broad daylight on 25 March 1966.

Very few journalists were working in Bastar in those days, which was the biggest district of the 10-year-old state and also a laggard one. And the few scribes of provincial papers who were present there were not allowed to file their reports.

Electricity, whatever little there was in the mid-'60s, was also reportedly cut off on the night of the massacre so that the bodies could be shifted clandestinely by the police in the dark. Reports said at least 55 people died in the firing but officially only 11 deaths were declared in the Assembly by Chief Minister Mishra on 26 March 1966. A senior and seasoned journalist, N. Rajan, of *The Hitavada*, a prominent daily from Nagpur, could, however, reach the spot only two days later and filed lengthy reports to his newspaper and also to Mumbai's famous weekly *Blitz*. They were almost like an eye-witness account. The *Blitz* gave the headline: 'Jallianwala Bagh re-enacted in Bastar.' The matter became a national political issue instantly. In his book, *Without Fear: A Journalist's Diary*, Rajan wrote:

> The palace presented a frightening picture. The walls were riddled with bullets and there were bloodstains everywhere. It was obvious that the police, in massive numbers, ran amuck. Pravirchandra Bhanjdeo, it appeared, was the target. His body was found... in his chamber, dragged by tribals after he was fired from behind. The police, right from the morning of 25 March, surrounded the palace. It was a well calculated siege. It is true that hundreds of tribals had gathered at the palace and they occasionally aimed arrows at the police. The tribals were there to protect their ruler. The police lost their balance seeing one constable killed and they went on firing. When exactly was the Raja was killed is not known. Presumably, he was done to death on 25 March evening.[12]

The Madhya Pradesh assembly was in its budget session at Bhopal when, on the last day, a dramatic and brief announcement was made by the chief minister and even as the opposition wanted to speak and sought the details of the police firing and the killing of the Maharaja, the Speaker adjourned the session leaving no scope for a debate on an issue of such an urgent importance that had rocked the nation. Of course, a judicial inquiry was ordered later and a commission under Justice Kanhiyalal Pandey conducted the inquiry.

D.P. Mishra, the chief minister, who was very active in national politics, was accused by the Opposition of eliminating Bhanj Deo in order to send a loud and clear political message to all the erstwhile princes and royal families to stay within their limits. Critical statements against the Chief Minister were not only issued from Bhopal but also from other parts of the country, such was the impact of the killing. The chief minister's direct involvement was never ever proved but charges flew thick and fast then. Mishra would abhor any opposition to his ideas and working style. And after Indira Gandhi had become the prime minister, D.P. Mishra became literally unassailable as the chief minister. And very powerful.

Ramchandra Guha, a renowned historian, has a different story about this unforgettable incident of Madhya Pradesh. He says:

Food scarcity in the district of Bastar, in Central India, had sparked a popular movement led by the deposed Maharaja, Pravi[r] Chandra Bhanj Deo. Chandra and his followers claimed that prosperity would return only when he, the rightful heir, was returned to the throne. The Maharaja was traditionally regarded as quasi-divine, as the key intermediary between the people and their gods... There were a series of protests asking for his restoration and then on 25 March, a several-thousand-strong people marched on the old capital Jagdalpur. A battle broke out between the tribals [sic], using bows and arrows, and the police using tear-gas and bullets...

Among those killed was Pravi(r) Chandra. This was, to quote the chief minister [of MP]—writing to the home minister in New Delhi—a 'tragic incident', 'shocking and regrettable'.[13] [Guha has repeatedly used the name as Pravi and not Pravir]

Rajmata Scindia writes in her autobiography that Bhanj Deo had come to meet her in the middle of February in Delhi but the two could not meet as she had left for Bombay. A few days later, a hoarding (such outdoor publicity by newspapers was unheard of then) of a newspaper in Delhi was read by her son Madhavrao Scindia and Bal Angre while they were driving in a car. It screamed 'Bastar Ruler Killed in Police Firing.' Both were aghast as it was just a few days ago that Angre had carried the Raja's message to Vijaya Raje for an audience which of course could not take place.

What kind of help did the tribal Raja want from the more affluent and powerful Rajmata? Was she in a position to help him? Could she have saved his life in some way? All these questions are unfortunately buried in history and have gone away with the slain Maharaja.

'What actually happened on 25 March 1966 no one will ever know. But one thing seems clear, Pravir Chandra was killed *inside* his palace, which means that his killers had entered the premises', Vijaya Raje later wrote in greater details in her biography under a chapter 'Tragedy in Bastar'. Shaken from within by the Bastar genocide, she, however, appeared to be in two minds at this stage about whether to continue in the Congress or not.

She further stated:

> but if what happened in Bastar shocked me, the indifference of my party's leadership shocked me even more. There were subtle pressures to sweep the whole mess under the carpet, to make out that it was an act of wholly justified by the circumstances. I made no secret of my disgust. But of course one does not quit lightly a political party of which one has been a member for nearly ten years.[14]

And what about Chief Minister Mishra? Was he suffering from guilt from within? Perhaps! His political memoirs, which speak of many events in greater detail during his tenure, including those in Delhi, surprisingly, have no mention of this major tragedy that took place when he was the head of the state! He is mysteriously silent on this episode.

The gory incident had a rippling effect on the other royals, especially those who were not getting along well with D.P. Mishra or with the Congress. Chief among them, of course, was Rajmata Scindia who had to protect her Gwalior interests at all costs.

VIJAYA RAJE'S SMART MOVE

Overcoming the grim nightmare of Bastar, which had badly shaken her from within, was not easy. Royal solidarity with the Bastar state and its young Maharaja notwithstanding, as a sensitive woman she was quite perturbed at the way he was killed inside his home by the state police machinery for no apparent fault of his.

Within weeks, the Rajmata got busy with the marriage of her only son. It was going to be a grand affair by all means and she was totally immersed in its preparations. Madhavrao Scindia's marriage was solemnized on 9 May 1966 with Madhavi Raje, the daughter of the Rana family from Nepal. The ceremonies took place in the Scindia house in Delhi where a large number of Indian and foreign dignitaries participated, besides most of the former princes and families in their Royal fineries. President Dr S. Radhakrishnan and Prime Minister Indira Gandhi, among many others, blessed the newly-wed couple.

The Rajmata writes in her autobiography that in a few days she was to meet Indira Gandhi at the famous hill resort of Pachmarhi during an Indian Youth Congress (IYC) rally. General elections were round the corner and thus the prime minister's visit was important to galvanise the rank and file of the party. All the bigwigs of Madhya Pradesh Congress were dutifully assembled there. She details in her book how D.P. Mishra attacked the princely families of Madhya Pradesh, specifically targeting her since she was present in the audience. He continued to blame the rajas and maharajas of not participating in democracy, effectively telling them that they were not worthy of being trusted. He sent a strongly worded message at a political rally on the eve of the elections. But that was D.P. Mishra, much less diplomatic than required of him on a forum like that. The Rajmata felt angry at being put on the spot by him but was determined not to get defeated.

The Pachmarhi gathering of the IYC, held sometime in May–June 1966, was organized by Arjun Singh, a protege of Mishra. He was the convenor of the IYC then, and went on to become a powerful chief minister (1980–85) of Madhya Pradesh. Mahesh Joshi, a former minister in Singh's cabinet who was also the first elected president of the IYC in Madhya Pradesh in 1968–69, recalls the Pachmarhi conclave and says 'CM would invariably go to the summer capital, near Bhopal and stay there for weeks together, something no CM can afford to do even in today's technologically much advanced times.' Joshi who was close to Mishra, although a much junior Congress worker, says direct elections to the frontal organisations would not happen then, appointments would be done in the state units from Delhi in consultation with CMs and as such Arjun Singh was the in charge of the youth wing. 'I faintly remember the spat between CM *Saab* and Rajmataji but frankly did not understand its political repercussions as I was a very young volunteer then,' admits an ailing Joshi, then 82 years of age.[15] Joshi passed away on 9 April 2021 in Bhopal.

On the political plain, this significant event did not augur well for an otherwise confident but high-handed Dr Mishra, and his government, which was sailing smooth and steady with no apparent threat looming over its head until then. Actually, many see the Pachmarhi incident, coming close on the heels of Bastar, as a major turning point in the political history of the state as it was from here that the sedate and religious-minded Rajmata got not only angry but decided that enough was enough. Yet another opportunity was waiting in the wings for her.

BROKEN GATE AND STUDENTS' AGITATION

Chief Minister Mishra may never have thought that a students' agitation in Gwalior, in which one lost his life, would eventually pull away his government from under his feet. But there was a history to it.

An innocuous incident of a truck accidentally breaking the entry gate of the Gwalior Polytechnic College had irked the students and soon arson and looting began. Law enforcement personnel, led by M. Natrajan, the superintendent of police, beat up the law breakers and this snowballed into a full-fledged agitation enraging the students no end.[16]

This had happened only a few weeks ago; a raja had been killed in police shoot-out and a number of innocent indigenous people had also fallen to police bullets in Bastar. In spite of the horrible happening, the mighty Mishra had remained unruffled. In the students' matter, too, he was in no mood to wilt under any pressure, as was his wont, and when the Gwalior MP, Vijaya Raje, tried to intervene, the chief minister asked her to keep her hands off it and let him deal with the agitation in his way. He even refused to meet a delegation of students.

'We had gone to Bhopal on the orders of the Rajmata to meet the CM and sort out things. When we went to the capital from Gwalior, the CM met us very causally and did not have the courtesy to offer of us a chair and listen to our grouse,' recalls 76-year-old Dhyanendra Singh, of the time he first visited Bhopal as a student. He, with his friends J.P.

Sharma, Dhirendra Singh Baghel and Chandrakant Mandhre, were active in the Gwalior agitation, among others. Dhyanendra Singh, a former BJP minister from Madhya Pradesh, is the half-brother of Rajmata Scindia—born to the same father but different mothers.

Students were expecting their elected leader to lend them support. Being a local MP, the Rajmata could not have afforded to remain aloof, so she had already rushed to Gwalior from Bombay upon hearing of the death of a student and was camping there to ensure that peace returned to the city. But that was not to be. As politics took over, she found herself in a catch-22 situation. While the police atrocities and use of force was growing by the day, the agitation soon spread in other areas of the state making things difficult for the government. 'I had an awful feeling that I had placed myself in the identical position to the Maharaja of Bastar,' she wrote at one place, while referring to the tight spot she found herself in.[17]

Old Congress leaders recall how the agitation spread like wildfire, finally forcing an agitated Vijaya Raje to take a students' delegation to meet the top leaders in Delhi, including Education Minister M.C. Chagla and Prime Minister Indira Gandhi. But nothing could move an obstinate Mishra. Not even a statement from leading Gandhian J.B. Kriplani in support of the student community.

Well after two months of the agitation and closure of education institutions and public opinion having turned against the popular government, the chief minister mellowed down a bit. As better sense prevailed, he ordered opening of the schools and colleges one after the other.

As far as Vijaya Raje was concerned, she was convinced that she was unable to do much, as a ruling party MP, for the welfare of people, in the given circumstances. She felt she was being pushed into a corner by the chief minister who did not like her at all. The Pachmarhi insult was also pricking her every now and then. She felt bad that she hadn't been able to prevent the Bastar tragedy, nor help the Gwalior students. She wrote about how she had made up her mind about the Congress, after her failure to provide justice to the student community, owing to a convoluted stand taken by the chief minister. She was feeling guilty from within and perhaps even weak and helpless.

4

The Scindias and the Hindu Right Wing

Politics in India has transformed in a big way over the past few decades, especially after the 1980s. Umpteen national- and state-level political parties with various ideologies and agendas have sprung up in almost every state. Convenient coalitions have also been formed from time to time, to oppose either the Congress or the BJP—the two main parties with a dominant presence on the political canvas since the last three decades. As a result, political workers and their leaders now have more room to go from one party to another—I would term it 'political portability!'

A political party's philosophy, position taken on issues, historical stands, manifestos, ideologies, etc., are no longer as sacrosanct as they once were. Parties are now as easily discarded or changed as one's clothes. Abiding faith in ideologies or strong following of a leader is a thing of the past, barring a few honourable exceptions. This is a stark reality, and no party can deny it. The 'Aaya Ram Gaya Ram' culture in politics, as it was jocularly called in Hindi after the Haryana episode when Chief Minister Bansi Lal engineered defections, was said to be actually first introduced by Charan Singh (1902–1987) in Uttar Pradesh. He had defected from the Congress in 1967 after his talks with Indira Gandhi had failed. In the process, he not only took along 17 MLAs with him, but he also formed the Jana Congress Party and succeeded in becoming the chief minister of the largest and most populated Indian state.

He was faithful to the Congress for over 35 years and then switched loyalties when he saw an opportunity to grow. The ambitious farmers' leader, a decade later, used the same tactic to become the prime minister after the Emergency—this time taking support of his bête noire Indira Gandhi. Charan Singh dislodged the ruling prime minister Morarji Desai in July 1979 and succeeded him. Shortly after that, Jayaprakash Narayan, the uniting force behind the quarrelling factions of the ruling coalition, passed away. Charan Singh remained in the office for just six months as the Congress pulled the plug when it suited them the most.

But such instances were still considered relatively rare compared to the politically unstable India of the '90s and later. Leaders like Sharad Pawar of the Nationalist Congress Party (NCP) and Mamata Banerjee of the Trinamool Congress (TMC) left the Congress to form their own regional parties in Maharashtra and West Bengal respectively and were decently successful. In 2021, both parties were in power in their states.

And in Haryana of the late '60s, it was a more hilarious story. In his book, *Behind Closed Doors: Politics of Punjab, Haryana and the Emergency,* seasoned journalist B.K. Chum states that in the house of 81 Assembly members, 44 per cent of the MLAs had defected—one five times, two four times, three thrice, four twice and 34 once during the political turbulence of 1966–68 in that small Jat land, carved out from Punjab in November 1966.[1] Bansi Lal (1927–2006), (three times chief minister: 1968–1975, 1986–1987 and 1996–1999), finally provided the much-needed stability when he was sworn in for the first time as the chief minister in May 1968.

Thus, making a decision to quit the ruling Congress for an option of sitting in the opposition ranks was a big and risky step for the Rajmata by any standard. When she mentally prepared herself to sever the ties with the Congress for reasons explained in earlier chapters, her real dilemma began to bother her. Which party to join? Who will accept her? Would she be able to adjust to their political ideology?

There are many accounts available in contemporary political history of Madhya Pradesh, suggesting that she pulled down the D.P. Mishra government soon after leaving the Congress and that too out of personal vendetta and to grab the most coveted post of chief minister. Her own accounts, however, contradict that theory. That she was not comfortable with the wily Mishra was an open secret in the political circles, but she made it clear that she found herself unfit in the Congress party only gradually and began looking for an alternative which came in the shape of an opportunity—the 1967 general elections, just after the Pachmarhi episode where a senior Angre had played a little role but had failed.

Veteran journalist Vir Sanghvi asks a few pertinent questions in his book, *Madhavrao Scindia: A Life*, co-authored by Namita Bhandare, such as, 'Why did Vijaya Raje Scindia leave the Congress? Why did she not stay and fight Mishra? And was her decision solely predicated on a factional fight within MP politics?'

'It is hard to say', he himself clarifies. 'It is true that she regarded it difficult to dislodge Mishra within the Congress, given his connections with Indira Gandhi. But it is also true that she never really subscribed to the Congress ideology with its emphasis on socialism and secularism. At heart she was self-confessed Hindu Mahasabhaite.'[2]

Her late husband Jiwajirao was a Hindu sympathizer and patron; Scindia's original seat of power for decades was the temple town of Ujjain, known to be a great ancient religious city that hosts Simhastha every 12 years. There is a strong relationship between the Mahakaleshwar (Lord Shiva) Temple, one of the important 12 Jyotirlingas in India, and the Scindia family. Present scion of the dynasty, Jyotiraditya goes to Ujjain each year to take part and perform the traditional religious duties, just like his forefathers did.

Sanghvi writes further: 'And even if she [Rajmata] was not sure where her sympathies lay, there was no doubt that Sambhajirao Angre, with his far-right-wing political views, was much happier outside the Congress.'[3]

In the mid-'60s, N.K. Shejwalkar (1923–2000), an exceptionally low-profile politician belonging to the Marathi middle class, was the Jana Sangh chief in Madhya Pradesh. He hailed from Gwalior and was an RSS activist with a clean image, unlike many of today's leaders, who are arrogant, ostentatious and corrupt. He went on to become Gwalior's mayor and then also its MP in 1977 and 1980. He knew Vijaya Raje well and when he got the first whiff of the news that the Rajmata was mulling the idea of quitting the Congress, he immediately consulted Kushabhau Thakre (1922–2003), the senior party leader who went on to become the BJP national president in late '90s when Atal Bihari Vajpayee was the prime minister.[4]

The two then met Sardar Sambhaji Angre (1920–2008), a descendant of the Maratha admiral Kanhoji Angre and Vijaya Raje's political advisor and her husband's distant relative, at Shejwalkar's Gwalior residence in the Lashkar area before meeting her to know her intentions for future elections. A fledgling Jana Sangh was desperate to have a toe-hold in the Gwalior region which was clearly under the heavy influence of the royal family as has been elaborated in the earlier two elections. An electoral alliance with the Rajmata was not easy, as some of her followers were not keen on joining the Jana Sangh.

But those who knew of the prevailing political conditions then aver something different. For example, Vivek Shejwalkar, N.K. Shejwalkar's son, recalls that it was the Rajmata's son Madhavrao who first took the membership of the Jana Sangh, at the hands of Vajpayee, later an MP from Gwalior (1971). After the initial rounds of talks, young Madhavrao was also involved in the confabulations with Angre and others about the future course to be taken by his mother.

The matter was finally referred to Pt Deendayal Upadhyaya (1916–1968), the then national president of the right-wing party and one who was overseeing the election management at the all-India level. It was he who gave the green signal for the talks and then for an alliance and seat adjustment, etc., which was eventually implemented when the Rajmata decided to quit the Congress. Chandikadas Amritrao 'Nanaji' Deshmukh (1916–2010), an RSS ideologue and Bharat Ratna recipient (posthumous) in 2019, who had set up the Deendayal Research Institute (DRI) in Delhi and the one who promoted rural development models, also played a key a role in taking the Rajmata to the Jana Sangh, local veterans in Gwalior recall.

The issue of funding the candidates in the elections was supposed to have been tricky but it was amicably settled, as the Jana Sangh candidates did not expect financial support from the Rajmata, something she was habitual of doing while being in the Congress.[5] She used to generously support other candidates of her party in the neighbouring areas by making Mahindra jeeps (perhaps the only brand of vehicles dominant in the markets then) available for campaigning. Arrangement of a vehicle or two for campaigning for a month was just out of bounds for an ordinary candidate of the Jana Sangh in those days.

Those were the days when the state assembly elections and the parliamentary polls used to take place generally simultaneously and at regular intervals of five years. On the eve of the elections in 1967, Vijaya Raje had to make the most crucial decision of her future political career—which opposition party to join after quitting the ruling Congress? It was not an easy task for a lady of her stature, and who had lost her husband a few years ago and had to look after a son and four daughters, besides managing sprawling properties and other riches. It was naturally not an easy riddle to solve.

In contemporary politics, there were not many such instances before this, showing what she actually did in 1967. Leaders normally junk and dump an opposition party to join the ruling party for the obvious advantages that come along— the trappings of the ruling party.

But Vijaya Raje performed a novel political experiment, an attempt more or less unheard of before! That year she fought two elections simultaneously—one for State Assembly (Karera constituency in Shivpuri district) to be an MLA and another for Lok Sabha (from Guna constituency) to be an MP! Well, the catch did not lie here but in what she finally did.

In what can perhaps be termed as a rare first, she fought the State Assembly polls on a Bharatiya Jana Sangh symbol and for the parliamentary polls, she chose a relatively new political grouping, the Swatantra Party (founded in 1959), also a right-wing outfit, supported by Mumbai industrialists and a few princes. Such a move, in those days, was an unparalleled happening and also suggested how opposition parties were ready to welcome her and adjust with each other despite the fact that she had not joined either of the parties as a formal primary member.[6]

The Jana Sangh could have objected to her standing on the Swatantra Party symbol or Rajaji could have put a condition that she could not contest on the Jana Sangh symbol in the same election. However, both parties were sworn enemies of the formidable Congress. Anti-Congressism as a political thought and a movement had already been born by then. Be it because of her stature or their own electoral needs, both parties bowed to her unique conditions. The election laws were not as stringent as they are today, a factor that also supported her make such a decision.

There are no prizes to guess the poll outcome.

She won both the elections with big margins. In Guna, she defeated D.K. Jadhav (Congress) by an astonishing margin of 1.86 lakh votes (about 79 per cent) and in Karera, her victory margin over nearest rival Gautam Sharma (Congress) was about 36,000 votes. These were the two elections in which her son Madhavrao alias Bhaiya and her daughter Usha, had vigorously canvassed for their mother. It was also during these elections that Madhavrao cut his teeth in politics at the young age of 22. The two young royal siblings managed to create a big wave in support of their mother, not wanting to take any chance, as she was fighting for the first time on two parties' symbols and none of them was the Congress for which she had won the two previous elections. Both Usha and Madhavrao turned out to be the star attractions among the crazy rural masses of the two constituencies as they had rarely come out of their palace to mingle with huge crowds until then. Sanghvi observed that at a national level, the Rajmata would be given more weightage as a Swatantra MP, but in Madhya Pradesh, it was the Jana Sangh that rose as a strong contender.[7]

A mention of Kushabhau Thakre (1922–2003) would not be out of place; in fact, it is essential to put things in the right perspective to help notice the subtle changes in the Indian political scenario over the years. He was an extremely simple, principled political leader of all times. Thakre was a quintessential organization man who led an exceptionally spartan life and represented the true RSS-Jana Sangh leader traits, which are almost extinct now from the public life at large. He would tour extensively across India, was media-friendly and had a great sense of humour (something rare in this party). He would go to any party worker's home and eat simple, homely food with them. Although a man with a serious outlook, he would also give in to hearty laughs when he was amongst journalists. He was a bachelor and a full-time Swayamsevak of the RSS who was later drafted to the Jana Sangh (which later became the BJP in 1980).

L.K. Advani, in his biography, has written about the interesting days when he, Vajpayee, Kushabhau Thakre, Sunder Singh Bhandari and others were busy raising the party from scratch. Kushabhau's organizational skills were unmatched; much of the existence that the BJP has today is owing to his hard work in Madhya Pradesh. He played a pivotal role in bringing the Rajmata into the BJP fold through his matured political understanding and stature. Thakre has gone on record to say:

> Rajmata Scindia did not leave the Congress because she wanted to become the chief minister which she could have easily become when she was at the height of her popularity. Her fight with D.P. Mishra was on principles and she did not want to be in a party that had a corrupt image.[8]

Incidentally, Kushabhau and the Rajmata both understood each other well and their association strengthened the BJP in Madhya Pradesh exceedingly well. Later, Sunder Lal Patwa, an RSS volunteer, (1924–2016) would also join them, besides Pyarelal Khandelwal (1925–2009). Patwa later became the chief minister twice and a union minister in the Vajpayee government at the Centre and earned a reputation of being a tough taskmaster and an able administrator in Madhya Pradesh, though a rung below Om Prakash Sakhlecha, an otherwise unsung BJP leader and ex-chief minister.

THE DRAMA

The Constitution of India and the prevailing electoral laws required Vijaya Raje, or any other elected politician for that matter, to quit one of the two seats she had won. Since she had bagged both seats, she could keep only one. Having been already to the parliament twice before, perhaps there was no craze in going there yet another time when in Madhya Pradesh, the Jana Sangh needed her badly in the Assembly. Hence, she gave up her Guna parliamentary seat, and fielded J.B. Kripalani on the Swatantra Party symbol in the by-election caused by her vacancy. He also registered a facile win despite being an outsider, defeating Subhadra Joshi of the Congress by over 1.38 lakh votes.

D.P. Mishra's majority in the Assembly was not precariously thin, with ruling Congress winning 167 seats out of 296 seats and the Jana Sangh bagging 78 with others having 42 MLAs.[9] But with the Rajmata deciding in favour of being an opposition MLA rather than being a Swatantra Party MP, Mishra began to have sleepless nights. Once she was sworn in as a member of the State Assembly, she instantly emerged as the towering leader and a rallying point for many disgruntled MLAs, thanks to her stature and new-found aura of political acuity who had left a party like the Congress.

One such 'disgruntled' MLA was the senior leader, Dr Govind Narayan Singh (1920–2005) from Baghelkhand. His father, Captain Awadhesh Pratap Singh, was the first chief minister of Vindhya Pradesh. Both father and son had been jailed during the 1942 Quit India movement, led by Mahatma Gandhi. As a staunch Congress leader, Govind Narayan Singh had initially supported Mishra in garnering votes in the Vindhya belt and other regions of the state. At one point of time, he had gathered as many as 105 MLAs in support of Mishra to help him become the chief minister.[9]

Singh was a deputy minister in Bhagwantrao Mandloi's ministry and as Mishra became the chief minister, Singh got the important portfolio of home department and later a cabinet berth. Both Mishra and Govind Narayan Singh were men of principles, well educated to boot, with an excellent command over English, albeit with fairly high egos and pride in themselves. Both were postgraduates and PhDs of the British time. But surely, Singh had a better ground-level connect with the party workers of the far-flung state than Mishra who would mostly live in his own 'glass house.'

What could have been expected of such talented and principled but 'political' people? Nothing less than a personality clash and tussle! And that's what happened. Due to differences in the working style and other political issues, an ambitious Singh was dropped from the Council of Ministers by Mishra in 1967. An angry Singh had written a detailed letter complaining to Indira Gandhi against his own 'boss' with a copy marked to Chief Minister Mishra himself. It was not a secret complaint. Clearly, politics in those days was a shade better than what it deteriorated to in the next decades—not in the Congress alone but in all parties!

'If roles had been reserved and Govind Narain Singh had been in his [Mishra's] place, frank talk with a few unliterary words interspersed would have cleared the air once and for all...but Mishraji was not Govind Narain Singh,' writes R.P. Noronha (only ICS officer selected in the CP and Berar cadre in 1938), who served as chief secretary under both the chief ministers—Mishra and Singh.[11]

Singh floated, among the first few of the Indian regional parties, his own group, the Lok Sevak Dal. He scripted his name in MP's political history after he shook hands with the Rajmata who was now a part of the Jana Sangh and defected from Congress to form the Samyukta Vidhayak Dal (SVD), thus upsetting the Congress applecart in an unprecedented move. The story goes like this: in a sudden move, many MLAs raised their hands at the behest of Govind Narayan Singh and announced that they were leaving the Congress and they crossed over to the opposition benches while the Assembly session was still on. A flabbergasted Speaker Kashi Prasad Pandey and Chief Minister Mishra tried their best to prevent it but could do little. Dr Singh's influence was such that those who were in two minds also could not say no and followed him from the treasury benches to the Opposition benches at the Minto Hall Assembly. The chief minister saw everything helplessly and then slowly walked out of the House. His government was toppled in a swift series of events that had been meticulously planned. He was down but not quite out, yet.

In this way, Govind Narayan Singh became the fifth chief minister of India's sprawling state of Madhya Pradesh with the support of Rajmata Scindia on 30 July 1967. This bolt rattled the world of politics and politicians not only in the state; but also came as a rude shock to Prime Minister Indira Gandhi, for whom Mishra was a close confidante at a time when she was a relatively new prime minister. Around that time, she was still reeling under the impact of a sudden revolt by Charan Singh that had taken place just a few months earlier, in May 1967 in Uttar Pradesh. Around the same time, she also had to manage the new and unstable state of Haryana. In Uttar Pradesh, it was an SVD government formed by rebels; in Madhya Pradesh, a few months later, in an almost similar coup 'Chanakya' Mishra was overthrown.

Interestingly, it was not Singh, the newly appointed chief minister who hogged the limelight. Vijaya Raje Scindia stole the march over Singh in this sensational game that had made national headlines. Without her support, Govind Narayan could not have dared do such an act; after all, he had lots of regards for Mishra who he occasionally called 'uncle.' But as Ashok Singh, his son, corroborates what journalist-editor Mayaram

Surjan wrote in his famous Hindi book *Mukhyamantri Madhya Pradesh Ke* (*Chief Ministers of Madhya Pradesh*), Govind Narayan Singh vowed to do the *terahvi* (thirteenth day ritual of the dead as per Hindu religious practice). In other words, Govind Narayan was out to unseat and politically finish Mishra. Ashok, an engineering graduate and a businessman in Bhopal, recalls the message his father gave out loudly in Bagheli, a local dialect, to his supporters, while starting off in his jeep on that June afternoon at Rampur Baghelan (Satna) soon after winding up the religious chores. Mourning period over, it was time to return to the real politic. His father gone, Singh now had no political boss to rein him in against the sitting chief minister 'Uncle Mishra.' Noronha has also briefly touched upon this topic.

The Rajmata had been upset with Mishra for not consulting with her on the Gwalior tickets—some 50–55 in all—among many other accumulated grievances, elaborated by me in the earlier chapters. She had an axe to grind and Singh was more than willing to do what was required. This is how the SVD was born, and history was made in the central Indian state. As Noronha writes:

> Hell hath no fury like a woman scorned. If Mishraji did not scorn the Rajmata of Gwalior, at least his procedures justified her belief that he did so. The Congress candidates for the 1967 election from the former Gwalior state were selected without consulting her and even her suggestion for a discussion on the subject was brusquely rejected. Considering that the only chance for Congress candidates to win in that area was through the support of the House of Scindia, her suggestion was not unreasonable.[12]

The result was such that Congress could not win a single seat, as Vijaya Raje had resigned from the party and had fielded candidates of her own choice. She made a clean sweep. The

Congress drew a blank in that area because of Scindia's impregnable dominance. While Mishra was opposed to feudal rulers, he conveniently took the help of the Rewa maharaja to win a few seats in the Vindhya region, thus exposing his hypocrisy. There is also an interesting story told to this author by a serving bureaucrat under D.P. Mishra. And I must mention it here. M.K. Ranjitsinh, a 1961 batch IAS officer, was posted as the district collector in what was categorized as among the 'first posting districts' of Madhya Pradesh at Dhar, in 1967. Since Dhar also fell under the old Scindia (Gwalior) state, Ranjitsinh, a scion of the Wakaner princely state of Gujarat, went to meet Shrimant Madhavrao Scindia who had gone to Dhar to campaign for his mother's candidates. The news of the collector meeting Scindia reached D.P. Mishra and in the next transfer list of officers Ranjitsinh was shifted from Dhar to another 'first posting district' tribe-dominated, rural place like Mandla, as a collector, against the wishes of the then chief secretary Noronha.

After his first posting in a backward district, an IAS officer would normally be moved to a better district as the collector. 'Clearly, my meeting with Scindia was frowned upon,' he said. That Ranjitsinh had always aspired to go to Mandla out of his passion for wildlife, was of course not known to the chief minister. Sinh, now 85, is India's leading wildlife expert today, who had cut his teeth in Kanha National Park, situated in the Mandla district in the '60s. 'Do I indirectly owe it to the revolt of the Rajmata that my boyhood dream was realized?' he wondered while recalling the days under D.P. Mishra, in a long chat with the author.

In the Assembly, no sooner had the MLAs made the announcement of joining the Opposition, than acrimonious scenes followed in the well of the house, drowned in complete din and chaos before the Congress MLAs staged a walkout. The remaining head count stood at 155, five more than the majority. Mishra was stunned. As the Rajmata, Singh and their MLAs went to see Governor K.C. Reddy at the Raj Bhawan, just across the road from the Assembly, Chief Minister Mishra also rushed there to complain against what had happened in the House a while ago. However, Reddy did not wilt under the pressure of a mighty chief minister and apparently told the latter that he had lost the majority which he (Mishra) was unable to see. The 'hearteningly independent-minded' governor not only advised the Rajmata to go and meet the president in Delhi as he could not accord her group any kind of recognition at that time, but he also adjourned the house sine die.[12]

Mishra's game plan abjectly failed much before he could draw out his chess board and play his next move.

The Rajmata, using a fraction of her massive resources, organized a fleet of buses to transport 160 MLAs (five more Congress MLAs had joined them a day later or so). All her MLAs were paraded before President Zakir Husain on 20 July 1967, in what was an unprecedented incident. Politically speaking, Madhya Pradesh was generally considered a tranquil, laid-back state. A coup of this kind was like an earthquake on a very high Richter scale. People, politicians and the press were aghast at such bizarre developments.

But the matter did not end on the Raisina Hills of New Delhi. The strength of the parties had to be counted on the floor of the House in Bhopal. Having sensed victory and appearing indefatigable to her colleagues, Vijaya Raje was in great form as she worked day and night. She again took a fleet of buses full of her new political partners back to Bhopal, braving futile physical attacks on the way near Beora. The buses were stopped on the way and Congressmen made efforts to hijack the MLAs, although in vain. In Delhi, she had made arrangements for all the MLAs at a posh Old Delhi heritage hotel, the Oberoi Maidens, and had 'looked after them very well' with the help of Sardar Angre.

On 28 July, the floor test had to take place and for that purpose the Assembly session was called again. Tension filled the air. The result of the fresh counting of the MLAs and their affiliation came out openly after the test could be done only on 31 July in which the Raje-Singh combo mustered up support of as many as 153 against Mishra's 136. Desperate to save face, he had mounted a vigorous campaign to have the House dissolved. Had the campaign been successful, he would have won that round of the battle and would have come back into the game. Noronha writes in his book that Mishra had no inkling of what was being done in Delhi and he largely relied on Indira Gandhi, who had made open statements about the possible dissolution of the Assembly. Little did he realize that he also had opponents within his own party. His party bigwigs in Delhi saw through the game and found that the 'Chanakya' had been defeated in his game; they did not permit him to dissolve the house. Y.B. Chavan and S.K. Patil tacitly supported the Rajmata—some believe it was the Maratha solidarity. A Goliath was being lethally attacked and finished. The spectacle was so rare that it galvanized all the opposition parties into a semblance of unity instantly and ensured a historic win for the newly formed SVD.

With Mishra's chips down, the Rajmata was on the top of the world. Soon demands began to be raised that she be made head of the government, that is, the chief minister. Sources known to her say she never had had that post in mind and when she was suggested and pressurized, she stood her ground and declined the offer steadfastly. Instead, she made the experienced minister of the Mishra cabinet and her new political friend, Govind Narayan Singh, the chief minister of the nascent Samyukta Vidhayak Dal (SVD), a grouping which was kind of a fashion of the day.

Singh remained as the chief minister from 30 July 1967 to 12 March 1969. But in an unprecedented move, the Rajmata was elected the leader of House, a post invariably meant for the chief minister to help control the Assembly proceedings, along with the Speaker. This has happened only once in Madhya Pradesh in all these decades. Whether it was a power-sharing formula or respect shown to the Rajmata is unclear. It can be assumed that mostly it was the latter as she had already declined to be the chief minister, a fact shared publicly by Kushabhau Thakre then and on many occasions later.

Singh, a traditional, seasoned and committed Congress leader would not have joined this coup but for his father's death around the same time. Had his father been alive (Captain Awadhesh Pratap Singh had passed away in June 1967), Govind Narayan Singh, despite sharp differences with Mishra, would still have been with the Congress, thanks to the ideological grip the father had had on the son. It's a different thing that two out of his five sons, Dhruv Narayan Singh and Harsh Singh, a four-time MLA, eventually joined the BJP and became MLAs at different points in time. Harsh, now 70, shifted to the BJP as he was denied a ticket by the Congress in 2003. Later, Harsh Singh's son Vikram Singh also became an MLA from BJP in 2018 from Rampur Baghelan—a pocket borough of the political dynasty of his late grandfather who always won from here.

◆

A story is often told that the Delhi leaders of the Congress party, despite having received a severe setback, showed great restraint and patience; they allowed the Singh government the requisite space and time. They knew it would fall due to its inherent contradictions. A few ministers and leaders were regularly in touch with the chief minister, trying to wean him away from the influence of the Rajmata in an effort to break the alliance at Indira Gandhi's behest. And when Govind Narayan Singh was assured of an unconditional entry back into the Congress by the leadership in Delhi, he did not blink twice and quickly herded back as many MLAs as he could to the Congress stable. The SVD government fell instantly in March 1969, under its own weight, as the MLAs switched their loyalty again to their parent party. The new political experiment proved a little too ephemeral. One of the reasons for Singh's return to the Congress fold was also the fact that he had found running the coalition government a very tough and tricky tightrope walk. He was not seasoned enough to take the diverse flock of birds along, especially the Jana Sangh leaders.

Naturally, the Scindia faction was downcast. They had to sit in opposition as the new chief minister, Raja Nareshchandra Singh, also a follower of the Rajmata and a former ruler of the Sarangarh royal family was anointed—just from 13 March to 25 March 1969. He too could not run the government. He was the sixth chief minister of Madhya Pradesh and had one of the shortest-lived chief ministerships of the country in those days.

MOTHER-SON IN JANA SANGH

In the meantime, the Rajmata had conclusively decided to join the Jana Sangh formally. Her son Madhavrao had already done so in the presence of Shejwalkar, Atalji, Thakre and others. Vivek Shejwalkar made available to me the important document of the Jana Sangh membership receipt of Madhavrao Scindia, dated 23 February 1970 bearing number 81122. He had paid ₹101 to be a member from Murar Mandal of Gwalior. The occupation shown therein was that of a 'farmer.' The person who had made him a member was none other than Atal Bihari Vajpayee. Both had signed on the membership letter, in Hindi. Sunder Lal Patwa, later to be the chief minister, was the state party treasurer, as per the receipt.

This was the time she had internally decided, perhaps after having tasted real political power from close, to remain in politics and would be with a party matching her values and ideologies. A deeply religious person, she would invariably go to saffron-clad saints and babas to show her obeisance; sometimes while going somewhere in her car, she would abruptly stop and take the darshan of a sadhu if spotted on the roadside. Rajmata, especially after having burnt her fingers with the SVD experiment and having been ditched by Govind Narayan Singh, felt that Jana Sangh, a Hindu party, matched with her political convictions. Old timers recall the fact that the Gwalior region was a major citadel of Hindu activists in the '40s through the '60s. There are many instances and events that adequately show that the Hindu Mahasabha and later the RSS had had visible influence in the Marathi belt of Gwalior. One of the earlier sardars of the Scindia durbar, Chandroji Angre was closely associated with the Hindu Mahasabha.

In the next few years, the Lok Sabha elections were round the corner. An astute Rajmata, now quite seasoned in politics, decided to field her 26-year-old son Madhavrao from Guna, her own safe seat and shifted to Bhind, near Gwalior, leaving Gwalior for Atal Bihari Vajpayee. That was in the year 1971. Elections had been advanced by one year as Indira Gandhi was not sure of any possible manoeuvring with a government that was in minority. Her gamble paid off. However, despite Indira Gandhi's popularity wave, the three seats—Guna, Bhind and Gwalior—besides a few others, were comfortably pocketed by the Jana Sangh. While elsewhere the party fared badly, in Madhya Pradesh, it won as many as 11 seats out of a total of 40. Across India, the Jana Sangh could win only 22 seats out of the 157 it had contested. And the lion's share was from Madhya Pradesh. This was a loss of 13 seats compared to the 1967 elections. Contrastingly, the Congress bagged 352 seats, up from 283 in the previous elections. It was a hugely impressive show by the Congress under Mrs Gandhi.[13]

Vajpayee, who hailed from Madhya Pradesh, defeated Gautam Sharma by over 70,000 votes; in the adjoining constituency Guna, Madhavrao humiliated Devrao Krishnarao Jadhav (Congress) by over 1.40 lakh votes and the Rajmata routed the Congress stalwart Narsingh Rao Dixit in Bhind by over 91,000 votes. Bhind was the third Lok Sabha constituency from where the Rajmata had registered a massive victory, the earlier three being Guna (1957 and 1967) and Gwalior (1962)— two of them on the Congress symbol. These were the same elections when she had persuaded Bombay-based press baron Ramnath Goenka to fight from Vidisha, formerly under the Scindia dynasty. She canvassed for him in Vidisha and he also won without much hassle, notwithstanding his 'outsider' tag. That was the Scindia influence.

The 1971 election success converted her permanently into a right-wing Hindu politician who went on to launch the BJP in 1980 as one of the founders and patrons and was immediately made its vice president. She was also anointed as the convenor of the Mahila Morcha (Women's wing) to mobilize women power under the new BJP banner. About this time, she had associated herself with the Vishwa Hindu Parishad (VHP), founded in 1963–64. She would profusely donate funds to them, what with her having a religious bent of mind. The Ram Janmabhoomi agitation had not warmed up then, but it was on the VHP agenda.

The Rajmata came into limelight once again in January 1980 when she contested, or was forced to contest by the Janata Party leadership, against Indira Gandhi from Raebareli Lok Sabha constituency in Uttar Pradesh. She was pushed into a battle royale without her consent, yet again. Across the country, the Rajya Sabha member suddenly became a star attraction who was set to take on Nehru's famous daughter. To her utter dismay, she heard about her being pitted against

Mrs Gandhi on a TV news bulletin. She was sent to Raebareli against her wishes. The Janata Party leaders perhaps assumed it conveniently (and wrongly) that since Indira Gandhi had lost from that constituency in 1977 at the hands of a maverick politician Raj Narain, fielding the Rajmata, a candidate matching Indira Gandhi in her resources and fame, would win them the prestigious seat. They were woefully off the mark!

The BJP was yet to be formed then and the multi-party coalition, with Jana Sangh still as its partner, had ruled the country post the Emergency for three years. But cracks had begun to show up. It appeared that the party, stitched up painstakingly by Jayaprakash Narayan, the saintly politician from Bihar, better known as J.P., was on the verge of a collapse due to ideological bickering and ego-related issues.

The Rajmata lost the multi-cornered contest of Raebareli, in which Charan Singh's party had also fielded a candidate. Indira won with comfortable majority, though she had also fought from Medak in Andhra Pradesh to be on a safer side. Her shrewd advisors had rightly suggested that if a Janata Party heavyweight like the Rajmata had come all the way to Uttar Pradesh to challenge her, it would be politically prudent to have another safe seat lest something goes wrong in Raebareli. Such was the clout of Vijaya Raje. Essentially a north Indian politician, Indira had moved south for the second time. Earlier, she had fought from the Chickmagalur constituency in Karnataka in 1978. Taking a leaf out of her book perhaps, her grandson Rahul Gandhi fought from two constituencies in the 2019 parliamentary polls—Amethi in Uttar Pradesh and Wayanad in Kerala. Quite expectedly, he lost from his family's traditionally-held seat of Amethi in the 'tsunami of Modi' that was witnessed by all in 2019.

In the meantime, for the Rajmata, the loss wasn't just that of the elections, it was a loss of face and stature! Many thought then that the election was heavily rigged, and booth capturing was rampant by agents of the Congress who were desperate to see Indira back as prime minister again. But political observers and writers many years later wrote that the Janata Party's internal bickering and the arrest of Mrs Gandhi (October 1977), among other factors, had swung the mood of the voters completely in favour of Indira, as if they had forgotten all her sins. She emerged as a martyr from just a day's jail term. Her stock suddenly went up in public eye. Morarji Desai, the then prime minister, had greatly fumbled in his political calculations by ordering her arrest, as it seemed then.

Indira was slyly coming back but political strategists of the Janata Party had completely failed to sense the pulse of the people. 'It was for the first time since 1952 that all candidates in Rae Bareli against the Congress had forfeited their deposits,' wrote M.L. Fotedar[14] in his book *The Chinar Leaves: A Political Memoir.* Fotedar, a veteran politician and former union minister, was a close associate of Indira Gandhi and had served as her political secretary from 1980–1984. He had also worked in Raebareli as a party worker deputed by Mrs Gandhi.

She had returned with a bang to be the prime minister once again, though unfortunately only for four years. She was brutally assassinated by her personal bodyguard in October 1984 at her home, resulting in massive anti-Sikh riots all over the country, mainly north India. Many commissions were appointed (and folded up halfway) to probe the riots and the Sikh genocide. A few Congress leaders like H.K.L. Bhagat, Kamal Nath, Sajjan Kumar (convicted by the court) and Jagdish Tytler were charged with leading and inciting mobs in Delhi to attack Sikhs and their families at their homes and in Gurudwaras.

The year 1980 was a landmark year. While the Rajmata chose to stay with the just-founded BJP, formed soon after the disintegration of the Janata Party in April 1980, her son Madhavrao, who had fought his first ever election of 1971 on the Jana Sangh symbol, had joined the Congress by the next election in 1980, with a stopover in 1977, as an independent. During the Emergency (1975–1977), Madhavrao had swiftly moved to Nepal—there are contradictory stories about how he decided to go there—and then perhaps to London. Upon his return, he fell apart, politically speaking, from his mother and, slowly, with his sisters in the years to come. As time wore on, the family divide widened and worsened.

For the first time, the mighty Scindia house was divided vertically.

5

Family Feud: A Mother and Son and their Divergent Political Paths

The sudden promulgation of a 'state of internal Emergency' by invoking Article 352 (1) of the Constitution and the swift use of an old, little-known law, Maintenance of Internal Security Act (MISA) of 1971—brought in to deal with situation during the Bangladesh War—to detain people indefinitely, had shocked not only Indians (activists, politicians, the common man) but also scores of civil liberties activists, lawyers and pro-democracy thinkers abroad. The reason? It was seen to be a very arrogant, high-handed show of suspending the fundamental rights of an individual's free speech and movement, among other things, by the Congress government in 1975. Prime Minister Indira Gandhi's defensive move of unbridled power play that witnessed unprecedented and unlawful actions had clearly throttled the very spirit of democracy in India.

Emergency was Mrs Gandhi's highly arbitrary response to the Allahabad High Court's historic verdict unseating her. The court held her guilty of various electoral malpractices (misusing Prime Minister's Office [PMO] official Yashpal Kapoor's services in the election, etc.) after hearing an election petition from her opponent Raj Narain who had lost the Raebareli parliamentary election of 1971 by over one lakh votes. He wanted to nullify her victory through his petition in the court of Justice Jagmohanlal Sinha who eventually invalidated her victory. Sinha's verdict was roundly criticized by Congressmen and others with all possible allegations that could be levelled against a sitting judge of a high court. Even his effigies were burnt. The Congressmen's harsh reactions were seen to be right to an extent in some sections as she was the first prime minister to have been dragged to a court of law. Congressmen saw an international conspiracy to dethrone her, some even mentioned the Central Intelligence Agency's (CIA) name.

'She stood disqualified through stealt,' wrote M.L. Fotedar, a senior Congress leader, adding, 'This was obviously a conspiracy to unseat her. She chose not to acquiesce to these conspiracies.'[1]

Hundreds and thousands were incarcerated in jails during the 21 months (25 June 1975–21 March 1977) for no rhyme or reason. Politicians, mainly from the Opposition, the rightists, the leftists, the socialists, students, writers, journalists, cartoonists, free thinkers, union leaders, RSS volunteers, the Anand Margis and a whole lot of others found themselves in one or the other jail. The Congress's chief ministers in states like Madhya Pradesh, Haryana, Punjab or Uttar Pradesh and the Lt Governor of Delhi, worked overnight to impress Mrs Gandhi and her son Sanjay by arresting more and more people. Sanjay had usurped the power of the prime minister. The country was completely terror-struck. Law abiding citizens experienced sleepless nights. The press was gagged; young men were forced to undergo vasectomies. The police and other administrative officers enjoyed sweeping powers—they could pick up any one and put them behind bars. No questions asked. Jails were full of 'criminals' whose 'crimes' were known neither to them nor to their family members or their lawyers. Prime Minister Indira Gandhi functioned, legally, as a virtual dictator, as political opponents were hounded by the state machinery.[2]

Rajmata Scindia, with whom Indira Gandhi had many differences, was on top of her 'hit list'. Others such as, Morarji Desai, Jayaprakash Narayan or 'J.P.', Atal Bihari Vajpayee, L.K. Advani, Arun Jaitley, Chandra Shekhar and Maharani Gayatri Devi, the dowager queen of Jaipur, and many MPs were picked up from different places from June 1975 onwards and imprisoned in different cities. The whole exercise was called a 'coup against the Constitution' or to use the words of H.Y. Sharada Prasad—once Indira Gandhi's trusted aide—'Emergency was Indira Gandhi's coup against the Prime Minister.'[3]

Vijaya Raje and Gayatri Devi, both Rajmatas of famous royal houses of Gwalior and Jaipur respectively, were housed in the dreaded Tihar Jail of Delhi during the dark days of the Emergency.

Many believed that the excesses of the Emergency era were not the handiwork of Indira Gandhi alone but of Sanjay and his cronies. Much has already been written on the Emergency and its 'architect.' I would therefore refrain from going into details other than the ones that throw a light on how it deeply affected the Scindias and their politics.

Indeed, if the Emergency had not been imposed—for whatever valid or invalid reasons it—the Scindia House would have perhaps been spared of the ordeal of political separation. An unfortunate, ugly family feud that followed and got blown out of proportion hurting all family members and their umpteen friends, in one way or the other, could have probably been averted. Many Scindia-watchers feel, even today, that the vested interests on both sides succeeded in driving a solid wedge between the pious Vijaya Raje and her son Madhavrao, an educated and sober politician, who was fast emerging as a bright star on the Indian political horizon in mid '70s, having already won his first election from Guna with an impressive margin.

◆

On 25 June 1975, the day the Emergency was declared, a big celebration, for an entirely different reason, was going on at 37, Rajpur Road in New Delhi. It was a sprawling campus, with lots of open space, a big double-storied house in the centre and forest all over inside the exclusive place. It was the twenty-first birthday of a young lady from a royal family. The evening was still young, guests were trickling in late for the party but settling down quickly to enjoy the heady pop music, choicest drinks and games and celebrate their friend's birthday in a style befitting a royal family.

The hostess was an elderly, warm lady accustomed to performing her puja (prayers) late in the evening daily before retiring to bed. Much before the party ended, she had retired for the day. Suddenly, her landline phone rang and she was hurriedly called to attend to it. In a cold, shivering voice, she was passed on the message of the Jana Sangh party General Secretary Madanlal Khurana, who later became the chief minister of Delhi. The message was serious enough for the lady to develop cold feet. 'Flee the place where you are, in the quickest possible time or else they will arrest you!' A loving mother was caught in a serious dilemma. She did not want to spoil the party of her beautiful daughter Yashodhara that night by breaking news she had herself found difficult to fathom. So, she quietly went to bed but only after having packed a bag with clothes, etc., for any eventuality. She could not sleep properly the whole night.

The next morning, she got to know from a newspaper *Motherland* that J.P. had been arrested and many other leaders were being hauled off into jails. The Emergency had been announced and brisk actions were happening, the newspaper told her. The lady, Gwalior's millionaire Rajmata, wanted to speak to her people in Gwalior from Delhi but could not, as phone lines had been cut. No party official was available in Delhi either for her to know more about it.

She was, meanwhile, advised by friends who had read the papers and had heard the shocking news on BBC radio, to quickly go underground. She was trying to contact Bal Angre, her political 'Man Friday'. He was in Calcutta to meet the *Indian Express* boss Ramnath Goenka. Vijaya Raje desperately wanted to take his advice about her next course of action in this trying situation. After they spoke, Angre somehow managed to hide his identity and reached Delhi by the next flight, courtesy of Goenka. Rajmata Scindia had left her Rajpur Road residence in the meanwhile and changed a few homes of acquaintances and common friends in New Delhi. She was also advised to change her now-famous attire of a spotless white saree, lest she be easily spotted. After several years, she wore colourful sarees borrowed from her daughters and Angre's wife, but it was only for a few weeks.

Her son Madhavrao was in Bombay, playing golf at the Wellington Club early in the morning on 26 June 1975. He was unaware of the happenings in the national capital in the days without 24x7 TV news channels and social media's unimaginable penetration that we experience today. As a Jana Sangh MP, he was almost certain to be arrested. He got the advice from his friends (famous industrialist Nusli Wadia, Ram Batra and others) to flee the country, which he did rather quickly. He went to Nepal and then sent for his mother and two sisters Vasundhara Raje and Yashodhara Raje to shift to Nepal where he had made all the arrangements for their safe stay. He had also conveyed that they could move to any European country from Kathmandu, if so required.

The Rajmata, having grasped the seriousness of the situation, began thinking differently now. She was, however, moved by the touching message of Madhavrao but her inner voice was saying something else. As a true Jana Sanghi, she was inclined to catch the bull by the horn. She was to follow her son and thus hoodwink the mighty Congress government in Delhi as per the original plan. After having almost reached the border of Nepal in the Himalayan Terai by car from Delhi, along with Bal Angre and others, such as Surinderlal Dewan and his wife, she refused to escape from the country.

She reportedly stayed on a friend's quiet and isolated farmhouse, far from where the actions were happening. For a few days, until 6 July 1975, she was there before finally deciding to return to her hometown, a move that, in retrospective, appears to be yet another turning point in the history of the Scindia family. Instead of crossing over the border, just about 40 miles or so to slip into Nepal, once her mother's country where her son was also eagerly waiting, she intensely thought of Gwalior after much of internal conflicts.

Angre, after listening to or observing Vijaya Raje, conveyed to Madhavrao his mother's message to take care of himself, before she left Delhi hurriedly, and that she would be looking after herself.

The Rajmata writes that Angre firmly believed that Madhavrao was left with no other choice but to remain in India and fight the injustice that the Congress had unleashed, exactly the way their ancestors had fought. 'Bal believed that Bhaiya's only course was to remain on Indian soil and to fight them (Congress) out as our ancestors had,' she further wrote. Those words... 'Let Scindia's erstwhile subjects say that their Maharaja chose to go to jail, but did not abandon them in their hour of need and that...it is his duty to come back here; not to take away his mother too'....were repeatedly ringing in her ears when she was caught in a crossroad between going to Nepal and returning to India. She was unable to decide, being much worried as she was about her daughters, her people and, above all, her duty and principles.[4]

But as Vir Sanghvi elaborates in his book, written a few

years after the death of Madhavrao, that until before leaving for Nepal via Calcutta, he was in touch with his mother who was always fine with the plan to go to Nepal—his mother's home, as also his wife Madhavi Raje's.[5] According to Sanghvi, it was logical for the Rajmata to join her son in Nepal. She was, however, conscious of endangering the safety of her hosts—the people who kept her safe in their houses one after the other in such trying circumstances. Rajmata was an hour's drive away from Nepal and the plan for her was to spend a few days at the farm before driving across the border to be with her son and be away from any threats that the Emergency had posed before her.

But she did not cross over the Indian border. Why?

There are different versions available. First, she did not want to be out of the country along with her son and leave the Gwalior, Delhi, Nainital, Pune and Bombay properties and its people to look after themselves during such turbulent and uncertain times. There were already reports coming in that those who had left the country would be treated as enemies and their possessions expropriated. 'There was no escape; every move was blocked off,' Scindia was quoted as saying in her autobiography.[6]

Second, Angre is believed to have impressed upon her, as mentioned above briefly, that it made political sense in the long term to return to Gwalior and publicly announce that they were giving themselves up to the police. So, they decided to go back to Gwalior, undertaking a risky and strenuous car journey from the Himalayan foothills.

Clearly, she was torn: who to choose? Her son or her daughters? Where to go? Nepal or Gwalior? She, after much thought that gave her sleepless nights, opted for the latter! Gwalior enticed her more than Kathmandu! Perhaps, Angre also may have shrewdly thought of keeping the mother and son apart, a feeling Madhavrao had gotten then.

Upon her return to her hometown, when she entered the Jai Vilas palace sometime between 7/8 July, she was told that an arrest warrant had been issued against her and Angre. But there were no police there, as expected, when her car entered the palace compound. After a quick bath to freshen up from the tiredness of a very long, arduous journey, she performed puja to her family gods inside the palace and asked Angre to call up the police officials, so that she could surrender herself. She was ready again for a long haul to unknown places with a lurking fear in mind.

The police, armed to the teeth, took her in a jeep that night to an unknown place but not before visiting Datia, on her request, where she spent some time with her Guru-Maharaj and came out 'much relieved and fortified internally.' She had been allowed by the government to take her old maid and her half-brother Dhyanendra Singh, alias Dhyanu, as company. They then proceeded to another direction, in the direction of her birthplace Sagar, and finally stayed in the Bison Lodge of the same hill station of Pachmarhi where she had taken up fight a few years ago with the then chief minister and, consequently, history had been made in Madhya Pradesh. Her time passed comfortably as 'Dhyanu' was always there to give her company and play cards to kill the time.

◆

Pachmarhi receives lots of rain each year. It also had beautiful forests in the '70s and '80s. After spending many weeks there in house arrest at the Bison Lodge, 'a pleasant little bungalow' in the sylvan settings of the summer capital of Madhya Pradesh, the Rajmata nonetheless got a little bored and she asked for a change of place. The request was almost immediately granted. The real reason, however, was that she did not want herself to be used for the government's subtle publicity campaign that the MISA detenues were like pampered guests and that the government was actually looking after them well.

Little did she know what was in store for her after Pachmarhi's rather cushy stay with Dhyanendra and a maid to accompany them day and night.

If one were to analyse her decision from any angle, it was one of her greatest mistakes, as she would also realize later, much to her shock. She was shifted from Pachmarhi to a prison, Delhi's famous prison. She became prisoner number 2265, having been housed in the Tihar jail—India's largest jail—without her maid and her half-brother. Solitary confinement in conditions that were adverse even for an ordinary citizen to live in, and she was elderly and diabetic, had to undergo the ordeal, nonetheless. It was there that Gayatri Devi of Jaipur was also brought in from different jails.

That way Vijaya Raje had been treated lightly in Madhya Pradesh. The then chief minister, Prakash Chandra Sethi, who was from Ujjain, had always held her in high esteem, a reason, Gwalior people say, no police force had been deployed at the palace to arrest her and later, when she was taken into custody and transported to Sagar and Pachmarhi, police officials behaved with her well—showing utmost humility and respect that she deserved.

Bal Angre, however, was kept away from her, at the district jail in Jabalpur for most of the 21 months of the Emergency. His 80-year-old father (also a Sardar in the erstwhile Gwalior durbar) was jailed in Gwalior as a common felon.

But as the Emergency days wore on, she started getting disturbing reports of income tax/customs raids conducted on the vast palace in Gwalior as also in Delhi, Pune and Bombay. Yashodhara Raje or Yesho, as she was lovingly called by her mother, was alone in Jai Vilas, Gwalior, confronting the unfriendly and probing tax sleuths while facing numerous other challenges of the authoritarian rule unleashed by Indira Gandhi.

Vijaya Raje explains that her youngest daughter Yesho had little or no inkling whatsoever of the accounts or the details of their properties and gems collection. As a mother, she was thus very worried yet totally helpless. Neither could she know anything about her daughters in India, nor about her son in Nepal. Madhavrao, being away from India, was equally helpless and was having sleepless nights.

The raids that continued in the palace in Gwalior went on for a very long time and taxmen went to every nook and corner of the expansive Jai Vilas palace and forced all rooms to be opened, keys of which were not with Yashodhara Raje. After a few days, Dhaynendra Singh returned from Pachmarhi to Gwalior to help her in facing the army of officials asking inconvenient and, at times, foolish questions; demanding very old documents and income tax related papers of past years and details about gold and jewellery as if it were all illegally acquired by the country's richest family and a deeply pious lady like the Rajmata.

One after the other, all the Scindia properties were raided. The authorities, according to Sanghvi, looked for a legendary Scindia treasure in Gwalior. The myth was that the Scindias had wells full of pearls—under the floor, hidden inside the thick walls and beneath the grounds. Most of the items scattered around the large rooms, verandahs and on their walls in the lobbies, were priceless antique pieces of art collected over the years through inheritance or received as precious gifts from foreign and Indian dignitaries.

Much of these costly items were reportedly taken away—either to their individual homes or submitted in government custody—no one would ever get to know where the precious possessions went away after confiscation by the individual officers from different departments. The indecorous officers would not let anyone know anything. Bank accounts of the Scindias had also been frozen as if they were economic offenders. Eventually, the Delhi mansion at Rajpur Road was also requisitioned by the government at a short notice of 48 hours and the family members could barely retrieve their possessions before an army of officials moved in with vengeance. They damaged it so extensively—the Italian marbled floor and beautiful furniture—that Vijaya Raje vowed not to enter the house that she loved so much, ever again. They later sold it to buy a large piece of land near Hyatt Regency hotel in New Delhi.

At one point, shockingly enough, Prime Minister Indira Gandhi told Usha Raje, the Rajmata's daughter, that her mother was being kept in prison not because of her political activities but for a graver offence of smuggling. This was like a bolt from the blue for the daughter.[7]

It was at this point, that Usha, who had rushed to India to help her sisters and her mother, used her good offices in Delhi to get closer to Mrs Gandhi to convince her of Vijaya Raje's innocence. Madhavrao, on the other hand, used his sister's contacts to send out feelers to Mrs Gandhi that he was prepared to give up his allegiance to the Jana Sangh and even give up politics. From the response she sent out, it seemed that Mrs Gandhi regarded this as a singularly welcome development. His sins forgiven, Bhaiya was allowed to return to India. But there was a deal Indira had in mind which she did not disclose at that time, a shrewd politician that she was.

Curiously, an important development was also taking shape in the Scindia household, simultaneously.

Usha Raje, after having met Indira Gandhi, could almost drive her point home with her mother that given the latter's health conditions and mental stress that the revulsive environs of the jail had caused, it was badly required to get her out of the place. The way out? Parole! That was the only alternative she had to get out of Tihar. Her daughters implored her to do what Mrs Gandhi was asking her to do, implying that she had no

other choice other than following her Mrs Gandhi's directive.[8]
'Amazingly, the Rajmata did as her children demanded. She agreed to give up politics and wrote a letter to Mrs Gandhi promising that if she were released, she would live life as a private citizen and not meet politicians', writes Sanghvi. Of course, in her autobiography, Vijaya Raje tells a slightly different story of the prison officer promising her that her parole application on health grounds would be accepted but she will have to keep applying for it every month for renewal of permission. There was no mention of a letter from her to Indira Gandhi requesting parole. The letter is not available in public domain but had been seen by Madhavrao Scindia during his lifetime and Yashodhara Raje knows about it as well. However, while Vijaya Raje may have agreed to come out of the jail on the insistence of her daughters, she had also sought guidance from her spiritual guru at Datia. He was a great influence on her, as will be seen in next chapters, in what was seen to be yet another important decision she refused to take.

Her admission in AIIMS was necessitated in the light of her health check-up before finally getting the parole and enjoying fresh air outside jail after so long. Her three daughters' doggedness worked well or else she would have spent the remaining days and months inside the suffocating, dingy cell of Tihar at the cost of her failing health. At one place in her autobiography, she mentions: 'I had gone to jail for political reasons but came out for domestic reasons.'[9] She admits that she had to do something to safeguard her family treasures and property—something anyone else in her place would have done under similar conditions.

◆

The Emergency seemed to have, for some time, united the Scindias, before they finally split. Madhavrao was allowed to return to India and his arrest warrant cancelled following an assurance from the top officials. He was reconciling to the fact he would quit politics, as had been decided before his return to India, and refocus on businesses in Bombay. His mother was also freed for a month on parole, subject to extensions; she had also started toiling with the idea of taking a sanyas. After the letter and her failing health, Indira Gandhi also did not wish to take the battle further. Frivolous cases started by various agencies were also not pursued by the government.

During the entire turbulent period, the whole family came extremely close. With politics out of their lives and the worst torments of that era behind them, the Scindias bonded again and Madhavrao would later refer to the time spent with his mother and his family as the happiest months of 1976.

He had a simple explanation for this: the absence of Sambhajirao Angre.[10] Angre, it seemed, always played a villain in the Scindia family feud. For Madhavrao, it was the Angre factor that became the tip of the iceberg. Without Angre, Vijaya Raje was the loving mother, doting on her children with care and affection. However, with Angre, she transformed into an overtly political figure for whom nothing else mattered as much as her and Angre's ideological cause, informs journalist Sanghvi, who was fairly close to Madhavrao and considered to be a friend.

Come 1977, elections were announced by Indira Gandhi. Madhavrao, who was wooed by Congress to stand on their symbol, instead chose to be an independent candidate from the same Guna constituency from where he had won as a Jana Sangh nominee in 1971. Congress did not field any candidate as a friendly gesture and thus with a lesser margin, Madhavrao won against a Janata Party candidate Gurbaksh Singh, who contested on the Bharatiya Lok Dal symbol, by 76,451 votes, despite a strong wave in the Janata Party's favour. In these elections, Vijaya Raje supported her son, though she had already joined the Janata Party.

Incidentally, Guna was a constituency from where Madhavrao won three consecutive elections but each one on different symbols and that underscores his immense popularity. After the 1977 victory and fall of the Janata Party by 1979, he had formally shaken hands with the Congress and contested the 1980 parliamentary election on their symbol; he won with massive margins, trouncing Naresh Jauhari of the Janata Party by over 116,000 votes.

During the 1977 election, the word was already out that while the mother had braved the Emergency and stayed in India and had even gone to jail, the son had 'run away.' This may have impacted his poll outcome as an independent candidate. Madhavrao was sad that this half-truth was being circulated by her mother and her camp followers. 'In fact, she had written in her letters praising Indira and that her children would also make up with the regime of Mrs Gandhi,' Sanghvi explains.[11]

Since right-winger Sardar Angre remained in jail until late 1977 and was released only when Indira Gandhi lost power, mother and son were together—politically and personally, during his absence. But once the 'Rasputin of the Scindia court'[12] was out, differences began to grow again and continued so until the death of the Rajmata on 25 January 2001 in Delhi.

Year 1980 was a watershed year in many ways for the Scindias. It was for the first time, after many years, that a Scindia scion was standing on a Congress ticket—the last Scindia to contest was the Rajmata in 1962. And in a reversal of roles, his mother was a Janata Party candidate against Indira Gandhi from Raebareli. The son fighting on a Congress ticket and mother contesting against the Congress supremo Mrs Gandhi resulted in widening the rift beyond repair. The Scindia political division was complete. They had taken divergent political paths that never joined again.

The family feud worsened with the divorce of political ideologies over the years. Sardar Angre was an indispensable character here too! Mother and three sisters were on one side and Madhavrao was on the other. Legal battles ensued at the cost of the image of the family. Newspapers and magazines got juicy stories, at times planted by Sardar Angre and at other times, by Scindia's opponents in the Congress. But Madhavrao was never heard speaking against his mother, though she had spoken and written against him at length, including in her autobiography. Many cases were filed against each other by both the sides in Gwalior District Court, Pune Civil Court, Delhi, Jabalpur and in the Mumbai High Court and continued for decades, ultimately spilling over to the next generations.

Sanghvi writes in his book about the time when the Rajmata took her son to meet with their lawyer and tax expert D.M. Harish, thus asking for a partition of assets among all family members:

> On October 12, 1980 Vijaya Raje 'celebrated' her 60th birthday. A few days before that she was in Nasik for organising a *yagna*. From there she drove *straight* to Mumbai to be at the small party hosted by her daughter-in-law, Madhviraje. No sooner than she entered the Samudra Mahal flat, she called for Madhavrao and forthwith took him into her waiting car downstairs, even as the guests were trying to figure out what was happening. She took her son to their lawyer and tax expert D.M. Harish. After a quick meeting there among the three in the evening, she allowed Madhavrao to go back to his home without her.'[13]

The Scindia assets were being divided. Vijaya Raje had asked for partition of assets. After this decision, which was taken on her sixtieth birthday, apparently after consultation with Angre, things never remained the same again.

A long pending case filed by Vijaya Raje in the Bombay High Court in 1984 (suit number 1861), for instance, went on for over 35 years, until 2021. She had also filed another lawsuit in 1985 in Pune.

It is significant to note that the years 1984–85 were politically very crucial for Madhavrao Scindia as he fought the toughest Lok Sabha election of his career from Gwalior against Atal Bihari Vajpayee and won with a handsome margin of over 1.75 lakh votes to become a union minister for the first time in 1985. 'It was ironical that Atal-ji who had given membership of the Jana Sangh to Madhavrao and in a way brought him into mainstream politics, lost at the hands of Scindia in 1984,' Keshav Pande, a veteran journalist of Gwalior, shared with the author, adding, 'it was another irony that while Atal-ji went on to be the prime minister, Oxford-educated Madhavrao could never make the grade.'

It would be relevant to mention here that Atal Bihari Vajpayee, born in Gwalior in 1924, was supported by Jiwajirao Scindia in his higher education and with a condition that after it was completed, he would work for the Gwalior state. But after completing his education, Vajpayee was attracted to the Rashtriya Swayamsevak Sangh (RSS) and became its full time pracharak (volunteer). He then requested Jiwajirao to free him from that 'contractual condition' which Jiwajirao immediately did. This reminds me of Dr Baba Saheb Ambedkar, who was supported by Maharaja Sayajirao Gaekwad of Baroda in his higher education abroad; Sayajirao's Marathi biographer Baba Bhand has written about it in several of his books.[14]

That was the contribution of the princely states of India to nation building. Of course, much more can be written about the royal families' efforts to promote education and their patronage to arts, culture and sports, among other fields. Both Scindia and Gaekwad, the Marathi-speaking families, were considered modern and visionary in their times. Today, the two major princely houses of yore are much closer than they were ever. Jyotiraditya Scindia's wife Priyadarshini Raje, daughter of Sangramsinh Gaekwad, a former cricketer, comes from the famous Gaekwad dynasty of Baroda. Both Gwalior and Baroda, the two illustrious Maratha families of the powerful erstwhile confederacy, were entitled to the 21-gun salute under the British Raj. Both were rich, people-oriented and globetrotters.

Meanwhile, Madhavrao Scindia was made the minister of state for railways in the Rajiv Gandhi cabinet and ever since, he did not look back. He quickly reached the dizzy heights in Congress politics and in public life. He is still considered to be one of the few most successful railways ministers India ever had.

LEGAL TANGLES

The two legal cases filed by the Rajmata in 1984 and 1885 were related to the huge property left behind by Vijaya Raje's late husband Maharaja Jiwajirao Scindia, who had passed away in 1961, without making a will. As the original plaintiff, Vijaya Raje prayed for partition and division of the moveable estate of the late husband on the ground that the said property belonged to the Hindu Undivided Family (HUF). She sought a share of 50 per cent in the property straightaway. In the Scindia family, a rule of primogeniture was always honoured, according to which the eldest male of the royal family gets the property rights.

'At the time of his death, Jiwajirao was a ruling Maharaja so it could be argued that his estate should have been disposed of following the law of primogeniture under which royal India—and royalty everywhere—lived,' wrote Sanghvi.[15] The landed property left behind by Jiwajirao, included: Jai Vilas Palace, Usha Kiran Palace (where the family once lived), Rani Mahal, Choti Vishranti, Hiravan Kothi, Vijay Bhawan and various smaller properties in Gwalior. In Bombay, there was the fabulous Samudra Mahal palace in Worli, an estate bought by Madhav Maharaj from Aga Khan, Vasundhara Building opposite the Mahalakshmi temple and Vijay Vilas on Warden Road. In Pune, the properties included the Padma Vilas and racecourse land and stud farms. In Delhi, Lekha Vihar (Scindia Villa) and acres and acres of prime real estate near what is now the Hyatt Regency Hotel. In Ujjain, Jiwajirao owned Kalideh Palace. In addition, there were also the Krishnaram Baldev Bank (acquired by SBI in 1974) and the Kusumpur Clay Mines with close to 300 acres of land behind Vasant Vihar in Delhi.[16]

Of course, many of the above-listed properties are not with the Scindias now—either they were converted into something else or disposed of. Usha Kiran Palace is now a hotel; Pune's Padma Vilas and the racecourse were sold off. There is no reliable assessment available anywhere about the priceless gems and jewellery collection the Scindias owned, barring the mention made by Vijaya Raje herself in her autobiography and some historical references given in that book at different places.

This long list of valuable properties became a bone of contention between Vijaya Raje and Madhavrao many years later. This could be attributed to the fact that soon after her husband's death in 1961, she had taken many decisions on her own. Madhavrao, then only 16, was too young to take part in important family matters such as these. One of the decisions was to ignore the primogeniture tradition of the royal houses and instead use the Hindu Succession Act to deal with the massive estate her husband had left behind. Under the law, three divisions were made, one each for herself, Madhavrao and the four sisters. Apparently, Madhavrao's father did not name any property exclusively in the name of his only son, a minor, when he suddenly passed away. One reason could be that in the '60s there was absolutely no indication of an end to the privy purses system, nor was there any threat to the institution of princes even if India had gained her independence. Jiwajirao may have naturally thought that Madhavrao being his lone heir, there would be no dispute over the inheritance. He was, however, proven wrong by his wife.

In any case, when both the Rajmata and Madhavrao passed away in 2001 within a span of about eight months, it became a legal dispute between the executor of Rajmata's will, S. Gurumurthy (plaintiff) and Madhavrao's only son Jyotiraditya Scindia, an MP. Gurumurthy was on the side of the three paternal aunts of Jyotiraditya, namely Vasundhara, Usha and Yashodhara who had filed written statements in as late as 2017, a newspaper report said, thus suggesting a legal tussle was still going on in the court.[17] A top lawyer of Gwalior told this author that 'most of the legal cases were still pending in 2021' in different courts, including in Gwalior, with Jyotiraditya on one side and his three aunts on the other. He also mentioned that the family relations were anything but normal.

In another major land dispute, BJP's top leader L.K. Advani was reported to have spoken to the then prime minister, Inder Kumar Gujral, on 12 December 1997, to help Vijaya Raje Scindia and her two daughters in resolving the dispute. It involved a high-value, 30-acre plot in New Delhi. Gujral wrote in his autobiography that he could help them only to a small extent.[18]

The plot of land brought in a dispute between the Scindia family and the Delhi Development Authority (DDA). The DDA had acquired the land after a long spell of litigation between the two parties. The land, measuring 30 acres, with the price running into several crores, belonged to the erstwhile Gwalior Potteries which later became Scindia Potteries Private Limited— also a Scindia family asset. But it became a matter of dispute due to ownership title. The open land located in Sarojini Nagar area, with big walls built around, is where at some point of time, the Jain TV Studios were erected and the TV channel functioned from there. J.K. Jain, a former Rajya Sabha member from Madhya Pradesh, was close to the Rajmata.

Ranoji Scindia (1700–1745), founder of the Scindia Dynasty
Photo Courtesy: Neelesh Karkare, Gwalior

Ranoji Scindia Chattri at Shujalpur in Madhya Pradesh
Photo courtesy: Dinesh Jain

Mahadji Scindia (1730–1794), one of the most prominent Maratha warriors
Photo Courtsey: Madhya Pradesh Archaeology Department, Bhopal

Daulat Rao Scindia (1779–1827). He was an art loving king of his times, credited with founding the famous Gwalior Music Gharana

Photo Courtesy: Kedar Jain

Jankoji Rao Scindia (1827–1843)
Photo Courtesy: Kedar Jain

Jayajirao Scindia (1834–1886)
Photo Courtesy: Kedar Jain

Jiwajirao Scindia (1916–1961), a modern Maharaja who detested politics but loved horse racing as a sport

Photo Courtesy: Kedar Jain

The Rajmata, Madhavrao and Atal Bihari Vajpayee at a political meeting of the Jana Sangh in Gwalior in 1971
Photo Courtesy: Kedar Jain

The Rajmata on her seventy-fifth birthday
Photo Courtesy: Kedar Jain

Sumitra Mahajan, later to be an MP, standing in front of the Rajmata at a BJP
meeting in Indore
Photo Courtsey: Bhalu Mondhe, Indore 1989

Early childhood—Madhavrao with his three sisters
Photo Courtsey: Kedar Jain

A family portrait with Madhavrao and his wife Madhavi Raje
Photo Courtsey: Kedar Jain

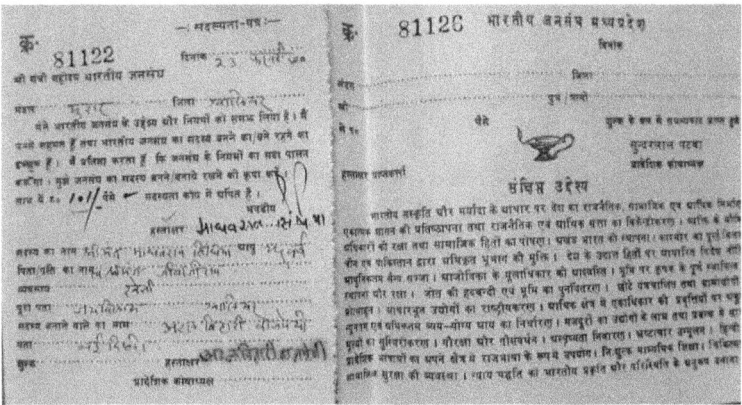

Jana Sangh original membership receipt of Madhavrao Scindia, February 1970
Photo Courtesy: Vivek Shejwalkar, Member of Parliament, Gwalior

Madhavrao Scindia (1945–2001) seen in traditional Gwalior
(Shindeshahi) pagri (headgear) with golden piping
Photo Courtsey: Kedar Jain

Madhavrao Scindia with sister Vasundhara Raje, who later became the chief minister of Rajasthan, in Gwalior, 1994
Photo Courtsey: Kedar Jain

Madhavrao Scindia, president Madhya Pradesh Cricket Association with former Indian cricket captain Sunil Gavaskar, in Indore in 1983
Photo Courtesy: Bhalu Mondhe

Pre-wedding ceremony of Jyotiraditya Scindia; Madhavrao seen in rare attire with wife Madhavi Raje, 1994
Photo Courtsey: Kedar Jain

Madhavrao Scindia and Madhavi Raje Scindia with their daughter Chitrangada (first left) and her husband (far right) Vikramaditya Singh on the occasion of son Jyotiraditya's wedding with Priyadarshiniraje of the Baroda royal family. The newly-wed couple is seen at the centre.
Photo Courtsey: Anil Mishra, Gwalior

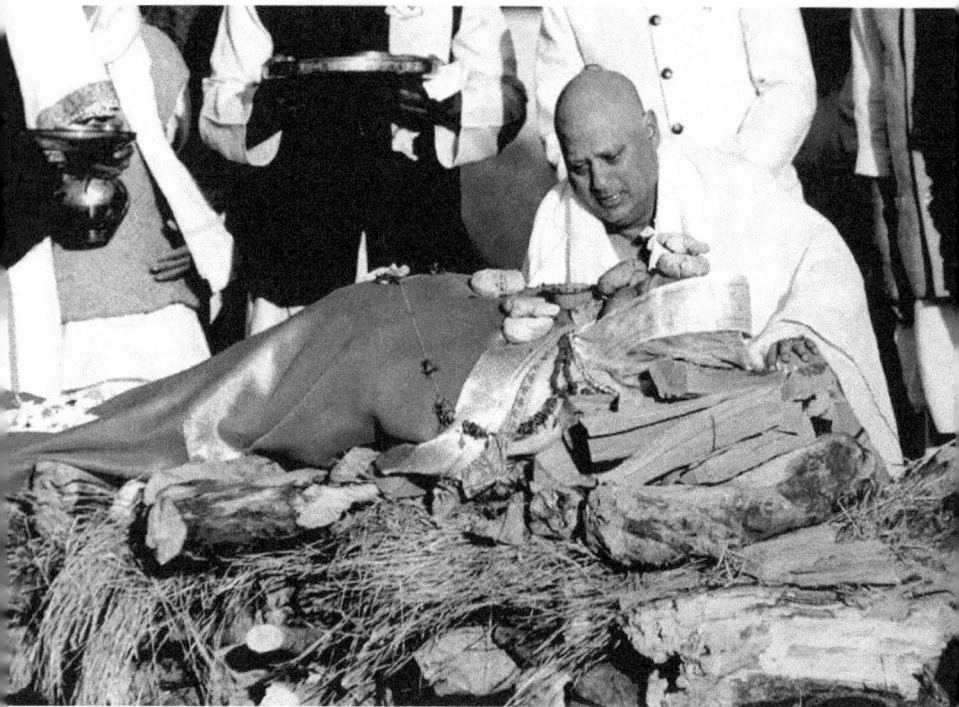

An emotionally-charged Madhavrao bidding final adieu to his mother in Gwalior, in January 2001
Photo Courtsey: Kedar Jain

Jyotiraditya in an open jeep with wife and father, accepting greetings of people in Gwalior soon after his wedding
Photo Courtsey: Kedar Jain

Jyotiraditya Scindia, addressing a mammoth crowd, during an election campaign in Guna, Madhya Pradesh
Photo Courtsey: Yogendra Lumba

Jyotiraditya Scindia with the Honourable Prime Minister Narendra Modi in
New Delhi in 2021
Photo Courtesy: Press Information Bureau

Family sources maintained that Jyotiraditya, the sole heir of Madhavrao, has been making efforts for out of court settlements in many of the cases as the open fights have maligned enough the names of all those concerned for a little too long. On 27 January 2021, a Mumbai High Court proceeding stated: 'By an order dated 12 March 2020, this court directed that the time to file compilation, affidavits and documents stands extended indefinitely as the parties have apparently settled the entire dispute.'[19]

An earlier report (August 2005) in the *Times of India* said:[20] Sisters fight nephew for control of charitable trusts. Two trusts—Krishna Madhav Public Charitable Trust and His Highness Sir Maharaja Jiwajirao Scindia Charitable Trust owned three multi-crore properties in south Mumbai. The trusts were set up by Vijaya Raje in 1966 and her three daughters were made the trustees in 1982, the report claimed. The BJP stalwart had reportedly received many precious gifts and thus, she needed a trust to be formed for their upkeep and management which she did and made her daughters the trustees, a common practice among the princely families of yesteryears. Her daughters moved an application before the commissioner charitable trust, Maharashtra, after the death of their mother that they be made the trustees. Jyotiraditya also submitted a similar application to gain control of the two trusts and wanted to be named as the real trustee.

Though the Rajmata had spoken and written against her son a lot, including in her autobiography and in newspaper statements—mainly about his political stand and family feud, available literature and documents show that Madhavrao, on his part, was never heard speaking against his mother. His restraint could be gauged from the following incident: in one of the election campaigns of the Lok Sabha elections in 1989, when he was contesting from Gwalior and his mother from Guna, from rival parties, he causally asked a group of four to five journalists including the author, just before boarding his chopper, parked on the lawns of Jai Vilas, 'what are the reports you people are getting from Guna?' To which, one of the over-enthusiastic journalists replied, 'Rajmataji is finding it tough there.' Madhavrao suddenly became serious, his facial expressions, behind the beautiful pair of imported goggles, changing noticeably. But he softly murmured: 'Don't tell me that, it is not possible.' And swiftly boarded the helicopter to go off for his campaigning.

This was despite the fact that his close aide, Mahendra Singh Kalukheda was the Congress candidate and pitted against his mother in Guna. Obviously, the son wanted her to win. That was the affection he had for her—sharp political and family differences, notwithstanding. Eventually, the Rajmata won the Guna constituency during the ninth Lok Sabha election by over 1.46 lakh votes.

Retired IAS officer Bimal Julka, a former private secretary to Madhavrao Scindia, then Human Resource Development (HRD) minister, recalls Scindia telling him that if ever a difficult decision pertaining to family property disputes arose, it should be decided and settled in favour of his mother and sisters.[21]

The vast Scindia estate is (also) vested in numerous trusts. Madhavrao once headed many of those created by the visionary maharaja, Jiwajirao Scindia to serve various social, cultural, educational, religious and developmental needs of the people of the erstwhile Gwalior state. These trusts included: Rani Usharaje Charitable Trust, Rang Mahal Charitable Trust, Mahadji Charitable Trust, Jai Vilas Charitable Trust, Gorkhi Charitable Trust, Mannu Raje Charitable Trust, Jyotiraditya Charitable Trust, Kamla Raje Charitable Trust, Padma Raje Charitable Trusts, Vasundharaje Charitable Trust, Yashodhara Raje Charitable Trust, Jankoji Raje Charitable Trust, Jayajirao Charitable Trust, Chinkoo Raje Charitable Trust, Scindia Rural Development Trust, King Edward Memorial Trust,

Samudra Mahal Trust (Mumbai), Maharaja Jiwajirao Trust (Mumbai), Amma Maharaj Chhatri Trust (Shivpuri), Sankhya Raje Dharmashala Trust (Ujjain) and Gangajali Fund Trust (Bhopal).[22]

After the tragic and untimely death of Madhavrao, Jyotiraditya Scindia is the sole head of the trusts and manages it through an army of managers and other trustees, most of whom are commoners, family members or trusted associates. Indeed, running of all these trusts, organizing their activities, maintaining properties under them, keeping accounts and giving salaries to the employees is not an easy task for any individual.

◆

That Vijaya Raje had lost to Indira Gandhi very badly, forfeiting her deposit, has been mentioned in an earlier chapter and does not need any repetition. But one thing became certain after that—the Rajmata further got firmly entrenched in the Jana Sangh and then the newly founded BJP whereas Madhavrao became very close to Sanjay and Indira from 1980 onwards.

Politics had sadly overturned blood loyalties in the Scindia family. Physical division of properties and staff of Usha Kiran, Jai Vilas, Rani Mahal in Gwalior and the Padma Vilas Palace and the huge racecourse property in Pune, among other landed properties and precious jewels and business companies, etc., was painful to the members on both sides. Young Jyotiraditya and his elder sister Chitrangada remember Madhavrao driving them from Mumbai to Pune where during the evenings the horses would be set free, and they would parade around the palace to entertain the owners. The public dispute over property and resultant animosities over political differences, however, resulted in legal cases over the next few decades. Properties in London, Delhi and some other places were disposed of due to pressing compulsions between 1980 and 2001, the year the Rajmata passed away. Many complicated litigations continued for many years during her lifetime and after that as well.

Indian Express had reported a little after Vijaya Raje's death in a Delhi hospital that the battle for inheritance was not for a few buildings or gems here and there but for a treasure worth a whooping ₹30,000 crores. The national daily had front-paged a banner story by Ritu Sarin, the then head of the investigative journalism team, covering contents of the will of the Rajmata and also quoting Sardar Angre, then 81 and one of the executors of the will. She wrote: 'Among other details of the jewels and jewelleries, that Angre had personally helped Vijaya Raje prepare list of moveable and unmovable assets which ran into 500 pages.'[23]

The 'will' had been released by Angre in public domain for the first time in the first week of February 2001, which of course ran into controversy then and was challenged by Madhavrao Scindia. The will was said to be written 17 years before her death, sometime in 1983. A second will, said to be more authentic, surfaced later.

A well-illustrated book, *The Palaces of India* by the Maharaja of Baroda on select few palaces, in its Gwalior section says:[24]

> Maharaja Jayajirao built his city-palace between 1872 and 1874 when the British were still occupying the Gwalior Fort after the disorders of the Mutiny. Jayaji had lived a relatively simple life which betrayed few signs of wealth and ostentation—he had even borrowed small sums of money off the British on the grounds of administrative necessity—yet after his death, officials stumbled on a series of ingeniously disguised hiding places containing wealth and treasure valued at sixty-two million rupees. It was quite simply the biggest hoard of precious stones in the world, including 'silver coin that could be counted by

millions, magnificent pearls and diamonds by the tens and thousands, rubies, emeralds and other gems by thousands, and wrought and melted golds by *maunds* [an Indian measure of weight].' In brief, it was patterned on the classic style of the world famous 'Palais de Versailles' in France. There are stories that suggest that to test the load-bearing capability of the palace ceiling, a number of elephants were made to walk on the terrace first and only after that the heavy chandeliers were hung. It is also said that 300,000 leaves of gold were used just for the 'reception-hall' decoration.

Maintaining the beautiful and vast abode indeed seems a challenge in modern times, even for people like the Scindias, considering the high costs involved and the typical workmanship that can hardly match the quaint styles.

Well, at the time of the Rajmata's death, Madhavrao was at her bedside in the hospital and had immediately dispatched Dhyanendra Singh to Gwalior to make arrangements for her funeral, which was to be as per the Scindia royal family traditions. As Dhyanendra recalls, he had been categorically told by Madhavrao not to allow Angre to come anywhere near her body. It was a tough task for Dhyanendra. Young Jyotiraditya, about 30 years old then, and his friends had successfully managed that task despite a huge crowd that had turned up from all directions in Gwalior to bid a tearful final adieu to their own loving Rajmata.[25]

Many years after her death Jyotiraditya still remembers vividly his 'pleasant days' spent with his grandmother. He told this author that his relations with his grandmother were 'very special'. He also said:

As a child, I have wonderful memories of the time spent with her in my childhood. She would have special meals laid out for me whenever I visited her in Gwalior. She would await eagerly for me. Her typically affectionate grandmother-like behaviour and special treatment for me is still itched in my mind; I could get angry with her at times and yet have my way but she would never get upset with me. I cherish the very pleasant memories of those days of my childhood.[26]

6

Vijaya Raje and the Ram Janmabhoomi Movement

The tumultuous saga of the Ram Janmabhoomi (the birthplace of Lord Ram) movement has gone through the long, uneven paths to the historic temple town of Ayodhya over the centuries. While it may have consolidated the Indian Hindus as never before, the fact is that the birthplace of Lord Ram was never a political issue as it has been made out to be since 1980 or so. The politico-religious campaign has now entered its last phase with a grand ceremony of bhoomi poojan for the proposed temple having been successfully held at Ayodhya on 5 August 2020 at the hands of Prime Minister Narendra Modi.

That Ayodhya is the birthplace of Lord Ram, going by all the available Hindu scriptures and archaeological as well as legal evidence, is a forgone conclusion. At one of point time, a few decades ago, the entire controversy revolved around the 'fact' of whether the place where the Babri mosque stood in Ayodhya was indeed the real birthplace of Ram or not. Arguments and counter arguments were given, archaeological evidence dug up, historians on both sides of the fence were engaged in bitter wordy duels to support their stand even as courts in the country kept adjourning the matter. After Partition in 1947, this was the time in late '80s and the '90s when the divide between the Hindu and Muslim communities widened and sporadic communal riots took place across India, killing scores of innocent people. In Bombay alone, 227 people were killed in the riots that broke out between December 1992 and January 1993.[1]

A Supreme Court order of 9 November 2019 finally paved the way for the ground-breaking ceremony, thus giving a clear message that the long-awaited temple would eventually be built at exactly the same place where, as many Hindus believe, Lord Ram was actually born. The five-member Supreme Court bench, headed by the then Chief Justice Ranjan Gogoi, post his much-awaited verdict, not only favoured construction of a temple but ordered the transfer of the 2.77 acres of disputed land to a trust to be formed by the Union Government. The religious ceremony (a puja) was performed by Narendra Modi with the RSS chief (Sarsangchalak) Dr Mohan Bhagwat sitting right inside the sanctum sanctorum along with a select few, including sadhus and members of the newly formed temple trust, and the VHP top brass associated with the movement, sitting outside at a distance. In addition to them, there were millions of VHP-RSS workers, men and women, sympathizers and Hindu leaders who remained glued to their TV sets to watch live the Ram temple ground-breaking ceremony on numerous Indian news channels. It was yet another golden-letter day in the annals of the movement, after 6 December 1992 when the mosque was demolished by a huge mob with saffron satin bands on their heads and shouting slogans.

It took over four decades for the movement to come of age, while simultaneously consolidating the Hindu vote bank for the BJP which entered the fray a bit late. The movement to build a temple at a place where Babri Masjid once stood for centuries was on the RSS agenda since the 1980s. It was

THE SCINDIA LEGACY • 119

eventually taken over by one of its 'affiliates', the VHP in a very aggressive manner. According to an authoritative book, there are 36 different areas in which the RSS has spread its social, political, cultural and religious work; the religious works are entrusted to the VHP that came into existence in 1964. According to Walter K. Anderson and Shridhar D. Damle:

> The RSS itself used the Ram Janmabhoomi issue during 1980s to galvanise the Hindu community and it looked to Moropant Pingle, a senior pracharak (full time worker) loaned to the VHP as a trustee in 1980, to provide strategic guidance to it, including using the Ram temple issue to mobilize pan-Hindu support. Pingle worked with pro-Hindu Congress leaders to support the building of the Ram temple and he conceived of Ram yatras (marches) in 1983–84 in Uttar Pradesh that portrayed Ram as a prisoner behind bars.[2]

There has been no such sustained campaign, of late, largely non-violent, for a religious shrine's construction anywhere in the world. The Ram temple movement was launched by the VHP in 1982; the BJP officially adopted the issue in June 1989 with a resolution passed at its national executive committee in Palampur, Himachal Pradesh, which said that 'The BJP holds that the nature of this controversy is such that it just cannot be sorted out by a court of law.'[3]

How such a vexed issue was adroitly sorted out by the apex court in 2019, just five years after Modi became the prime minister, could be a juicy matter for a separate book. But it made RSS a much bigger fan of Modi, himself a former *pracharak*. The RSS always wanted a Ram temple in Ayodhya as it was seen to be a step forward towards their dream of creating a Hindu Rashtra.

The movement has been a heady mix of politics, religion, faith, history, archaeology, complex legal tangles and so on with the first legal suit dating back to 1885. Mahant Raghubar Das had filed suit No. 61/280 of 1885 in the court of a sub-judge, in Faizabad, seeking permission to construct a temple on the Ram chabutara (raised platform) adjoining the Babri structure in Ayodhya.

The Babri mosque was built by Emperor Zahir-ud-din Muhammad Babur's general Mir Baqi in Ayodhya in the year 1528. Babur was the founder of the Mughal dynasty and enjoys a distinct place in Indian history. Many believe that Baqi had demolished a Ram temple in order to build the mosque. There's a long history associated with the bitter controversy about his birthplace but the limited point that I am making here is that apart from any ordinary villager who was seen to be a devout disciple of Ram, there have been many others who worshipped him. Most of the important Hindu princes of their times, politicians, industrialists and women among others have been genuine worshippers of Lord Ram. He cuts across genders, economic strata, political ideology and social dynamics. The ancient epic written by Valmiki—Ramayana—in Sanskrit is a highly revered book in Hindu society. In India, Ram Navami continues to be celebrated in North India with much fervour since centuries.

Rajmata Vijaya Raje Scindia was one of the many strong followers of Lord Ram. She used to take part in the VHP activities in every possible manner and in later days, was a leading figure of the Ram Janmabhoomi agitation. In fact, soon after leaving the Congress party, she got associated with the Jana Sangh and gradually espoused the cause of the VHP— the two sister organizations having the same goal to achieve, under the big umbrella of the RSS. Until her death in January 2001, she was the vice president of the VHP, according to the Indore-based Vishnu Sadashiv Kokje, the international president of the Parishad since April 2018. He contested an election and won with majority after having served the organization as its vice president for three years before this.

But then she was not just a decorative office-bearer. There are many known and unknown incidences which hold testimony to the fact that she was involved in the movement from the bottom of her heart. It is also said that after an RSS meeting held in Jai Vilas Palace, Gwalior, in which the then Sarsanghchalak Guruji Golwalkar had also participated, the Rajmata was deeply impressed with the personality and aura of 'Guruji', not to speak of his thoughts and commitment for nation-building.

Rajendra Sharma, a veteran journalist and editor of the right wing, lowly-circulated daily *Swadesh*, recalls how much she was involved with the VHP for many years since after she had joined the Jana Sangh. Sharma had been associated with the Rajmata since the late '60s as a young journalist. He had come from Mandsaur, his native place, to join the newspaper *Hamari Awaj*, in Gwalior, which was supported by the Scindia family. It was bought from one Jhamanlal Sharma by a Scindia trust—Srikrishna Madhav Trust, in July 1967. Rajendra Sharma worked very closely with Vijaya Raje and wrote extensively about her political and other activities. He would also accompany her on her tours, frequently.[4]

She would support the cause of the Sangh Parivar. Vir Sanghvi, in his book, mentions that many years ago, Vijaya Raje had sold her precious property in Mumbai to buy up Helicopter Services Pvt. Ltd which owned seven to eight helicopters that were available for private charters. Of course, by then, Vijaya Raje had become a leading light and principal financier of the Jana Sangh, so the choppers were mainly used to ferry the Jana Sangh leaders from one public meeting to another. Naturally, the Jana Sangh never paid for the charters and Helicopter Services ran up huge losses. But Vijaya Raje was never an RSS karyakarta (volunteer) but was definitely a staunch Hindutva supporter by thoughts and actions.

Late Acharya Giriraj Kishore (1920–2014), a sandal-smeared, bearded ex-school teacher in Morena, once under the erstwhile Gwalior state, was senior vice president of the VHP. The term 'Acharya' in Hindi means a schoolteacher which went pretty well with his new avatar of a vociferous torch-bearer of Hindutva. He is said to have caught the attention of Vijaya Raje Scindia in the '70s who then promoted him in the VHP. And with zealot Hindu image and acerbic language used in his public speeches to provoke Hindu sentiments, he soon became the popular face of the aggressive organization.[5] He died at the age of 94 at the VHP office in Delhi.

The available VHP literature mentions in many places that Vijaya Raje was also associated with starting the cow protection wing (Gow-Raksha Vibhag) within the VHP. When her repeated reminders failed in forming an opinion, she moved a resolution, which she wrote in her own handwriting, in the meeting of the Kendriya Pranyasi Mandal in Bhopal in 1986 in favour of cow safety. Cow conservation and cow rearing were some of the agendas included in the resolution for anti-cow slaughter. Those were the days the VHP was busy with such non-political agendas.

The Bhopal meeting not only passed her resolution, but Vijaya Raje was also made the president of a newly formed committee—the Bharatiya Gou-Vansh Rakshan Evam Samvardhan Samiti—to promote cow protection across India. Devki Nandan Agarwal and Purshottam Das Jhunjhunwala were made members of the committee with Narasimha Joshi as its convenor.

Much later, the VHP created a dharma sansad (religious parliament) and according to an India Today report, the BJP's association with the sansad became more obvious when Vijaya Raje participated in its meeting on 4 April 1991. It was this meeting which decided that future kar sevas would be aggressive and that violence could not be ruled out.[6]

She was also present at the kar seva which began in July 1992. Among those transporting raw materials for the construction of the platform (at Ayodhya) were Rajmata Scindia, Ashok Singhal, Acharya Giriraj Kishore, Mahant Nritya Gopal Das, Sadhvi Uma Bharti, Sadhvi Rithambhara and Vishnu Hari Dalmia.[7]

Sadhvi Uma Bharti, another firebrand Hindutva leader who went on to become union minister in the Vajpayee government and then the chief minister of Madhya Pradesh in 2003 was incidentally brought into the BJP by Vijaya Raje in 1984 and later in the VHP; she had also advised young Uma to go to the famous 'math' of Udipi's Pejawar Swami. He later became Uma's religious guru, philosopher, and guide until his death in 2019. Uma wrote in her article after Vijaya Raje's death that upon hearing her religious discourse at Damoh, an impressed Rajmata had invited her in 1970 to Gwalior and extended her patronage to the young but wonderful speaker.[8] Uma would speak with rare authority on a variety of topics; her magical oratorial skills and in-depth knowledge of Indian culture and religious aspects was astounding. Even though she had little formal education, she would cast her spell binding the audience in magic within seconds when she was not even 10 years old. The saffron-clad sadhvi always maintained that without Rajmata Scindia's blessings she would not have been what she became in public life. That Vijaya Raje had passed away just two years before she became the first woman chief minister of Madhya Pradesh, always pinched Uma Bharti.

The Rajmata had become such a votary for the cause of the Ram temple construction, that in spite of being an MP and vice president of the BJP, she stepped up her involvement in VHP activities like any other ordinary kar sevak (volunteer). P.V. Naramsimha Rao writes in his book, 'In one of such kar seva programmes on 28 October 1990, she was arrested by UP police while leading about 15,000 kar sevaks across the border of Madhya Pradesh at Sitapur Ram Ghat in UP.'[9]

Koenaard Elst, a Dutch author, writes at one place in his celebrated book *Ayodhya and After: Issues before Hindu Society,* that Vijaya Raje Scindia felt that it was not Mr Advani's place to make any such promise on behalf of the Hindus. To give context, Advani, had on 13 August 1990, suggested that Muslims leave the site of the Ram temple to the Hindus, and promised that in return he would persuade the VHP leadership to even renounce its demand for the hand-over of the disputed sites in Mathura and Varanasi. It was on this statement that Scindia had reacted more vehemently than any other VHP leader, which goes to underscore her strong bond with the right-wing movement.

The political situation in the country had suddenly changed in the late '80s. The V.P. Singh-led National Front (NF) government, a coalition of many parties, was installed at the Centre by December 1989. Neither BJP nor Congress was able to form government in Delhi. The Third Front cobbled together an ephemeral government. It had the outside support of the BJP, led by L.K. Advani. Advani had also announced the BJP's support to the kar seva openly, having sensed the huge response to the VHP's clarion call given earlier for temple construction. In his memoir, Advani, then the BJP chief, writes:

> By now, I was fully convinced that this movement was not only about building a temple in Ayodhya. It was not even merely about reclaiming a holy Hindu site from the onslaught of a bigoted foreign invader in the past. It was equally about reclaiming the true meaning of secularism from the onslaught of pseudo-secularism. It was about reasserting our cultural heritage as the defining source of India's national identity.[10]

Koenaard Elst further wrote in his book, under the chapter 'Ram Janmabhoomi Politics':

The centuries-old struggle over the Babri Masjid-Ram Janmabhoomi came in a critical phase on November 9, 1989, when the first stone of the Ram Janmabhoomi Mandir was laid, in a grand shilanyas ceremony. The actual construction had been announced for February, but then the VHP leadership decided to give the new Prime Minister VP Singh, who at that time enjoyed a lot of goodwill, four months' time to work out an amicable agreement among all the parties concerned. But during these four months nothing was done. This forced the VHP to announce, in July 1990, that it would start temple construction on 30 October 1990.[11]

He further said that to divide the Ram Janmabhoomi movement, Prime Minister V.P. Singh, without consulting his allies and other political parties such as the BJP and the communist parties, etc., announced, on 7 August 1990, to implement the recommendations of the Mandal Commission* Report, giving 27 per cent reservations in government jobs to the OBCs.

That was about the time Advani was contemplating a pad-yatra (journey on foot) from Somnath to reach Ayodhya on 30 October for the kar seva. Pramod Mahajan, the party's firebrand general secretary had then reportedly improvised the idea and made it into a rath-yatra, since the distance was over 10,000 kilometres and walking all the way to Ayodhya in Uttar Pradesh from Somnath in Gujarat would have been too tiresome. Mahajan and Modi, then a promising young leader, became co-travellers of Advani on the rath. Rajmata Scindia, along with Sikander Bakht, both party vice presidents, had flagged off the prestigious Rath Yatra from Somnath to reach in time to Ayodhya for the crucial kar seva. The Yatra

---

*The Mandal Commission was appointed by the Janata Party in January 1979 with a mandate to identify socially or educationally backward classes of India. It was headed by an MP, B.P. Mandal.

had created an unprecedented buzz across the route and with national media covering the first such event with much more enthusiasm, it got tremendous publicity to the Ram-Rath as it rolled out of the famous temple town of the Saurashtra region. Clearly, Advani was the cynosure of all eyes then as the first such political show, timed to meet the kar seva at Ayodhya, turned out to be a huge success. He was much pleased with the turn out on the way to greet him all the way. International media too gave him a place of prominence. But on 23 October 1990, the yatra was suddenly halted in Samastipur in Bihar, by Chief Minister Lalu Prasad Yadav. Advani was arrested and the yatra could not reach Ayodhya. The political atmosphere became extremely surcharged and Advani, overnight, became a more important and prominent leader due to his arrest. Many political pundits and writers believe that thanks to the Advani yatras, Hindus were awakened and together as a robust group they ultimately helped the BJP grab power at the Centre with Vajpayee as their prime minister, three times, including one term of just 13 days.

For the readers' convenience, it may be clarified here that during those days when the VHP had become very impatient with various governments in Uttar Pradesh and Delhi, it had also become much more aggressive. Between 1989 and 1992, a number of small and big kar sevas were announced, cancelled and rescheduled. All were aimed at mobilizing more and more support for the Ram temple from across India.

Finally, when the 465-year-old structure of Babri mosque was demolished on 6 December 1992 by the mob comprising lakhs of frenzied Hindu kar sevaks drawn from all over the country shouting slogans like 'ek dhakka aur do, Babri Masjid tod do' (push once more, break the babri Mosque) and 'Ram Nam Satya hai, Babri Masjid Dhwasta hai' (Ram's name is the truth, Babri Masjid has perished) the VHP, RSS and BJP leaders heaved a sigh of relief. It created an unprecedented patriotic wave nationwide. Muslims were naturally very upset and scared; the Congress was completely crest-fallen because 'their' prime minister Narasimha Rao had miserably failed to protect 'secularism.'

Curiously, Rahul Gandhi, a few years later on 19 March 2007 to be precise, said in Western Uttar Pradesh's Deoband: 'Had the Gandhi family been there in politics [at that time], Babri Masjid demolition would not have taken place,' inviting all-round criticism and some defence.[12] But political analysts back in Delhi dubbed it a display of political naivety and immaturity on part of the Congress leader and nothing beyond that.

The former Rajmata of Gwalior was among those seen seated in the front row along with L.K. Advani, Ashok Singhal, Atal Bihari Vajpayee and others witnessing the historic mosque come down brick by brick on 6 December 1992. This was despite the fact that the Uttar Pradesh government, led by the BJP chief minister Kalyan Singh, had given in writing an undertaking to the Union Government that it would not allow any damage to the mosque during the proposed mega kar seva. The hyped-up atmosphere all over the country, especially in the Uttar Pradesh towns of Ayodhya and Faizabad, had to be seen to be believed. Some said it was a brutal attack on India's long-standing secular image, while others maintained that it was the first step towards actualizing the 'Hindu Rashtra' dream of the RSS.

Whatever it was, in Delhi, Prime Minister Narasimha Rao watched the entire episode unfold, rather helplessly. He trusted BJP's Kalyan Singh in a little too much and then faced unending criticism from his Congress colleagues such as Arjun Singh, Madhavrao Scindia and M.L. Fotedar (all cabinet ministers in 1992) and the international press. It was quite a political contrast that while the mother was right there in Ayodhya, supervising the demolition of the mosque, her son, as a cabinet minister in Rao's government in Delhi, was helplessly watching the structure crumble as his political boss Rao could not decide upon any preventive action plan well in advance.

Most Congress leaders accused Rao of being hand in glove with the BJP, the seers and the VHP to ensure that the masjid was pulled down. Though the fact had been that he had made several efforts to a establish dialogue with the RSS headquarters at Nagpur and had utilized his ministers such as Vasant Sathe and V.N. Gadgil and also some of his religious gurus. Prime Minister Rao's passive approach may have made him the darling of the Sangh parivar, but he soon became a persona non grata within the Congress in the following years. After he demitted office as the prime minister, he was not even given a ticket by his successor Sitaram Kesri to contest to which he had once philosophically responded: 'Man gets what he deserves.'

After his death, his side of the Ayodhya story, in his own words, was published as a book called *Ayodhya: 6 December 1992*. The former prime minister had put a condition to the publishers that while the manuscript would remain with them, the book should come out only after his death. He died in December 2004 and Penguin brought out the 317-page well-written, factual book in 2006.

Rao was forced by his colleagues to act in the matter. The Central Bureau of Investigation (CBI) had then lodged FIRs against most BJP and VHP leaders, including Advani, Murli Manohar Joshi, Uma Bharti, Vinay Katiyar and Vijaya Raje in the Babri mosque demolition case. In all, 32 accused persons faced charges and even after decades, the CBI could not prove anyone guilty despite having named them in the chargesheet. The court case dragged on for almost three decades, inconclusively. The original FIR was against 49 people, but 17 of them passed away during the long period of hearings, including Shiv Sena supremo Bal Thackeray and Rajmata Scindia. The trial kept on dragging for years.

The special CBI court finally pronounced its verdict on 30 September 2020 in which all of the accused were acquitted—a full 28 years after the national disaster! It was deemed as shock or a celebration; it depended entirely on which side of the fence you were on!

THE RAJMATA'S FIRM REFUSAL

Despite her total devotion and commitment to the cause of Hindutva and right-wing BJP, why was the Rajmata not considered in the fray as the president of the Jana Sangh/BJP? This was a puzzle to many, including her son Madhavrao, who showed some concern for his mother despite their strained relationship. Once, while discussing politics of the BJP with the author in the late '90s, he angrily wondered why on earth 'they' weren't making his mother the president of the party even though they were championing the cause of reservation for women.

L.K. Advani, however, did know about this, much earlier. And so did Atal Bihari Vajpayee! Much before the BJP came into being, the issue had been settled already! When there was a search for the president of the Jana Sangh, headed by Vajpayee, Advani was asked to replace the incumbent president but he refused, saying he was not a good orator, and suggested another name. He writes in his memoir:

> Atalji agreed to my suggestion and we went to Gwalior to persuade her [Rajmata] to accept the post [president]. After a lot of persuasion, she finally said 'Yes'. Relieved and happy, we thanked her for her assent. Just then, she said, 'But please wait... As you know, I don't take any important decision in my life without seeking the approval and blessings of my Guruji at Datia.' The same day she went to Datia, a small district town in Madhya Pradesh,

and returned the next day with the bad news. 'My Guruji has said "No"'.[13]

While Dhyanendra Singh, her brother, remembers this incident vividly, Advani writes that they (he and Vajpayee) had then approached, after the refusal of the Rajmata, Dr Bhai Mahavir who too declined to take over as the Jana Sangh's president, as his wife did not approve of it. Mahavir later became the Governor of Madhya Pradesh (1998–2003) courtesy of the then RSS chief, K.S. Sudarshan, and had made life miserable for Digvijaya Singh, the then chief minister, who was said to be involved in such governance practices which were, according to Mahavir, unethical and smacked of corruption.[14]

Their fights used to provide juicy stories to the media and intelligence sleuths would keep an eye on the journalists who visited the Raj Bhavan to meet its wonderfully straightforward occupant. Mahavir was a nationalist, an RSS member and an upright, simple politician who passed away in Delhi in December 2016 at the age of 94.

When the Rajmata's centenary celebrations concluded in October 2020, amidst the COVID-19 threat, Prime Minister Narendra Modi, a staunch Hindu hardliner of the BJP, not only paid a glowing tribute to Vijaya Raje, but also released a ₹100 coin in her honour.

7

Madhavrao Scindia and the Congress: A Love-Hate Relationship?

Winning an election is a tricky business. Not everyone is cut out for it. In a democratic set-up, particularly, with a very wide range of voters, whose numbers run in the millions, it is a task which is much more than what people generally term as humungous.

And if you are in India, the world's largest democracy, it's all the more challenging. You can thus imagine how difficult it could be for an individual to win election after election, from one constituency to the other and from one party's symbol to a new one. It becomes more complex a process given the fact that elections in India are ridden with caste calculations, illiteracy among the electorate, rigging possibilities and many other issues that add up to the ground-level perplexities for an individual candidate.

And this applies to almost all candidates, irrespective of their party affiliations. 'In some parts of India the rule of law has been compromised by an increasing criminalisation of politics,' wrote Christophe Jaffrelot, a political scientist and author in reference to some of Indian states. 'Gangs associated with candidates (if not parties) during elections, intimidate voters and/or capture ballot-boxes in the polling stations of constituencies deemed hostile...' to the candidate commissioning the operation called booth capturing, he concluded.[1]

In the light of this very brief introduction to the convoluted process of the Indian elections and the in-built challenges, especially in the Lok Sabha elections where the voter base is very broad, readers would recall that even towering personalities like Indira Gandhi of the Congress (R) (in 1977) and Atal Bihari Vajpayee of the BJP (in 1984 and before that as a Jana Sangh candidate too), had to swallow the bitter pill of defeat.

They lost at some point or the other in their long and eventful careers despite their immense popularity. Indira Gandhi was the prime minister before and after the defeat while Vajpayee rose to occupy that highly coveted office after his losses in Gwalior and other places. This is just to indicate and underscore the uncertainties of any election outcomes governed by local conditions which cannot be compared on any common scale. Since I have covered many elections myself, being a political journalist, I can say, with absolute confidence, how tough it is in the Indian context to keep winning election after election despite the rapidly evolved methodology of scientific election management put in place by various political parties and candidates.

Madhavrao Scindia, the 'prince charming' of the Indian politics, was an exception. He was a star dazzling on the Indian electoral horizon, winning every single election of the nine polls he contested from two constituencies and three parties, without a break. He never contested from the two constituencies simultaneously to keep a 'safer' seat, as did Indira, Vajpayee (he once contested from three seats and lost two), Advani, Narendra Modi and lately, Rahul Gandhi.

That is precisely what makes Scindia stand apart from the rest despite him being an erstwhile maharaja of one of the largest and richest royal states of India. Not all maharajas who contested after Independence met with successes the way Scindia did.

Curiously enough, however, his mother Rajmata Vijaya Raje faced the ignominy of losing one election, not in her home state but in Uttar Pradesh against the mighty Indira Gandhi, and much later, his son Jyotiraditya experienced a shock defeat from the traditional Scindia family seat of Guna in Madhya Pradesh in 2019. In between the era of the Rajmata and Jyotiraditya, the other Scindia who had to taste the defeat was Vasundhara Raje. She lost the 1984 Lok Sabha election from the Bhind-Datia constituency of Madhya Pradesh to Krishna Singh, also a member of a small princely state of Datia, by a big margin of over 87,000 votes. Interestingly, Vasundhara was pitted by the BJP and supported by Vijaya Raje, and Krishna Singh Judeo was supported by Madhavrao Scindia. The Congress won that seat too.

Guna was first represented by a Scindia family member way back in 1957 when Vijaya Raje had been forced to contest on a Congress ticket. That was her first election. Between 1957 and 2019, in all 18 general elections/by-elections that took place, only thrice a non-Scindia family member stood from Guna and won—Ramsahai Pandey (1962), J.B. Kripalani (1967) and Mahendra Singh Kalukheda (1984). In the rest of the 15 polls, it was one or the other Scindia!

Madhavrao's track record as the people's representative remained unbeaten throughout his long career spanning three decades. That makes rare history when one looks at the colourful yet tricky Indian political kaleidoscope. What made him so popular? What did he do to develop his constituencies? How did he maintain relations with his constituents? I shall tackle it later. But for now, to gain a better perspective of electoral politics, as far as Madhya Pradesh is concerned, we need to know the only other such political personality who matched the aura of Madhavrao—Sumitra Mahajan.

She is a part of BJP and represented Indore, the commercial capital of Madhya Pradesh and once a seat of power of the Holkar royal dynasty. She contested her first election for the Lower House of the Indian Parliament in 1989 and then kept winning each election until 2019 when she was denied the party nomination by the BJP after she completed a very impressive tenure as the Lok Sabha Speaker (2014–2019), the first BJP woman to occupy this high seat. In all, she won eight consecutive polls, from the same party and the same highly urban and literate constituency. Needless to say, she became the darling of the voters as her victory margins were always sizeable every time she took on a new Congress candidate.

Only once, in 2009, did she have a 'narrow escape' when her own party's local leaders and moneybags openly sabotaged her, throwing party discipline to the wind, to bring down her margin of victory to the lowest at 11,480 votes. The BJP, the party with a difference, however, took no action against the known group of Indore dissidents who had supported the Congress candidate almost openly. That she finally managed to clinch it is credit to her popularity borne out of her love for the development of Indore city, her simplicity, accessibility and, above all, a clean image.

Oxford educated Madhavrao Scindia, on the other hand, contested first from a rural, farmer-dominated segment of Guna which was dusty, poverty-stricken and backward. But he was equally at ease with the voters here as he was with those of the urban areas of Gwalior, his other constituency, represented almost alternately with Guna, for close to 30 years. Yet, he maintained his unbeaten record. He won four elections from Guna and five from Gwalior. From a debutant candidate of the Jana Sangh in 1971, to an independent candidate in 1977 and then a Congress nominee in 1980 to being his own regional party's (the Madhya Pradesh Vikas Congress [MPVC]) candidate in 1996, his graph went up and up, barring the last election of his life, in 1998, which he won with a narrow margin against a BJP candidate Jaibhan Singh Pawaiya. The distinction the ex-royal ruler thus achieved remains unparalleled—representing three different parties and registering victory as an independent. In India, having a party symbol in an election matters the most but Scindia took that risk too—of being an independent—and could overcome it early in his political life.

Elsewhere, L.K. Advani, the BJP patriarch, is another tall leader who also remained unbeaten throughout his long and chequered political career in one political party, just like the communist leader Indrajit Gupta who won many more elections from different places in the left-wing-dominated West Bengal.

But there is a slight difference here.

While Advani, a former deputy prime minister, won seven Lok Sabha elections from two different constituencies of Delhi and Gandhinagar, with a break in 1996, due to Hawala scam controversy, the former union home minister Gupta lost just one election in 1977 and won as many as 10 terms, beginning with a by-election in 1960. Like Scindia and Advani, he too changed constituencies and emerged victorious. In India, where the roots of communism as political ideology did not spread much deeper, Gupta's victories stood out, so did his performance in the parliament. In Mahajan's case, she is the only longest serving woman MP, although from one single constituency and a single party, the BJP.

◆

Madhavrao was born with a silver spoon in his mouth. He was not only royal by birth but also by nature. There are umpteen examples which bear testimony to the stories narrated by people from different walks of life underlining the fact that Scindia's dealing with laymen or his former 'subjects' was straight, simple and gentlemanly. Raghuraj Singh Chordia, a former Congress-affiliated mayor of Neemuch for 10 years, says, 'I had met "Maharaj" a number of times in Neemuch, Gwalior, Guna, Delhi and Bhopal and always felt that the Gwalior scion was quite down to earth, helpful and with absolutely no iota of arrogance...he was a true gentleman.'[2]

Jyotiraditya Scindia, his son, in an interview with the author, said:

> What I have learnt from my father is that more important than anything else is to be a 'good human being' rather than being called a good politician... My father always valued his relationships with people. He would say most important in life is not any post or position or yash (success) or kirti (fame) but maintaining genuinely good human relationships. He was extremely truthful in his relationships with people, and tried to forge parivarik sambandh (family relationship). I have always been inspired by the way my father dealt with people. If I find some little place in people's heart, I would consider myself saubhagyashali (fortunate).

Madhavrao had the golden opportunity to be a businessman in Mumbai (many of those who knew him well believed he would have been a failure because money never fascinated him much), looking after family treasures which he did for some time with his bosom friend and Bombay's industry tycoon Nusli Wadia who was ever willing to guide him when needed. Scindia had also invested in the Bombay Dyeing and Manufacturing Co. Ltd, the leading textile group of the country and had become its director for a few years. He even started sitting in the posh office at Neville House, the headquarters of Bombay Dyeing in the Ballard Estate area. He also tried his hand at developing a classy real estate project—an elite, high-end, multistoried residential apartment at the ancestral Samudra Mahal land, designed by one of the top Parsi architects Beji Billimoria, a high-rise specialist of his time, when people were wondering if such a project would at all make profits. Nusli Wadia is reported to have said in Vir Sanghvi's book that Madhavrao's decisions were taken more with emotion rather than practicality, in reference to an investment he had made in Wadia's company in the '70s.

But Scindia soon gave up business and was caught up in the vortex of politics and shifted from Bombay to Delhi. He then devoted himself completely to public life throughout to emerge as a national-level, mass leader. He was an affable, accessible, rich and extremely popular maharaja of the erstwhile Gwalior state who was known the world over as a dynamic politician with a variety of interests from horse racing to cricket and flying to making friends. He was an excellent pilot and at shortest temptation would slip into the cockpit and be the captain of a chopper or a small plane and fly it with an ease that could match any other professional pilot having clocked hundreds of hours of flying. There are many instances one finds after talking to a number of people across the country that narrate stories of his forays in the air even as the minister.

Arjun Singh, former chief minister of Madhya Pradesh, echoing similar sentiments of what Jyotiraditya told me, once recalled, as mentioned in the *Indian Express*, (reproduced from *Shrimant Madhavrao Scindia—Sansamaran-Smrutiya: 1945–2001)* after his death, that Madhavrao would always look after his friends and never ignored anyone.[3] Years later, when he was forced to form a political party, interestingly enough, Scindia thought of his school friends to lead it, which is a testimony to what Arjun Singh had stated. Jyotiraditya maintains that his father would always give priority to his family relationships—something Madhavrao showed in this case too.

The year 1971 was in way a major milestone in Madhavrao's political and personal life. He became father to a son—Jyotiraditya—on the first day of the year in Bombay. Then, as an obedient son of Vijaya Raje, he fought his first election that year on the symbol of the Hindu right-wing party the Jana Sangh (later to be known as the BJP) from Guna, which, ironically, turned out to be his last constituency in 1999, as a Congress candidate. He, however, had started campaigning much before he entered the electoral fray himself; available records suggest he held his first election rally outside Gwalior, in 1966–67 at Ujjain and Khachrod (Nagda) when he was just 22. He accompanied his mother on election tours then and read out speeches written by her.[4] He was an instant hero among the crowds then.

That election was for the Madhya Pradesh state Assembly and the most prestigious one for his mother. A major political history was waiting to be written after those elections and has been narrated in an earlier chapter.

While Scindia may have entered the political arena via the Jana Sangh, he was always meant to be a committed Congress leader, as it seemed from the later developments. A leader with a difference who served the grand old party in various capacities inside the parliament, outside it and in the government. He, like many other senior Congress veterans, had the opportunity to work with Indira Gandhi, Rajiv Gandhi and his widow Sonia.

After Scindia had made his decision to join the Congress, he did not bother much about his family's political lineage or affiliation. He is said to have always harboured secular credentials and the Congress was the right party for him. The difference thus can be explained in that some of the elections he fought were against his mother and sister's party, the BJP, and against a towering BJP leader such as Atal Bihari Vajpayee. Madhavrao Scindia's career touched its zenith in 1984 when at the very last moment the Congress leadership sent him to Gwalior to take on the national leader Vajpayee and where he managed to defeat the all-time great of Indian politics who also had strong links with Gwalior. Scindia recorded a massive victory of a staggering margin of over 1.75 lakh votes much to the surprise of his all detractors. Scindia had pulled out all the stops and had made history in the process.

Those days a story was doing the rounds—right or wrong, no one knows for sure—that Arjun Singh, the chief minister, had managed to shift his rival from Guna to Gwalior with a twin objective: if he lost to Vajpayee, his political career would be finished and if he eked out a victory, chances of which were considered very low, he would go to central politics in Delhi. Rajiv Gandhi liked the idea and sprang a surprise at the eleventh hour. Some historians say that Vajpayee tried to run to Bhind to file the nomination but could not reach there and complete the formalities before time.

The Scindia-Vajpayee contest was the most talked about election of India that year, covered by national and international media for days together. The Congress wanted to pin down Vajpayee to Gwalior so he could not go elsewhere for campaigning, what with him being the star campaigner of the BJP. Hundreds of Indian and foreign journalists had descended upon Gwalior to write about the mega-fight which the 39-year-old Scindia had dramatically won and got his name written with golden letters in the annals of Indian politics.

That was the year the BJP, then just four years old, displayed its worst ever electoral performance. The party could send only two MPs to the Lok Sabha: C. Janga Reddy, the giant-killer in politics from Hanamkonda in old Andhra Pradesh who defeated P.V. Narasimha Rao and A.K. Patel from Mehsana in Gujarat. Since Indira Gandhi had been assassinated only a few months ago in October 1984, there was a massive sympathy wave, riding on which the Congress won highest number of seats in its history—404 MPs. Advani, who was a Rajya Sabha member and had not contested in the election, termed it as a 'Shok Sabha' (a gathering of mourners) and not a Lok Sabha, election.[5]

But then, look at the beauty and endless possibilities of Indian politics: Scindia defeated the same Vajpayee, who had held his hand when Madhavrao took his first baby steps in politics, who gave him the membership of the Jana Sangh just about 13 years ago, in Gwalior itself.

Well, the other difference, and it could be considered a major one, was that despite being in 'politics' Scindia was not a typical 'politician' in the popular sense of the term. You get the hint of the same in what Jyotiraditya has said about his father above. He was not cunning, he was not corrupt, nor was he clever, as is required in Indian politics to survive and go places. He was intelligent, highly educated, cultured and a leader full of genuine empathy for others. The absence of these three Cs in his character made him a great leader with a pan-Indian image, but it had a flip side too!

His attractive personality, ready wit, willingness to help the poor and the downtrodden with an approach towards development made him what he was. He would often say that he would do politics from his heart and not from his mind, and that showed that he was essentially an emotional person rather than a shrewd politician or a manipulator that one sees around in umpteen numbers today in all parties, especially in the Congress. Madhavrao was also an administrator par excellence. His record as the railway minister is unmatched even 30 years after he demitted office. D.S. Mathur, an IAS officer of the 1971 batch, who was already working in the Railway Board when Scindia became the minister in 1985, says:

> Madhavrao was open to new ideas and was very fast in implementing decisions if found them to be useful for public at large. If the metro trains are plying in India today, the credit must go to Scindia who had picked up on the idea I had suggested to him, as his OSD, just as an off the cuff remark on Delhi traffic congestion. He liked the

idea and then immediately convened a meeting with the Chairman of the Railway Board to explore possibility of Delhi Metro train service and then pushed for the same. The other major contribution he made was of starting computerisation of railway ticketing system and other digital reforms in the department. He put both works on fast track.[6]

The real the icing on the cake was his decision to start a one-day train that leaves in morning and returns the same evening. Shatabdi Express was started to commemorate the Nehru centenary and the first super-speed train was started between Delhi and Jhansi which was later extended first to Gwalior and then to Bhopal. Prashant Mehta, his close aide, recalls how he and Scindia travelled sitting in the engine with the driver to personally test the ride and the speed. Railway officials had apprehensions about the high price of tickets and they wanted to wait for six months to revise rates after seeing the response to this kind of novel experience. 'But the train was fully booked on the fourth day itself, reflecting that the gamble had paid off early in the day, making Scindia not only happy, but also a hero among Rajiv's cabinet colleagues,' Mehta told the author. The bullet train that has been the talk of the Modi regime, was also on Scindia's mind in the '80s. He had made a visit to Tokyo in 1988 to explore the possibility of bringing the technology to India.

Late O.P. Khanna, Scindia's long-time private secretary, had once told me that Scindia would invariably go through the timetables of major trains every evening and pull up those senior zonal managers from where delays were reported; that was the level of commitment he had for his sarkari job. It was quite unheard of in those days of the mid-'80s for a minister to sit in his office until 2.00 a.m. to dispose of files and hold meetings with officers. Of course, a separate book can be written about his eventful stint at the railway ministry because he was the first minister who made it mandatory to give bed rolls to the passengers in air-conditioned bogeys. And when top railway officials offered a small excuse of creating a space to keep all the bed rolls in a compartment, Madhavrao went all the way to Perambur Railways Coach factory in Tamil Nadu to see the design of the new bogey and ensured that the problem was sorted out. 'So much concern for passengers was a rarity from a minister,' observed Mehta, underscoring the zeal of his boss towards ensuring passenger comfort and thinking about the minutest details.

As a journalist during my visits to Gwalior, I remember having seen the modernized Gwalior Railway Station, absolutely spic and span. He also utilized an abandoned railways land to convert it into a world-class hockey stadium with expensive Astro turf laid down. A *Free Press Journal* report,[7] lauding him then, had said 'India needed 10 more Scindias to improve the sports facilities.' He also gave many sportsmen jobs in the railways. Injecting punctuality into the Indian railways system was the other priority area he had fixed for himself, as far as his contribution to the department goes.

Following in the footsteps of Lal Bahadur Shastri, he too had offered to resign from his post after a train accident in Kerala in 1988. Before leaving for the accident site in a small plane, he had sent in his resignation to the prime minister. Rajiv Gandhi did not accept it, but that was Madhavrao Scindia, an emotional politician who took the moral responsibility upon himself, instead of making a General Manager or a Railway Board traffic member the proverbial scapegoat. Jyotiraditya believes that his father set a rare example of leadership by taking the ownership of the incident when he tendered his resignation though he was not directly responsible for the mishap.

Motilal Vora, former chief minister of Madhya Pradesh, once wrote that Scindia's administrative efficiency was such that he would issue orders for work to be done, if he was convinced of the same, then and there. 'The rail-road bridge is one facility which was the need in most of the smaller towns. In my constituency of Durg one such bridge was pending for 30 years. After I requested him, he not only sanctioned it, announced the date for its stone-laying ceremony so that the department began working speedily,' Vora recalls in *Shrimant Madhavrao Scindia—Sansamaran-Smrutiya: 1945–2001,* penned by Dr Anil Mishra and Rajendra Bharti.

This was the reason that the people of his constituency were happy with him. First, by always trying to be with people when they needed him and second, by working for the development all the time and third paying personal attention to people from the Gwalior-Chambal area, made him extremely popular.

Yogendra Lumba, former District Congress Committee (DCC) chief of Guna, says that Madhavrao had always nursed the constituency well. He implemented cent per cent electrification scheme and had launched Guna-Etawah rail line besides many other schemes such as irrigation projects, that helped generate direct or indirect employment and created public facilities, but as Bimal Julka, his former aide, put it in a conversation with the author:

> During Digvijaya Singh's rule in MP between 1993–2003, Scindia had to struggle hard to elicit necessary and natural support from the State Government machinery in implementing his vision and programmes for the benefit of the people.

Guna was a common political turf for Digvijaya and Madhavrao who were contemporaries in politics but were political opponents despite being in the same Congress Party for many years. Raghogarh, where a quaint little fort stands today that belongs to Digvijaya Singh's ancestors, is an Assembly constituency in the Guna district (but not part of the Lok

Sabha constituency) represented by Digvijaya, a former vassal of the area, much smaller than the Gwalior state. Historical documents of British time state that the Khinchi Rajputs had fallen to the Gwalior Marathas (Scindias) and that the two did not get along well for over 150 years.

Now Digvijay's only son, Jaivardhan Singh, a former urban development minister in Kamal Nath's 15-month government, is the sitting MLA from Raghogarh.

What Julka, a former secretary in Government of India, felt was true. Madhavrao was no match against Singh's Machiavellian manoeuvres in which the latter was engaged at all times. Many political writers, analysts and his party men, therefore firmly believed that if Madhavrao could not reach the destination he deserved in his political journey, it was due to the absence in him of the 'C' factor—cunningness, corruption and cleverness.

After his death in 2001, an editorial comment in *Hindustan Times* said: '...A shattered nation can only mourn the best prime minister India never had.' The *Deccan Herald*, Bengaluru, had observed '.... He was considered a leader who was made for bigger things and responsibilities.' The *Hindu* wrote,

> To say that the death of Madhavrao Scindia is a loss to the Congress is to understate the overwhelming tragedy of his sudden unforeseen departure. Scindia's death is a loss of the polity itself-a fact that is accentuated in these distressing times when a dismal mixture of mediocrity and manipulativeness seems essential for political success.

Towards the late-'90s, post the Hawala scam cases, many party leaders and journalists in Delhi had started seeing and talking about him as a future prime minister from the Congress. Dr Manmohan Singh, the latter-day 'accidental prime minister' was nowhere on the horizon, though he was definitely on the top of 'king maker' Sonia's mind, but few had the inkling of the same.

In one of the conversations, his senior friend and former union minister Natwar Singh had told him in the Parliament soon after Scindia was made the party's deputy leader of Lok Sabha: 'Madhav, wait for some more time, she [Sonia] has many more things for you in her mind, this is just the beginning...' It was then seen in political circles, rightly or wrongly, that Sonia was grooming him for a much bigger role. Scindia, with other select leaders, was close to the Congress supremo and was a leader of the anti-Rao faction. 'Natwar, Arjun Singh and Madhavrao Scindia had once wondered why Rao was not disciplining V.C. Shukla, the parliamentary affairs minister, who had told the Lok Sabha that the Bofors papers were on way to India.'[11] That was the Rao style of politics to keep Sonia under check, using the Bofors scandal off and on.

It was the time all three were important ministers in the Narasimha Rao government but were close to Sonia who was not even the party president. Both Singh and Scindia as Union Human Resource Department (HRD) ministers one after the other had left clear instructions that the Rajiv Gandhi Foundation (RGF) proposals be dealt with on priority, a sign of their importance attached to '10 Janpath' (a synonym for the famous Delhi address Congress workers would use informally for their boss who lived there).

Both Singh and Scindia belonged to the same state but did not like each other much when Scindia was a new MP and Arjun Singh was a powerful chief minister and was close to Indira Gandhi. 'It had more to do with the temperament of the two, than anything else. Scindia was a straightforward, regal politician but Arjun Singh was just the opposite,' observes a veteran politician from Indore who knew them both.

There was a real incident during an international cricket match at Indore's Nehru Stadium where Madhavrao Scindia, being the president of the MPCA, was watching an ODI (one-day international) and message arrived that Chief Minister

Arjun Singh would also come for some time to enjoy the game as he was in the town. Scindia, as the host of the ODI, quickly readied himself to welcome the chief minister at the entry and take him to his presidential box in the Nehru Stadium.

But Arjun Singh kept him waiting for about an hour and then word came through the district collector that the chief minister would like to buy a ticket for himself and sit in the pavilion with the paying public and not in the VIP box with Scindia. Madhavrao then went down to the pavilion and sat there and kept a seat next to him reserved for the chief minister; watched the game sitting in the pavilion with public for another half an hour or so. Eventually, when the chief minister possibly learnt that Madhavrao was waiting there in the open pavilion, Singh cancelled his visit to the cricket venue all together.

Those were the days when mobile phones were not in use in India and VIP communication would happen through field officers' wireless gadgets. This story, howsoever insignificant, shows how crafty Arjun Singh could be in his politics and how he used to behave with his party colleagues. Scindia, on his part, was magnanimous enough to extend every possible courtesy, as a cricket administrator and host, not just as a well-bred maharaja, a leading Marathi paper from Mumbai had commented then. That was in December 1988.

At one point of time in the Congress, both were very powerful, courtesy of Sonia Gandhi, who trusted them for their respective capabilities and image. 'What impressed me [about Madhavrao] was that he never gave up or took the easy way out; his answers were straight and advice always good,' the Congress president had said in a speech on the occasion of the release of a book on Scindia in Delhi, sometime in 2009.[12]

Back in 1993, Arjun Singh was at it again. He had played a backward card to promote Subhash Yadav, an MLA from the Nimar region, as chief minister of Madhya Pradesh. But it was for the optics than for a genuine urge to help the cause.

Actually, the move was to stop Madhavrao and S.C. Shukla from becoming the chief minister, which Yadav, Shukla and Scindia all realized much later when Digvijaya Singh, Arjun's original protege, became the chief minister. That was the original, real game plan of Arjun Singh.

That within the next few years Arjun Singh found himself isolated and was ditched by his chela Digvijaya, is a long and different story, too well known in Congress politics.

Madhavrao was also made the All India Congress Committee (AICC) general secretary in charge of several states such as Maharashtra, Goa, Odisha, etc., by Sitaram Kesri in an effort to strengthen the party apparatus. While he was known to be an effective administrator in the government, in party organization he was equally impressive. In an interview of August 2000, to well-known TV journalist Karan Thapar, Madhavrao is seen batting well to defend the party leadership and Sonia Gandhi, a new MP.[13] From Congress ideology to issues in the states, to the allegedly weak opposition in parliament to the Vajpayee government and his own role there, to that of the BJP's failure, he articulated like a seasoned Congress man. It showed how deeply he was involved in the party politics, especially after having won the Congress Working Committee (CWC) post, alongside Pranab Mukherjee and Ahmed Patel.

There is another interesting story that needs to be shared here, the one that highlights the twists and turns of politics in India that have been so normal in the Congress.

Makhan Lal Fotedar, without giving much background, claims:

> Indiraji summoned Rajivji in mine and Arun Nehru's presence. During the course of the conversation regarding parliamentary elections, she categorically told her son two things he should never do in future. She said: Do not ever bring Teji's son—Amitabh Bachchan—into electoral

politics and do not induct Madhav Rao Scindia in your cabinet if you ever become the prime minister.[14]

That Rajiv Gandhi did the exact opposite of what his mother instructed, on both accounts, is inexplicable. In fact, if Rajiv got some good grades in his government's report card in first five years, it was due to the extraordinary performance of Scindia as the railway minister for the full five years from 1984 to1989, whose achievements I have mentioned above.

Why could not he get what he was 'meant for' in the later part of his career? Most Congressmen—those not even attached to him—always felt that he would have been a very effective chief minister of Madhya Pradesh and a successful prime minister too.

Even Karan Thapar once instigated him by asking on a TV show directly the reasons for not taking over party leadership, given his good credentials. He was the deputy Opposition leader under Sonia Gandhi in the Lok Sabha. But Scindia, in his heart, knew (a fact he had shared with his close aide from bureaucracy) that Sonia would not make him the prime minister. The officer Prashant Mehta (IAS 1975) had told Scindia in a lighter vein that he would like to move up from the civil aviation ministry to the PMO along with Scindia, to which the latter had instantly said, 'She will never make me the PM.' Scindia's reading of Sonia was right because when the opportune time came, she had already thought of Dr Manmohan Singh as the prime minister—perhaps because of his meek character. Of course, Scindia was not alive by the time the United Progressive Alliance (UPA) came to power after a surprising defeat of the Vajpayee-led National Democratic Alliance (NDA) in 2004.

The youthful leader's life was cut short by an extremely tragic plane crash in September 2001. The cruel hand of fate intervened at the wrong time in the fortunes of his family, his party, his followers and the nation. As for the prime ministership, many of his fans and independent observers have always felt that he would have gotten it one day as he was considered young then; but to lead the state of Madhya Pradesh, he was perfectly suitable. 'There he surely suffered because he did not belong to the category of a crafty politician', says a former bureaucrat who had worked with him in Delhi.

Some of the contemporary politicians from his state always played dirty with the gracious Maharaja and through deceit, double speak and other deplorable means prevented him from becoming the chief minister of Madhya Pradesh, more than once. Laxmikant Markhedkar, his school mate and former president of the Madhya Pradesh Vikas Congress (MPVC) recalls that Scindia had been offered the opportunity:

> I was privy to the telephone call prime minister Rajiv Gandhi had made to Madhav Maharaj when he was at his friend and minister Balendu Shukla's official residence in Bhopal. I was standing next to Maharaj; Rajivji was imploring him to take over as the CM but he kept saying that if he was being made the CM unanimously, only then would he accept the responsibility.[15]

The other factions led by Arjun Singh and the Shukla brothers were deadly opposed to his candidature. They did everything to deny him his rightful claim as the chief minister, being a senior Congress leader with unimpeachable reputation.

In 1989, Arjun Singh was forced to quit after the Jabalpur High Court gave a scathing verdict against him in the Churhat lottery scam in which was found guilty. First, Singh refused to step down, but when party high command got reports from observers Buta Singh and Makhan Lal Fotedar that Singh was obstinate, the party took a tough stand and threatened to expel him and his supporters. The entire drama went on for four to five days in Bhopal in January 1989. Only after the strict line adopted by Delhi, did Arjun Singh agree to quit but put a rider:

Motilal Vora be made chief minister and not Scindia. Party high command had reportedly sent observers with instructions to make Scindia the chief minister but the machinations of the Arjun Singh group did not let that happen.[16]

Even his critics would agree that Madhavrao Scindia always kept the bar high for himself as far as political ethics were concerned. He never stooped low to conquer, nor did he come in the way to deny others their due. Motilal Vora is an example. When Arjun Singh steadfastly opposed his (Scindia's) candidature for chief minister, Scindia instantly lent his support to Vora who remained obliged to Scindia for life. Scindia could have put a spanner in the wheel to deny Vora and create problems for party leadership as well. The 'Moti-Madhav Express' later became famous in Madhya Pradesh politics after Motilal Vora was anointed as chief minister for the second time. Vora once ruefully wrote that 'Scindiaji would refer to "Moti-Madhav Express" often but how can I recall it when he is no longer around...that was our golden period together!' Vora as the chief minister and Scindia as the union railway minister, had teamed up to launch a number of policies and programmes for the development of Madhya Pradesh and hence the duo was dubbed as the 'Moti-Madhav Express' by the media.

◆

The way he had entered the Congress in the '80s and had come out with flying colours after each election, it was in the same dramatic manner that Scindia had left the party under prime minister P.V. Narasimha Rao's regime. A principled politician who had once quit as minister of Civil Aviation, while taking responsibility for an air crash IN 1992 in which none died, he once again resigned when false charges in the Hawala scam were hurled at him in 1996. He did not want a stigma on his 'Mr Clean' image at any cost. He also wanted to keep the Scindia family's long-standing and spotless prestige, intact. This was the third resignation of his career—all given to protect his honour!

In early 1991, the Jain diaries had appeared from nowhere, triggering a political landslide which rudely rocked national politics in the mid-'90s. Surendra Kumar Jain, a businessman from Madhya Pradesh, was arrested on charges of running a hawala (black money operations) racket with others. The two diaries seized from him by the CBI had details of alleged payments made to as many as 115 politicians and bureaucrats. The amount was said to be between ₹60 and ₹70 crores—big bribe by the standards of the '90s. The loose pages of personal diaries maintained by the Jains, had names among others, of BJP president L.K. Advani, Madhavrao Scindia ('MRS'), Rajiv Gandhi, Arif Mohammad Khan, Chandra Shekhar and Balram Jakhar—they were all shown to be the beneficiaries.[17]

Scindia was the HRD Minister in Narasimha Rao's cabinet. He was initially hadn't taken it seriously when his name had begun to circulate in Delhi's top circles but when the CBI and the Intelligence Bureau (IB) sources confirmed that the prime minister was going to prosecute everyone named in the Jain diaries and that the law ministry was preparing the chargesheets, something that even Rao confirmed reluctantly, Scindia was taken aback. But then he was not alone in this fight. When the CBI finally filed the chargesheet, names of two of his ministerial colleagues Balram Jakhar, later to be the governor of Madhya Pradesh and V.C. Shukla also figured in it. And Shukla was from Rao's own camp, unlike Scindia. Others included Advani, Arjun Singh, Motilal Vora, Ajit Panja, P. Shiv Shankar and Yashwant Sinha.

Those following Indian politics closely did not ever believe the two of the names on the list of accused—Advani and Scindia. That they would take bribes was beyond even the common man's comprehension. Sanghvi mentions in his book that Advani always maintained a clean track record and that Scindia was one of the richest politicians of his time and that he tried to maintain an honest image among the people.[18]

The CBI, despite several meetings between Scindia and PM Rao to thrash out the issue, went ahead with filing the chargesheet. In one of the meetings, apparently, an incredulous Prime Minister Rao told Madhavrao that the CBI director (Vijaya Rama Rao) did not listen to him. Weak on evidence, the chargesheet said that between November 1989 and April 1991, ₹1–1.2 crore were paid as bribe to Scindia. Although the chargesheet mentioned that as an MP and as railway minister he had taken bribes for awarding tenders to Jain's company, Beco Steel Castings, a sister concern of the larger Bhilai Engineering, it was sloppy on account of facts and figures.[19]

While Scindia and other Congress and BJP leaders knew he was above board, the descendant of the great Mahadji Scindia, the pride of the Maratha warriors who had humbled Mughal rulers, was deeply hurt by the very fact that such an aspersion had been cast on him, his honesty and his public image had been sought to be tarnished by his own party's leaders. Many of those who were in this 'Hawala Group', shocked as they were, refused to contest the impending parliamentary elections of May 1996, including Advani, Kamal Nath and Vidya Charan Shukla for their individual reasons. The Congress was out to deny them tickets, with them being 'tainted' leaders.

Kamal Nath, for instance, fielded his estranged wife, Alka, to keep a firm grip on the Chhindwara fiefdom though she was reluctant to fight, not having been in politics and for other personal issues. Arjun Singh, who had already formed a separate party under N.D. Tiwari's leadership after his earlier expulsion by Rao, contested from his home turf Satna on the ticket of the All India Indira Congress (Tiwari), better known as the Congress (T) but shockingly finished third behind the

BSP and BJP candidates. The official Congress candidate had finished fourth. In Delhi, Advani had quickly decided how to react; he called a press conference the same day at Ashoka Road party headquarters and announced his resignation from the Gandhinagar seat and said he would not contest until and unless he was discharged by the court. This was on 16 January 1996.[20]

Scindia took an entirely different route. He decided to go to the people's court.

Linking the whole hawala insult and conspiracy to defame him with 'the pride and prestige of Gwalior and of the Scindia family,' he played a master stroke. He left Delhi for his erstwhile seat of power by road, receiving a tumultuous and historic welcome all the way after he entered Madhya Pradesh from Dholpur in Rajasthan on 9 February 1996. Banker Abhay Paprikar, son of veteran Congress leader Raghunath Paprikar of Gwalior, recalls:

When Madhavrao arrived in Gwalior from Delhi after the hawala bombshell, the crowd response was seen to be believed. He got a hero's welcome at Morena-Chambal border. Thousands of people had spontaneously descended upon Gwalior from all over MP to express solidarity with their beloved Maharaja. People firmly believed that there was some kind of *shadyantra* (conspiracy) in framing him.[21]

Scindia chose his hometown to break his silence and spoke against the CBI and against those who had falsely implicated him in the corruption case. Several national newspapers reported his fiery speech, which was a direct attack on the Prime Minister Narasimha Rao, though without naming him, initially. 'I don't need a certificate of honesty from any agency to prove my innocence in the Hawala scandal in which I am implicated deliberately. Your faith in me is the certificate of my clean conduct,' he thundered, amidst loud applause of '*Hamara neta kaisa ho, Madhavrao jaisa ho'* (What should be our leader like, like Madhavrao)' or '*Maharaj aage badho hum tumhare saath hai'* (King you move forward we are with you).

Scindia was successful in making his fight the 'fight of Gwalior' over the next few days. Every Gwaliorwala felt humiliated along with Scindia. That was the command Scindia had on the city and its people for whom he had done a lot as railway minister and before that as an MP. Through his acerbic speeches he could convince people of the conspiracy theory and they instantly believed. Whatever he was saying in Gwalior was being heard keenly in Delhi, nay, it was being said for them to hear.

But what was the next plan? The elections were approaching fast. Scindia's fight wasn't with the entire Congress leadership; he was simply very upset with one individual—the prime minister. He wanted to teach him a lesson and prove his honesty, which, of course, was never in doubt in the minds of the people. The only way to go back to people and seek their mandate was to enter the electoral fray.

Thus was born the MPVC, with a small door kept ajar, if required to be used in future. And it proved to be a very prudent political move later. A lesser-known politician from Ganj Basoda (Vidisha district), Dr Lakshmikant Markhedkar, was overnight summoned by Madhavrao to Delhi and made its president and the party was registered in Delhi with the Election Commission of India (ECI). Jayant Khanna from Rewa was made its secretary. Both were Madhavrao's school friends from the Scindia School, Gwalior; while Markhedkar was from Madhav House and played cricket with Madhavrao; Khanna shared the Jayaji House dormitory of the famous boarding school in late '50s with him. Anil Somani was made the treasurer.

There was no other close follower of his in the party, as a part of a well though-out strategy. Balendu Shukla, Mahendra Singh Kalukheda, both ministers in Digvijaya Singh's cabinet, and many others were deliberately not asked to join the new party, lest they invited wrath and were 'disciplined' by the Congress leadership. Nonetheless, they all worked for him on the sly, day in and day, out ensuring his victory.

The MPVC fielded two candidates—one was Scindia and the other was Mahendra Karma, from a tribe from faraway Bastar. Both won the 1996 Lok Sabha polls. The debutant party had a cent per cent result. Scindia had gone to Bastar to campaign for him, leaving Gwalior behind for his entire family to do the campaigning. Jyotiraditya, who had earlier campaigned in a few elections, was again there with his newly-wed wife Priyadarshini Raje in the family's most prestigious election at Gwalior.

Scindia was sure of his victory, given the enthusiasm he saw among the cheerful crowd, but was unsure of the state government led by Digvijaya Singh. Because while earlier Digvijaya Singh had agreed to field a 'weak' candidate, he later changed the plan, as has been his wont, and fielded a former MP (Khargone and South Delhi) Shashi Bhushan Bajpai, who had earlier contested against Rajmata Vijaya Raje and had lost in 1991 from Guna. He was considered to be an anti-palace politician eyeing the large chunk of the Brahmin vote bank of Gwalior. Why Singh, either under pressure from Delhi or on his own, pressed Bajpai into the field never became clear. It was obvious from his move that he wanted to create more problems for Scindia, just as he had back-stabbed Arjun Singh, once his political guru, by promising him full support for Congress (T) but ultimately did not allow MLAs and MPs to join the state-level Jabalpur convention of the Tiwari Congress in 1995 and held most of them back from going to Delhi for the National Convention. Only two or three MLAs, including Indrajeet Patel, attended the Delhi gathering of the new outfit.

Soon after filing his nomination papers at the collectorate in a huge rally, Scindia returned to the Jai Vilas Palace to meet the waiting people and a large number of enthusiastic workers. He called me to the first floor's beautiful, ornate and large living room to grant an interview. His favourite orderly Chavan was quick to bring cold drinks, as Scindia removed his shoes and slipped his feet into more comfortable Kolhapuri slippers. It was rare that a journalist was permitted in the private portion of his palatial residence where, after offering a cold drink, a relaxed Scindia causally asked if I knew how the returning officer was. He was asking about SPS Parihar (IAS 1986), the newly appointed collector of the district. Incidentally, he was known to have been an upright and an impartial bureaucrat. I told Scindia, from my modest journalistic understanding and information of Madhya Pradesh, that the returning officer would not possibly play any foul game given his spotless track record and integrity. Scindia did not doubt him but he had CM Digvijaya and his potential to create trouble in his mind for sure.

The election result was as per expectations, and Scindia defeated Phool Singh Baraiya by a huge margin of over two lakh votes and Bajpai by over three lakh votes. It was a testament to the fact that Gwalior clearly stood by its leader as never before. The BJP, was also stung by the hawala politics of Rao, had decided not to field a candidate against Scindia, who was once their own man. Needless to say, the Congress candidate's deposit was forfeited; he got some 27,000 odd votes. Surprisingly, Bajpai still moved an election petition in the high court which was dismissed.

Around the same time, provoked by Rao's move to establish an alliance with Jayalalitha's All India Anna Dravida Munnetra Kazhagam (AIADMK) in Tamil Nadu without having consulted them, other noteworthy Congress leaders such as P. Chidambaram and G.K. Moopanar had also quit Congress. They formed the Tamil Maanila Congress (TMC), following which Chidambaram came all the way to Gwalior to address a public gathering at the Bada area in support of Scindia at the peak of campaigning.[22] Scindia's fight against Rao got bolstered, as another stalwart joined him. Both were birds of same flock—anti-Rao crusaders, but Congressmen to the core of their heart.

In Delhi, no party got clear majority in 1996; the elections produced a hung Parliament, first time in that decade.

The BJP and its allies—the Shiv Sena, the Samata Party, the Haryana Vikas Party and the Akali Dal, (Shiv Sena and Akali Dal quit the NDA alliance in 2020–21) won 194 seats, followed by the Congress plus allies with 139 seats. Other splinter groups were in two digits, such as the Samajwadi Party, the Dravida Munnetra Kazhagam (DMK) and the Telugu Desam Party (TDP). President Shankar Dayal Sharma naturally invited the largest group led by the BJP. The BJP had sought Scindia's support, but he refused. Atal Bihari Vajpayee somehow formed the government, but it turned out to be a '13-day wonder' as there was no majority.

The United Front (UF) then cobbled together a government, led by the Janata Dal (43 seats) and 12 other smaller parties. That government lasted for just about 11 months under the leadership of H.D. Deve Gowda, the first non-Congress prime minister from a southern state. Scindia seconded his name after Biju Patnaik suggested him for the prime minister's post in the UF meeting. The MPVC had supported the UF from outside, with Scindia as a member of the steering committee. As a principled stand, he did not take a ministerial berth with the Hawala sword still hanging on his head. He was waiting to be exonerated but the case was dragging on and on. The Delhi High Court had quashed the charges of corruption against Advani on 8 April 1997. But case was still on.[23] Other chargesheets were also quashed and Scindia and the others were acquitted in the next few days.

Upon the Gowda government's fall, Inder Kumar Gujral,

a gentle, soft-spoken politician from Punjab became the prime minister on 21 April 1997, after lots of politicking within the Front parties and leaders. Both Mulayam Singh and Lalu Prasad Yadav's ambitions sprung up at the last moment; they wanted to be the prime minister and were pitted against each other. Then they also tried to be the deputy prime minister which also did not happen. The MPVC supported this government too, as it was technically the same government with a United Front 'head surgery' done. Gujral mentions in his autobiography:

> CBI was thinking of appealing in the Supreme Court against the Delhi High Court verdict in favour of former union ministers, including V.C. Shukla, Madhavrao Scindia, Kamal Nath and BJP Chief Advani. This was a Catch-22 situation. Either way, I stood to lose politically.[24]

Curiously, a month later, he further wrote,

> on 16 June 1997 I granted permission to the CBI to file an appeal in the Supreme Court in what came to be known as the 'hawala case' on which I had been applying my mind for some time.[25]

The prime minister had taken advice from Ashok Desai, the Attorney General, who was then holidaying in the US and faxed his opinion to the PMO to go ahead and let the CBI appeal against the Delhi High Court judgement which had let them off the hook. This was despite the fact that Gujral was known to be a good friend of Advani and that the MPVC was supporting his United Front government, although with an insignificant number. The prime minister got good press on his 'bold' decision. But even the Supreme Court dismissed the appeal for want of adequate evidence. All were acquitted, bringing down the curtain on a sensational scam that was not to be.

About the same time, Congress, in a dramatic move,

THE SCINDIA LEGACY • 159

removed P.V. Narasimha Rao from its presidentship, holding
him responsible for the 1996 debacle and because corruption
charges began catching up with him. Rao suddenly became
a liability for the party. His long-time private secretary Ram
Khandekar, in series of articles written in Marathi, has said how
badly Rao was treated by Gandhi loyalists. Sitaram Kesri, in
charge of the Congress coffers, was swiftly made the Congress
president, much to the comfort of Scindia, who, though he
did not have friendly ties with Kesri, felt that Kesri was much
better than having to deal with Rao, whom Madhavrao would
not even like to look at, let alone talk politics with and or
seek favour from. Kesri, on the other hand, took a great liking
to Scindia.

On 5 November 1996, Kesri, apparently after consultation
with other leaders, held a press conference to announce the
MPVC's merger with the Congress, with Scindia seated on the
dais with him. Newspapers reported then that the Congress chief
waited in the porch of 24, Akbar Road, to usher Scindia in. Such
optics and photo ops are significant in politics. Scindia had a
very real smile on his face, after a very long time. S. Bangarappa,
former Karnataka chief minister, was also reinducted into the
party the same day.

Scindia was back where he deserved to be, just about a
year later, but not before going through a huge mental trauma,
a blot on his clean image and having to undergo an avoidable
process of forming a new party and taking on the Congress,
something he had never have dreamt of doing.

What did P.V. Narasimha Rao gain from trying to implicate
his own party men the way he did? Was that an offensive
move or a defensive one?

Well, that is all debatable. What became clear to all was
that Rao had made a futile effort to finish off the opposition
shrewdly but that it had gotten him neither the honourable
tag of an anti-corruption crusader nor strengthened him in

his ongoing war with Sonia and her supporters. In fact, the hawala move badly boomeranged on the so-called 'Chanakya.' First, all of the accused were acquitted by the district court and then by the Supreme Court. Second, his son Prabhakar, having been involved in a urea supply scam and Rao himself embroiled in a-first-of-its-kind scandal of buying out Members of Parliament to save his own government, in July 1993, amply proved he was anything but 'Mr Clean.' So Rao had failed in his targeting of, among others, Advani and Scindia—the two original 'Mr Clean.'

Scindia's commitment to the Congress was never ever in doubt. Was he not the person who, just three years ago, had organized an impressive show of unity among the warring Congress factions in Madhya Pradesh? In political circles of the state, a small sleepy town Dabra, near Gwalior, became famous because of Scindia's initiative. On the eve of the Madhya Pradesh Assembly elections of November 1993, his unity efforts saw Arjun Singh, Digvijaya Singh, the Shukla brothers, Motilal Vora and others coming together on a common platform to challenge the BJP which had been in power from 1990–92 with Sunder Lal Patwa as the chief minister.

The Madhya Pradesh government, along with Rajasthan and Himachal, had been sacked in the wake of the Babri Masjid demolition, by Prime Minister Narasimha Rao. But when elections took place in 1993, Congress romped home and much of its credit went to Scindia who not only criss-crossed the huge undivided state but also held the party together like a sailor who controls the shaking ship. The 'Dabra spirit' was like the much-needed sugar coating on the bitter ties of the warring regional satraps. Dabra town's only claim to fame so far had been its lone sugar factory, set up in 1940.

Well, when the Congress won the majority, and a chief minister was to be elected, Scindia was kept waiting in Delhi and Digvijaya, the Pradesh Congress Committee (PCC) chief was made the chief minister, with Arjun Singh supporting him. Scindia's return to the Congress fold brought a full circle to a close. The brief sojourn outside the Congress and with a serious charge of corruption slapped against him, Scindia, an otherwise simple politician, learnt a lot about the many crooks who run the Indian political system and the double speak of most of its leaders in all parties. He had become a toughened and rounded politician now.

♦

Scindia watchers always feel that the scions of the Gwalior House are destined to struggle to achieve great things. They don't get them easily. Madhavrao, and later Jyotiraditya, have been examples of it. Even for a post of the MPCA, a small membership-based sports body, Jyotiraditya had to contest twice (2010 and 2012) in a direct election with a BJP strongman from Indore. The he won it with sufficient margin is another matter.

Come 1998 Lok Sabha elections, it was yet another test of Scindia the senior. The Gujral government had fallen in November 1997 on the issue of the DMK's participation in the Government. The CWC, under Sitaram Kesri, had issued an ultimatum to the prime minister to remove three ministers for the party's alleged links with the Liberation Tigers of Tamil Eelam (LTTE), following the Jain Commission of Inquiry's interim report's tabling in the Parliament. It was a detailed probe into Rajiv Gandhi's assassination. But a principled Gujral put his government on the stake and refused to remove them, saying that the DMK had not been found to be directly involved in any conspiracy and that a final verdict in the matter from Supreme Court was still awaited.[26]

The fall of the UF government necessitated yet another election, costing the nation about ₹700 crore as per the estimation of the ECI.

Madhavrao had no choice, like most others, but to contest all over again. His natural choice was Gwalior. Within a space of less than two years he was facing the electorate again, but this time as a Congress nominee. The mood of the nation appeared to be upset with coalition experiments which had been failing in Delhi. V.P. Singh had also failed a few years ago. The BJP fought the election again under the leadership of Vajpayee and the NDA alliance made impressive gains to record a majority by winning 182 seats as against UPA's 141, a gain of just one seat over the last tally. Vajpayee managed to garner enough support from other parties and formed what looked like a 'stable' government.

But in Gwalior, owing to a combination of factors, Scindia struggled a lot against a local BJP candidate Jaibhan Singh who had strong links with the VHP. He was quite vocal against the palace, its people and their politics; he launched a blistering personal and baseless tirade against Scindia during his campaigning. Singh did not offer any plan for development of Gwalior or any programme for the betterment of people, yet they seemed to enjoy his diatribes against the Maharaja and the 'feudal family.' Since in the earlier election of 1996, the BJP had withdrawn a candidate against Madhavrao, the BJP rank and file in Gwalior was a little angry with their seniors. This time around, they got a chance and put up a united face against the Congress.

Scindia was completely unaware of the ground realities, as it seemed, he took the election lightly. The problem with such big personalities seems to be that, in most cases, they don't get the real picture of a situation or facts about people, especially during polls. They listen to what people close to them feed them. Party workers would invariably partake in apple polishing and would say only what the maharaj would like to hear, not the ground reality. So, no one had reportedly made him aware of a tough fight on hand. A Delhi journalist had, however, told someone very close to Madhavrao that the election was going to be tough for him after the former had taken a round of Gwalior and had chatted with a cross section of people in the streets.

Digvijaya Singh was the chief minister who had his staunch supporters in Ashok Singh and others, the anti-Scindia faction within the Congress, in Gwalior. Jaibhan played on the nerves of the people and that made quite an impact. He managed to narrow the victory margin to just 26,279. This was a shock for Scindia, an alarming signal. He had never ever won an election with such a slender margin, not as a MPVC candidate in 1996 nor against the towering leader Vajpayee in 1984. Apparently, many Congressmen had clandestinely supported the BJP candidate against Scindia.

Was his popularity on the wane? Was a Scindia getting less popular in Gwalior? Perhaps! The result was there for everyone to see and analyse in their way. But the writing on the wall was clear.

That Madhavrao managed to win that election is an altogether separate matter; the narrow victory margin was a big worry for him. As an MP he had to again sit in the opposition benches with nothing much to do. Not for long, though.

The Atal Bihari Vajpayee government had lost the confidence vote after completing one year in office, by just one vote. He could have easily made an effort to buy out MPs, the way his friend Narasimha Rao had allegedly done. Yes, Vajpayee and his ministers tried to win over leaders like Ram Vilas Paswan and Inder Kumar Gujral to support the NDA, but that friendly move miserably failed. On 17 April 1999, Vajpayee's government stood down again, only to be elected again the same year.

The 1999 elections, the third in almost three years, saw Scindia returning to Guna. The reasons were obvious. In any case, he had won from there on earlier occasions but the last three elections, 1991, 1996 and 1998, were all contested by the Rajmata from Guna.

In their entire struggle, the Scindias always made sure to follow one sound principle: they have taken extra care of not hurting each other in electoral matters and times. Despite political and personal differences, they have shown respect for each other in public. Clearly, they always wanted a Scindia, standing in any election, from any constituency, to win. So Guna was vacated for Madhavrao by his mother in 1999 who did not contest that election due to illness and advancing age. Alas, that turned out to be Madhavrao's last election.

A tragic plane crash on 30 September 2001, in Mainpuri district of Uttar Pradesh claimed his life, along with his private secretary, a few journalists of Delhi and a crew of a private plane of the Jindal group. The ill-fated aircraft flew into a cloud on an afternoon around 1.25 p.m. on its way to Kanpur, but what came out a little later was a big fireball. What was more tragic was that he had had no plans to visit Kanpur but since Sheila Dixit took ill and another leader backed out, Scindia had to fill in the gap. As if Yamraj (the God of Death, as per Hindu scriptures and beliefs) had called him there.

Madhavrao Scindia was 56. By Indian political standards, he had easily 20 more years of active politics left in him. But that was not to be in his destiny.

On an earlier occasion, Scindia had a narrow escape in a plane that had crashed, luckily, without him being on board in 1980. Sanjay Gandhi, Indira's son and Madhavrao's buddy, died in that accident early in the morning. Madhavrao, a flying fan, was to join Sanjay on the joyride. There are many stories that were circulated on why he could not join Sanjay that morning. Perhaps, he was destined to have more years to live his life for society and the nation.

Incidentally, Madhavrao was the first of the Scindias in many decades to have lived to see a third generation and cross 50 years of age. A few years before he was killed in the shocking plane accident, he was fortunate enough to have seen his grandson, Mahanaryaman, son of Jyotiraditya and Priyadarshini Raje, born in November 1995.

Most of the males in the illustrious Gwalior dynasty died before they reached 50 years of age, including Madhavrao's father Jiwajirao and hence when Madhavrao got to see his grandson, he was the happiest. He almost cried in jubilation on seeing the little new Scindia, family sources confirmed.

Earlier, I had referred to what Natwar Singh, the former union minister had once told Madhavrao about the future plans of Sonia Gandhi for him. Let me now share what Madhavrao had replied then. He had gloomily replied to Singh: 'But who knows whether I will be around by that time.' When the Congress candidate Dr Manmohan Singh took oath as the thirteenth prime minister of India, in 2004, the party had returned to power after about eight years. Madhavrao had already left the world about 32 months ago.

When Scindia was cremated in his hometown with full state honours on 4 October 2001, more than two lakh people had turned up in Gwalior, making a record of sorts, thus proving his popularity as a mass leader. They had tried to participate, by overcoming all odds of security and other issues, in the last rites of their loveable Maharaja. A large number of leaders and ministers, cutting across political lines, had made it a point to be in Gwalior for the last rites of a truly great leader and a greater human being. Suddenly, Gwalior felt orphaned and enveloped itself in a pall of gloom for several days.

His overwhelming popularity and the shocking incident which had claimed his life so suddenly made the people sob inconsolably. There was probably not one person, from a VVIP Vajpayee the prime minister, to an ordinary three-wheeler autorickshaw driver and a paan shop owner, who did not weep that day in Gwalior upon seeing Scindia's mortal remains go up in flames.

The most famous son of Gwalior was gone forever.

In the funeral procession, Bombay Dyeing scion Nusli Wadia, Maharashtra Chief Minister Vilasrao Deshmukh and Indian cricket board chief Jagmohan Dalmiya were slowly walking out of the quiet precincts of the Jai Vilas Palace with a heavy heart and wet eyes and were exchanging notes in a low voice about their just-departed friend. All three shared how he had called them just a few days before his untimely death, chatting with them without any special reason.

All were unanimous: Madhavrao had had a clear premonition before his death.

He had spoken with many of his dear ones across India and abroad by calling them on the landline phone over the past one week preceding 30 September 2001. In Indore, he had graced a long-pending dinner party on 25 September at the house of J.S. Anand, a member of the MPCA. Those who had attended the big party recall how jovial Madhavrao had been that evening. He was the president of the MPCA at that time.

Elsewhere, in most cases, he had dialled the number himself without the help of an operator or a personal secretary, including this author. He called me up at my home in Bhopal from the Residency Kothi in Indore on the morning before departing for Delhi after he had changed his original programme of going to Neemuch.

Had he not changed his prior schedule of tours within Madhya Pradesh, maybe he would have lived much longer.

Is destiny changeable? Perhaps, no.

8

Daughters as Political Heirs:
Two Daughters, Two Stories!

Politics in India, for many years, has veered around dynasties: be it royal or non-royal. While women's participation has been relatively less, curiously, it was India—not even modern superpower America or populous China—that had a woman premier as the top executive of the country, way back in the '60s who ruled for many years.

The most famous Indian political dynasty is, of course, that of the Nehru-Gandhi family, with no princely background. Between their three generations, members of the family ruled India as prime ministers for more than 35 years. Jawaharlal Nehru, the architect of modern India, ruled for 16 years straight. He took over the reins of the nation soon after India gained Independence and remained as prime minister until his death in 1964. Indira Gandhi, his only child, ruled with a break between her two stints of 1966–1977 and then 1980–1984 and then the youngest occupant, at 40 years, was the pilot-turned politician, Rajiv Gandhi, who was at the helm of the affairs of the country for just five years, 1984–1989. He then got embroiled in the Bofors gun scandal, and his party badly lost elections, after which he tragically lost his life to a LTTE terrorist attack in 1991. No Gandhi came to power after 1989, though the Congress, led by P.V. Narasimha Rao and then Dr Manmohan Singh, formed governments at the Centre and ruled the nation for 15 years. There were also years when none of the Gandhis were present in the Parliament after Rajiv's cruel assassination.

Besides the Congress dynasty there have been many other families in Indian politics representing different parties who ruled the roost for decades. And continue to do so. Chaudhary Charan Singh, Mulayam Singh Yadav, Bal Keshav Thackeray, Chaudhary Devi Lal (Chautala), Sheikh Abdullah, Bansi Lal, the Karunakarans, M. Karunanidhi and the Badals are among those, besides others, who have been successful political families with at least three generations or a large number of the close clan (Mulayam) winning one election after the other and sustaining their political hegemony for decades. A noted columnist giving many of the above families' examples, and more, in his *Times of India* article wrote:[1]

'Election after election, politics of the progeny kept flourishing across the country because people continued electing the political offsprings without having any qualms about it. This has been true from Kashmir to Kerala.'

Among the royal dynasties, it is the Scindias of Gwalior in Madhya Pradesh who are the only family to have not only engaged in but have also ruled politics since decades, mainly in two parties—the Congress and the BJP—and continue to toil hard in more ways than one and, in the process, enjoy the fruits of power till the present day. They left behind the regal splendour and cosy private life to join the rough and tumble of tricky Indian politics. Interestingly, there have been three women leaders from this famous family belonging to the same party who have dominated politics in some measure over the last few decades.

I have earlier written about Vijaya Raje and her political contribution to the two different parties, first the Congress for about a decade and then the BJP, with an interlude with the Jana Sangh. She, as the head of the famous family after her husband's untimely death in 1961, decided to remain in politics, being an MP and MLA and then her son, Madhavrao and much later her two daughters, out of the four, also followed suit one after the other. These two daughters are now established politicians in the two adjoining states of Madhya Pradesh and Rajasthan. Both belong to the BJP, the party their mother helped promote to some extent. While Vasundhara Raje, married into a neighbouring princely family of Dhaulpur (Dholpur) in Rajasthan in 1972, went on to become the chief minister twice, her younger sister Yashodhara Raje is a long-standing cabinet minister in the Shivraj Singh government in Bhopal.

Both sisters divorced their husbands and charted their own independent and fairly successful course in life. Vasundhara's successor, her only son Dushyant Singh with Rana Hemant Singh, has been an MP for over two decades now, representing Jhalawar-Baran, a constituency his mother vacated after she shifted back to state politics from Delhi.

Vijaya Raje, who had brought down the powerful chief minister D.P. Mishra's government in one stroke, in 1967, had the Madhya Pradesh chief ministership's offer almost ready on the platter. She chose not to take it. Had she accepted the mantle for herself rather than just being a kingmaker, the former queen would have been the only second woman chief minister in the history of the country after Sucheta Kripalani (1963–67) of Uttar Pradesh, and first one from Madhya Pradesh. Kripalani that way was senior even to Indira Gandhi—a junior minister in Prime Minister Lal Bahadur Shastri's cabinet in June 1964.[2]

Women's participation in politics was a rarity in the '50s and '60s, although Indira Gandhi had become the prime minister by 1966 after Shastri's sudden death in Uzbekistan. The other prominent woman politician making the news then was the chief minister of those early times, Nandini Satpathy, of the Congress who ruled the state of Orissa (now Odisha) from 1974 to 1976.

Later, many other states such as Goa (Shashikala Kakodkar), Tamil Nadu (J. Jayalalithaa), Assam (Anwara Taimur), Uttar Pradesh (Mayawati), Madhya Pradesh (Uma Bharti), Bihar (Rabri Devi), Delhi (Sushma Swaraj and Sheila Dixit), Gujarat (Anandiben Patel) and Jammu Kashmir (Mehbooba Mufti) saw the fairer sex dominating the political scene as powerful chief ministers.

There were a few others too. The last one fighting her lone battle for survival in the first half of 2021 was Mamata Banerjee of the Trinamool Congress Party (TMC) in West Bengal who won that tough battle rather easily against a mighty and resourceful BJP which had put up aggressive campaigns with no less than the prime minister making a number of visits to the coastal state to address mammoth crowds. The BJP literally left no stone unturned in trying to defeat Mamata. Though the chief minister herself lost narrowly against her own former colleague from the Nandigram constituency by around 1,700 votes, her regional party recorded a third straight victory and hoisted her as the chief minister for the third time in a row the first time having been in 2011. She was the first woman chief minister of the once communist-dominated state where two left party chief ministers—Jyoti Basu and Buddhadeb Bhattacharjee—ruled the state for over three decades.

VASUNDHARA RAJE

What Vijaya Raje did not achieve, or rather, did not want to achieve, her next generation managed to do it with aplomb. Her elder daughter Vasundhara Raje became the first woman chief minister of Rajasthan, a state historically dominated by patriarchy. Her flourishing political career got a shot in the arm when she became the president of the state BJP unit and then the chief minister for the first time in 2003; it was the same year Sadhvi Uma Bharti became her counterpart in the adjoining state of Madhya Pradesh; Uma did not last even a year in office and resigned over a court case.

The BJP was then divided over the issue—many in Delhi and Bhopal wanted her out as her style of governance was highly controversial. She too was the first woman chief minister of the large state, though bifurcated three years ago. Uma was like a daughter to Vijaya Raje who would have been extremely happy to see her two 'daughters' annexing the chief ministership in the same year in two adjoining states. Alas, before she could bear witness to such an event, she passed away in 2001.

Vasundhara's style of politics has been unique. A domineering character, she has a large number friends and staunch followers and also political foes. But her political rivals would also agree that she worked hard for her party and was the sole face of the BJP in Rajasthan for over two decades. Her progress has been meteoric and eventful, unlike her younger sister, who was essentially accommodated by the BJP in Madhya Pradesh due to her mother's obligation on the party.

Starting her career as an MLA (she also served the party organization) in 1985–90 of the eighth Rajasthan Assembly, Vasundhara Raje never looked back and went on to win four elections from Jhalra Patan constituency with big margins, touching 50,000 at times. Before that, from 1991 until 2003 she stood as an MP from Jhalawar, once part of the Scindia state, and won five times straight to become a junior Union minister in the Atal Bihari Vajpayee government, where she held many crucial departments with an independent charge. She was also minister of state for External Affairs in 1998–99, considered an important charge, reporting directly to the prime minister. Having been fluent in English and with global exposure, she came in handy for Vajpayee whose expertise in foreign affairs has been well known.

But her claim to fame was her first stint as the chief minister of an otherwise difficult and caste-driven state. Leaders like Jaswant Singh and Bhairon Singh Shekhawat had propped her up. She was made the BJP state unit chief in November 2002 and by May–June 2003, she embarked upon her rally for change (Parivartan Yatra) which brought rich dividends to the party in elections later that year, thanks to her magical touch.[3] The other plus point weighing in her favour was that she was from a royal family. Rajasthan is full of princely families, local vassals and royalties.

In Rajasthan, early growth of the Jana Sangh was halting because of its refusal to cater to the feudal agenda of the ruling Rajput class that had lost land in the wake of the abolition of the jagirs.[*] This influential class—angry with the Congress— shifted its allegiance to the Swatantra Party.[4] So Vasundhara Raje naturally got a head start in the first elections that she led her party into. She mesmerized her voters with her bold personality and aggressive political speeches. There were other factors too such as the emergence of a dynamic leader called Pramod Mahajan, a smart conductor of yatras and an expert in organizational matters. He was close to the then prime minister and also to L.K. Advani.

Shekhawat and Singh, on their part, by promoting a young female, removed their own contemporaries and competitors like Lalit Kishore Chaturvedi, Harishankar Bhabhra or Raghuveer Singh Kaushal from the chief minister's race, in one stroke and the 'victims' could not even complain.[5] Raje had a triple advantage at her disposal and made intelligent use of the opportunity provided to her by party high command. She was the daughter of the 'Maratha' Scindia family, daughter-in-law

---

[*]A type of feudal land grant in the Indian subcontinent.

of the Dholpur (Jat) princely family and her son married into a Gurjar family in the year 2000. All these factors worked in her favour, in addition to her oratory skills, hard work, leadership skills and regal style. The Rajputs and Jats together held the key to power in Jaipur, and both lent their support to her in 2003.

Of course, 2003 was a special year for the BJP and its strategists (Mahajan, Arun Jaitley, Venkaiah Naidu and others) as well, since the party could form three state governments in Madhya Pradesh, Rajasthan and the newly-created Chhattisgarh with a thumping majority under the leadership of Uma Bharti, Vasundhara and Dr Raman Singh, respectively. This was also the time that the BJP (NDA) government was in power at the Centre under Vajpayee. In Madhya Pradesh, it was the worst ever performance of Congress under Digvijaya Singh who had ruled the state for 10 long years and the BJP won on the promises of providing good roads, quality of power (electricity), water for irrigation to farmers and a clean government. Firebrand Sadhvi Uma Bharti had lured women voters to the BJP in a big way. The Congress was reduced to 37–38 seats in a House of 230 MLAs.

The trio of Uma-Raje-Singh, being the second generation of leadership that the BJP had calculatedly groomed and thrown up at the right time, represented the new face of the saffron party. Senior leaders such as Kailash Joshi, Sunder Lal Patwa, Vikram Verma (both Union ministers in the Vajpayee government), Lakkhiram Agarwal and Bhairon Singh Shekhawat, a towering leader from Rajasthan, had been given different roles and responsibilities or were shifted to central politics to the pave way for younger leaders.

That was the BJP's successful strategy of establishing a second line of command. Vasundhara was first given the charge of the party affairs as the president of the Rajasthan unit and then, in the next year, she won the chief ministership, thanks to her pre-poll 'Parivartan Yatras' in 2003 and then again in 2013, before her second term. Her ability to criss-cross the dusty villages of Rajasthan just like a commoner and mingle with people easily had a lasting impression on the rural voters of the BIMARU (Bihar, Madhya Pradesh, Rajasthan, and Uttar Pradesh) states.

A decade later, with the emergence of Narendra Modi on the national scene, there was a further build-up of an army of new leaders to take control of states. Devendra Fadnavis, Trivendra Singh, Tirath Singh Rawat, Yogi Adityanath, Manohar Lal Khattar, Jai Ram Thakur, Sarbananda Sonowal and others were promoted to take charge of the BJP's increasing number of states. Shivraj Singh Chouhan, Uma Bharti's and veteran Babulal Gaur's successor in Madhya Pradesh, was the choice and find of Pramod Mahajan in 2005 and continued until 2021 and beyond. Chouhan became chief minister when Modi was his counterpart in Gujarat. As an all-powerful prime minister (unlike Rao or Gujral), Modi gradually sidelined ageing leaders, caring little for the criticism within his own party and outside it. Advani and M.M. Joshi were dumped into a newly formed 'Margdarshak Mandal (advisory group)' and effectively consigned to history while simultaneously pushing up fresh faces.

In Rajasthan, it was indeed a golden-letter day in the state' modern history when its first woman chief minister was sworn in on 3 December 2003. The land of warriors and businessmen saw the BJP trouncing the party in government—the INC— with consummate ease. The BJP bagged 120 seats out of 200 against 56 of the Congress, led by the outgoing chief minister Ashok Gehlot. Newspapers carried headlines such as 'A royal win for BJP.'[6] The anti-incumbency wave was so forceful that the party which had won 153 seats five years ago in 1998, was decimated to just 56 seats. 'Of course, the Congress was a faction-ridden party but the other fact is that Vasundhara Raje, projected as the chief minister, fought the election methodically to come out with flying colours,' said veteran journalist Sunny Sebastian, former state correspondent with *The Hindu* (Jaipur), recalling 'the well-woven and aggressive campaign aiming to garner women's votes; it was a master stroke of the BJP to declare her as the chief ministerial face.'[7]

The chief minister-designate Vasundhara Raje herself won with a big margin defeating the local MP Rama Pilot, wife of Congress leader, the late Rajesh Pilot, by over 27,000 votes. The party office at Sardar Patel Marg in Jaipur wore a festive look and party workers were seen dancing and shouting slogans in favour of Raje who was able to turn the party campaign into a referendum on development or lack of it. 'The election results have made it clear that "Governance and Development" gained salience at the hustings, and the BJP's core issues like Ayodhya, Bhojshala, Hindutva and so on seem to have lost the relevance,' wrote a political researcher, N.S. Gehlot.[8] The BJP had managed to keep its vote share between 33 and 38 per cent.

Her first stint as a chief minister was expected to be extraordinary because of two reasons: first, as a graduate with honours in Economics and Political Science from Mumbai, she had gained good knowledge of the workings of the administration at the Centre, thus attaining a good stature in the BJP. Second, corruption and misrule of the Gehlot government (1998–2003) had been such that the angry, frustrated citizens of Rajasthan were expecting a transparent and honest government under her and thus voted in hordes for the BJP. They had elected Vasundhara with high hopes. As Sebastian says:

> She had no competition from within her party with stalwart Bhairon Singh Shekhawat already out of state politics and had become the Vice President in 2002 for five years and with the Congress, people had been bored

and were upset. She heralded a welcome change in the northern state.

The first few years were relatively smooth, and she brooked no political opposition, or so she thought. Jaswant Singh, who had supported her, soon became a political foe. In the book *Political Profiles of Cabals and Kings*, author Aditi Phadnis mentions:

> Those close to him say he could not have made a bigger mistake by backing her initially. Raje's political trajectory was all her own. The breach between the two leaders grew, mainly on the issues of governance and development of Rajasthan. Things went to the extent that the state bureaucratic machinery registered against Singh a case under the Narcotic Drugs and Psychotropic Substances Act (NDPSA) for offering opium to community chieftains on the occasion of '*riyan*'—considered an old tradition in that state. Singh and his wife Sheetal also went public against the CM's supporters portraying her as 'Goddess Durga'.[9]

Irrespective of these skirmishes which began after about two years of her rule, she had already become the tallest and most powerful leader of Rajasthan and continues to be so even today—the only face of BJP recognized at the national level from the state. In the 2004 Lok Sabha polls, her charismatic leadership got the BJP 21 seats out of 25 in the state but in Delhi, it was the UPA with Congress as the main party and not the NDA with the BJP as its lead party, which formed the government with Dr Manmohan Singh as prime minister. Slogans like 'India Shining,' 'Feel Good,' etc., did no good for the BJP at an all-India level. Vajpayee had to step down despite giving what was then touted as sushasan (good governance), after many years of (mis)rules of various political combinations in New Delhi.

Vasundhara tried her level best, as the chief minister, to devote herself to the socio-economic development of the state which has smaller regions (Mewar, Marwar, Shekhawati, Hadoti, etc.) with different cultures rampant caste and tribe equations. She formulated many programmes such as rainwater harvesting (rules framed for the first time), separate feeder line for agriculture, special attention and financial allocation for creating road networks, free textbooks for girls in all classes, employment for youths and tripling of the agriculture budget, among scores of other policies and initiatives that any new government does with the help of the same set of bureaucrats, with some changes here and there. In an *India Today* report dated 10 July 2017,[10] she explained how participation of the public in general helped her government in fighting and resolving the water crisis in the state despite facing financial setbacks. She also credited the success of the Mukhyamantri Jal Swavlamban Yojana to the help received by the Army, religious organizations, the bureaucracy and political people. She started one Adarsh School in every panchayat and with the 'Skilling India' scheme a staggering 10 lakh jobs were claimed to have been created.

Frankly speaking, all such welfare programmes for different target groups and beneficiaries are anyway launched by the incumbent governments and there was no novelty in the programmes that she had initiated one after the other. However, what people liked most about her was her work ethic, her continuous work across the length and breadth of the state; a state that had suffered from inadequate rains for centuries. People were awestruck watching from close a 'Maharani' ruling the state for the first time. She did a lot for industries, and in the beginning of 2008, it was claimed by the government and others that Rajasthan was sprinting towards its goal of shedding the tag of a backward state, if not getting totally out of the BIMARU club.[11]

Yet, surprisingly Vasundhara lost the 2008 assembly elections. Why did that happen? How did she lose? More importantly, how was it possible for the Congress to have bounced back, given that she had run her government so well? Had the Maharani's charisma faded away so quickly?

Raje was shocked beyond doubt and so were the BJP bigwigs in Delhi. While Congress got 96 seats, BJP could manage to win only 78. It was said to be result of, among other issues, her decision to give reservations to the Meenas at the cost of the Gurjars who had then launched a massive agitation in Rajasthan blocking highways and creating problems for other states while protesting. In the police firing, 31 Gurjars were reportedly killed. Eventually, neither the Gurjars voted for the BJP nor did the Meenas, political analysts then said. Faction-fighting in the BJP began soon; the daggers were out. Party leaders began baying for her blood, including the Jaswant Singh faction. Surprisingly, she had united all the castes in the states and had won five years ago but the same caste equations had gotten horribly disturbed in 2008, resulting in a debacle for the BJP government.

Ashok Gehlot, besides levelling many corruption charges, had made other serious personal accusations about the chief minister's daily consumption of alcohol in the evenings and thus remaining inaccessible to people. ('8PM, no CM' was a frequent barb that she suffered at the hands of Gehlot, a teetotaller, and by the Congress; 8PM is a popular whisky brand). Gehlot had also tried making, rather cheaply, political capital out of her foreign trips while being in the opposition.[12]

A little short of the majority, the Congress swiftly swung into action and formed the government on 13 December 2008, with the help of the BSP and BJP dissident Dr Kirodilal Meena's faction of MLAs and was sworn in as the chief minister. The BJP was, of course, far behind the magic figure of 100 seats and could not have formed the government under any circumstances. Ironically, despite her popularity, that was the first major dent Raje suffered in her career. Another followed in 2013.

The same year, in Madhya Pradesh and Chhattisgarh, under the leadership of Shivraj Singh Chouhan and Dr Raman Singh respectively, the BJP was successful in returning to power with a clear majority. Dr Singh continued his 15-year long three uninterrupted stints before suffering a humiliating loss in 2018. He was also a union minister of state with Vasundhara in Delhi and was packed off to his parent state to take on the incumbent Congress chief minister Ajit Jogi in 2003. He did wonderfully well encashing upon the voters ire against a corrupt regime of the bureaucrat turned chief minister, Jogi.

Shivraj Singh, extremely hard-working and a shrewd yet overtly simple politician, on the other hand, continues to be in power after a short break of 15 months between 2018 and early 2020 when the Congress leader Kamal Nath was the chief minister. After his loss in 2018, the BJP high command did not make Shivraj the leader of the Opposition in the Assembly and instead picked up Gopal Bhargava, a former senior minister from Bundelkhand.

But Chouhan has had his ways; he is also the only successful mascot in Madhya Pradesh that the BJP has been projecting since 2007–2008. He possesses great survival instincts, coupled with political skills to 'adjust' to the demands and styles of functioning of different regimes within the BJP. He was once very close to L.K. Advani, to the extent that he was 'considered' as prime minister material. Advani had gone on record to say this when the BJP founder was openly opposed to Modi's anointment to the prime ministership. Advani had compared the development of Madhya Pradesh state (sic) with that of Gujarat under Modi and had favoured Madhya Pradesh while singing paeans for Chouhan.[13] The fact is that there is no comparison between a modern Gujarat and an ever-developing Madhya Pradesh where health and education remain stressed sectors. Corruption has grown manifold in the BJP regime, as people in general and industrialists in particular point out. Corruption in the bureaucracy is big-time and remains unchecked under Shivraj Singh, a fact he probably knows well but either turns a Nelson's eye or is under compulsions or is helpless.

Chouhan, 62, is still considered to be in the race for the country's top job. People close to him claim that age and experience are on his side and he is a popular brand now, notwithstanding the Vyapam scam slur on his image or the rampant corruption cases that are unearthed in Madhya Pradesh with shocking frequency. The *Indian Express* included him among the 100 most powerful people of India in 2021 at the forty-second slot, below Priyanka Gandhi and above Gajendra Singh Shekhawat, another anti-Raje leader and Union minister from Rajasthan.

Returning to Rajasthan, 2008–2013 was a time for struggle for Vasundhara, as the opposition leader. The defeat had resulted in the BJP state unit chief O.P. Mathur's resignation; he had to immediately step down. Her opponents then began clamouring for her to quit as the leader of the Opposition. She was, however, obstinate, and refused to heed to any such hint from the top. Raje drummed up support of over 60 MLAs who were all in a defiant mood. The party's all-India chief Rajnath Singh's suggestion in this regard was also ignored. The BJP state unit was divided and intense faction fighting began. Many accused her of being 'too autocratic' and blamed the former chief minister for her 'firm style of leadership 'which had caused the defeat.' Eventually, after Advani's intervention in October 2009, she resigned, only to be reinstalled in the same position a few months later—a clear sign of her victory and indispensability. It added to her stature. The party's senior leaders in Delhi also realized that Vasundhara was indispensable in Rajasthan even if she had lost a year ago. Clearly, she had grown bigger than the boot—both the RSS and the BJP had been dwarfed.

Another time that proved difficult for her as the leader of the Opposition was in 2009. In the parliamentary polls in

2004, when she was the chief minister, BJP had won 21 seats, but in 2009, the scenario had completely changed. The BJP's tally had slid to single digits—just four seats!

Yet, former prime minister Atal Bihari Vajpayee, in a surprise move, declared that the next state elections would be fought under Raje's leadership, creating commotion and unease in the rival camp within the BJP. She was then formally made the party president of the state unit and her opponent Gulab Chand Kataria was made the leader of the Opposition in the Assembly but not before both were called to Delhi and properly admonished by party seniors. Kataria, her former home minister, was a big leader of the Mewar region but was sulking as his proposed Mewar Rath Yatra of May 2012 had been vehemently opposed by Raje and others. The matter went to the high command in Delhi, Raje was called to party headquarters and as per her wont, she showed her red eyes to Delhi; 'they had to rein in Kataria who had to eventually cancel his Lok Jagran Yatra.'[14] With these appointments, both top leaders buried their hatchets. The party was now united. The efforts of Rajnath Singh and others brought about a permanent truce in the warring factions which led to the BJP and Raje's victory in 2013. There were many other political developments between 2009 and 2013 but they aren't of relevance here.

She became the chief minister for the second time from 2013 to 2018. Soon after, she was caught in another controversy. Well, the unseemly controversy was not about poor governance or corruption or police firing but mainly about helping her family friend and cricket administrator Lalit Modi of IPL fame. The IPL boss apparently got into serious trouble when his fishy deals in the Board of Control for Cricket in India (BCCI) started tumbling out; it was during this time that Vasundhara is believed to have supported him flee the country in anonymity. The letter she apparently wrote for him in 2011, surfaced a few years later, giving a handle to the Opposition to beat her with when she was the chief minister. They immediately demanded her resignation in 2015. Her party leaders in Delhi were also baying for her blood but she managed somehow to insulate herself. After all, Vasundhara is a gritty woman, a good fighter. She had repeatedly shown signs of emerging stronger after a crisis.

Lalit Modi is yet to return to India, 12 years after he fled the country after the BCCI disciplinary committee accused him of many wrongdoings and the Enforcement Directorate (ED) wanting to interrogate him.[15] Modi could not face the charges of embezzlement and ran out of the country to London, sometime in 2010–11. Considering his proximity to Raje, Modi was royally dubbed as 'Super Chief Minister' of Rajasthan by the Opposition, which none ever denied. It's very easy to level such charges against politicians, especially those with a high profile, said a political observer.

Yet, Vasundhara could not have been charged with any kind of proven corruption during her two stints, being from the one of the richest and most famous family of the country. She did face political accusations of favouring one lobby or the other and faced some unprintable loose charges, but nonetheless remained a leader of the highest order.

Her administration had been generally good, though some communal riots had taken place killing 60 people in Jaipur during her first stint and raising questions over her art of good governance. Industry was a vital sector in which Rajasthan had slid as per *India Today's* State of the State study[16] of the Hindi heartland states, done in 2017, a year prior to the elections.

Her claims to good welfare work thus got her nowhere as after five years she lost to the Congress, the party she had wrested power from in the earlier elections, emphatically.

Interestingly, Rajasthan is one state where in the past 25 years people opt for the rival party roughly every five years. It is an interesting political phenomenon which may need a detailed analysis by political scientists on how the voters intelligently use the right franchise to oust the incumbent government every five years. This keeps the politicians on their tenterhooks; if they don't perform, they perish. That way the wise Rajasthan voters have punished both the main parties. Seems anti-incumbency is easily sensed by the people here, unlike in neighbouring states where Sheila Dixit or Dr Raman Singh or Shivraj Singh successfully completed 15 years of unbroken stints.

Picture this: in 1993 it was the BJP under Bhairon Singh Shekhawat; in 1998 it was the Congress under Gehlot with a resounding margin; in 2003 the BJP was under Vasundhara Raje; again in 2008 it was the Congress under Gehlot, and in 2013 it was the BJP led by Vasundhara Raje and finally in 2018 veteran Ashok Gehlot returned, once again at the age of 68 as the chief minister of this politically unique state. The anti-incumbency factor thus worked in a very justified fashion against both parties, thanks to the uncanny Rajasthan voter's political acumen.[17]

In 2018, the Congress won despite internecine struggles within the party factions of senior versus youth—Gehlot versus Sachin Pilot. Rahul Gandhi favoured Gehlot over the PCC chief Pilot who was accommodated as the deputy chief minister. But he revolted in vain in 2020 and resultantly lost his ministry and party's top post. He did not play his cards adroitly. The Congress watchers said Rahul did not really want to make Gehlot the CM, or so he made people believe through his statements, and was favouring younger leadership but an old coterie around his mother Sonia forced him to do so in the case of Rajasthan. In Madhya Pradesh at the same time, another old war horse was installed as the chief minister who knew nothing about Madhya Pradesh.

Vasundhara, the second-time chief minister, was a bit different in her administration. She did not like to toe the line of the Centre. During 2013–2018, she took up many fights with her own party's powerful leaders in Delhi. Given her nature and political height it is not surprising that she can take up cudgels in her defence at the shortest provocation.

By the time she had completed her first years in office, Narendra Modi had taken up prime ministership in May 2014 in a dramatic manner after a big win with the NDA allies. She was said to be in two minds about whether to attend the grand oath-taking ceremony of May 2014 at Delhi. She was reportedly upset that even after managing to send all 25 MPs from her state, Modi had not given more cabinet berths to Rajasthani MPs. In the first team, the PM included a minister of state, upsetting Raje. She had let her annoyance known, openly, in her own way. Though in an interview on Aaj Tak, she had clarified that 'she was not angry,' and that inducting a minister was the prerogative of the prime minister.

After losing the elections in 2018, when she was being side-lined by Delhi, she sought to flex her muscles again and showed her strength in very many ways. In 2021, she met party supremo Amit Shah after a gap of almost two years.

When asked about rumours floating about the possibility of her quitting the BJP, she retorted saying: 'Me and leave the BJP? I can never leave the party that my family built with blood and sweat and our wealth. We even split up over it [a reference to her late brother Madhavrao Scindia joining Congress]. The BJP is the only family I have other than my own.'[18] Yet, in the Assembly by-polls in April 2021, she refused to campaign and party high command rushed Jyotiraditya Scindia, the new BJP campaigner, at the last moment after he had been sent to West Bengal once. Her equations with party supremo Amit Shah and others remain anything but cordial.

YASHODHARA RAJE

Compared to her elder sister, the Madhya Pradesh minister of Sports and Youth Welfare, Technical Education and Skill Development and Employment has kept a low profile and is politically a lightweight. She returned from America in mid-1990 due to personal and family reasons; she had gone to the US after her marriage to Mumbai-based cardiologist Dr Siddharth Bhansali. Although initially her mother had reservations about the match, she later reconciled to the situation prevailing in the family then and approved the nuptial ties of her youngest daughter.

In her autobiography, she says, 'As her mother, I should have found a husband for her earlier. She was twenty-one. Now she had fallen in love with someone whom I did not think was at all suitable.' The Rajmata had wanted to marry her off to a family 'of their own caste and background,' as per her autobiography.[19] But Vijaya Raje's dreams remained dreams! There used to be lot of tension in the family those days on this issue and eligible scions of princely families were found for her, but the pair's 'mutual infatuation' did not fade. The two finally got married on 9 March 1977.

Once Yashodhara Raje, born in London in 1954, was back in India from the US in 1994, she entered politics and joined her mother's party just about two to three years before Vijaya Raje passed away in January 2001. Yashodhara fought her first election from Shivpuri, the traditional seat of the Scindia's, in 1998 when Madhya Pradesh was under Congress rule. She defeated the Congress heavyweight Hari Vallabha Shukla by about 7,300 votes. In the next election in 2003 she stood from Shivpuri again and trounced Ganesh Ram Gautam by a bigger margin of 25,734.

The party made her the minister for tourism and sports but before she could establish herself as a successful minister, she was shifted to Gwalior to contest a parliamentary by-election. Being a 'Scindia', she won hands down in 2007 and then repeated the performance in the 2009 general election. On both occasions, it was Ashok Singh of the Congress who was at the receiving end. The Jyotiraditya faction of the Congress remained passive and obliquely supported her, as has been the tradition of the Scindia household—no Scindia family member opposes the other on political lines and loyalties, notwithstanding the differences and disputes about inheritance going on in the court of law. All parties always knew of this 'healthy arrangement' and perhaps none of the senior leaders objected to this.

Largely a private person in Bhopal and Gwalior, she is said to be popular in Mumbai and Delhi party circles of the rich and famous. In a long chat with writer Malavika Sangghvi in *Sunday Times* of the *Times of India* (cover story, 29 May 2005), she allows readers a peek into her personal world. She told the columnist on record: 'I don't think there's a single one of us who's had an easy life.'[20]

It was Yashodhara who had faced Indira Gandhi's army of probing officials during the Emergency when she was all alone in Jai Vilas Palace, Gwalior. He mother was in jail, her brother had left the country and many of her ancestors had died young, including her father. But several years later, as a ruling party MLA in 2005, she told the columnist: 'I have not disappeared or run away or been cowed down. I have met life head on. You are dealt certain cards and you jolly well learn to work with them,' she had explained the philosophy of her life with no special context. The interview had appeared just after four and half years of the death of her mother and then the tragic plane crash of her brother, Madhavrao Scindia alias Bhaiya, which had pushed the entire family in a state of unbearable shock. But her quote was seen to be linked to her ongoing legal fight over property matters with Jyotiraditya who was then in Congress. At one point in the interview, she comments that 'her mother [the Rajmata] saw me as the man in the family.'[21]

Yashodhara, after the two parliamentary polls victory, returned to the state politics and in 2013, was made in charge of the Commerce and Industries department, considered to be an elite and heavyweight department, by Chief Minister Shivraj Singh Chouhan. It was a decision he later regretted immensely as he received several complaints against her. Senior bureaucrats, while working in her department, were largely upset with her style of functioning and had even termed her finicky. Even the industrialist lobby was said to be not too happy with her treatment to them and her tardy, convoluted mechanism. Secretariat officials would often disclose to journalists visiting the state secretariat and covering the beat that she would sit on files and delay the decision-making process for reasons best known to her.

She was then removed summarily after a spat with a bureaucrat who had been the blue-eyed boy of Shivraj Singh. Baghelkhand's wealthy politician Rajendra Shukla, a close confidante of the chief minister, was given the important portfolio of Commerce and Industry in 2016, following repeated complaints against the former Gwalior princess, the political grapevine believed. Major part of her ministerial responsibilities thus remained tourism and sports portfolios. She is also known to make digs at his colleagues in cabinet meetings. When she became a minister in 2020, after the sudden fall of the Congress government, caused by her nephew Jyotiraditya, with whom her relations remain lukewarm, she was again allotted the Sports and Youth Welfare portfolio along with Technical Education.

After joining the BJP in March 2020, among the first things that Jyotiraditya did was to go and call on her at her residence in Bhopal to seek her blessings. They spent some time together but their cold formal relationship didn't seem to thaw, at least publicly.

In Bhopal, a story goes around repeatedly about an order she had gotten passed from the government. As per a *Times of India* report, she was caught up in a controversy over her repeated insistence of using the title 'Shrimant' even in the government's official correspondence. 'More than 55 years after royal titles were abolished under the Constitution, the BJP government in Madhya Pradesh has said that one of its ministers will be officially addressed as 'Shrimant'—a title of Scindia royal family.' The newspaper report further added, 'on 19 October [2006], the Madhya Pradesh government approved tourism minister Yashodhara Raje's demand. It slipped out an official gazette notification that… henceforth be addressed as 'Shrimant 'Yashodhara Raje Scindia.'[22] Contrastingly, Jyotiraditya had given special instructions not to use the word 'maharaj' on his official letter heads when he was elected the president of the MPCA. That a large number of people call him as maharaj out of their personal deference, is a different matter. His title was made into an election slogan by Shivraj when the two were in opposing political parties in 2018.

There were many adverse reactions to this demand made by Yashodhara Raje who, after her marriage, had become Mrs Bhansali, having married a common man outside a princely family. After she separated from her doctor husband in 1994, she returned to India and began using 'Scindia' as her surname, something that surely helped her in her elections in Shivpuri. After all, she was the youngest daughter of Jiwajirao and Vijaya Raje who had commanded huge respect during their lifetime and after too. She has remained unbeaten so far.

9

Third Generation of Scindias in Politics

Not too many political families manage to survive for several decades in the adverse, uneven and complex conditions of Indian politics and yet earn a name for themselves. Things don't always swing the way you want them to in the political system of this country and therefore sustenance over a long period of time for politicians remains ever challenging. Many examples can be cited in support of what I am saying.

The Scindias, for one, have survived the tumultuous travails of politics with grace and dignity and are thriving!

They are robust politicians, are popular and are already into their third generation of public service or politics—whatever adjective you may like to give to one of the most sought-after 'professions' in this country, of late. Numerous election rallies that were taken out in the later months of 2020, as also in the first quarter of 2021—the times of the dreaded Corona pandemic—bear testimony to the fact that political workers remained undeterred by the world's most fearsome disease. Be it the Madhya Pradesh by-elections to the Assembly or Bihar, Assam, Bengal or Tamil Nadu elections, everywhere, the picture

190 • ABHILASH KHANDEKAR

was the same. What did the surging of large crowds, showing scant regards to social-distancing protocols and guidelines of the central government and the states indicate? Answer to this is simple: the irresistible urge to be part of the political process at all times—for whatever it's worth! Many political experts and social scientists have written that the common man's interest in politics has increased manifold after Narendra Modi's ascent to power in 2014. That is another vast subject in itself.

Many who know the Scindias even distantly believe that given their rich historical family background, they are in politics to give something to the society and not 'take' from it. Vasundhara Raje, former chief minister of Rajasthan, for instance, said in a televised interview that the Gwalior royal family had given ₹54 crores (in 1946–47) to the new Indian government soon after Independence.[1]

Politicians, of course, are naturally dictated by the 'rules of the game' but the Scindias have largely succeeded in keeping a clean image, while setting the bar high in the given conditions of the Indian political theatre. Critics and others, however, say that one of the reasons for them to join politics, one after the other, is to protect their family riches and treasures. And this could be true. Some hints of the same are available in Vijaya Raje's writings when she appeared worried about her vast property during the Emergency days and wanted to secure it.

The contrary is also true: her son Madhavrao Scindia, after 20 years of the Emergency, had taken on the government single-handedly and had sharply reacted to the corruption allegation against him by his own party men and government agencies in the Hawala scandal (which turned out to be a damp squib). Scindia had locked horns with the most powerful man of the time—the prime minister—in 1996, all alone. Had he not weighed the side effects of such an act before deciding his course of action? He must have calculated the pros and cons but had placed his honour and integrity ahead of everything else, as we have seen earlier. And that amply displays how the Scindias have gone about protecting their image and stuck to values such as probity in public life and the family esteem, least bothered about the dangerous repercussions of their political move.

After the departure of Rajmata Vijaya Raje Scindia, a first generation politician, from the political scene, her son Madhavrao and two daughters—Vasundhara and Yashodhara Raje—kept her and the family's flag flying high in two different national parties and two states. In fact, two of them had already earned a name for themselves during the Rajmata's lifetime. Much of it has been said earlier at different places and with different references.

The Rajmata was one politician who did not seek 'power' for herself despite being in a public figure for a fairly long time. On principle, and to protect her own standing, she had dethroned a powerful chief minister in the '60s. 'But beyond that there are not many instances which even indirectly suggest that she was ever power-hungry,' says 65-year-old journalist Keshav Pandey of Gwalior who has seen all three Scindia generations from up close.[2]

Veteran political analyst Lalit Shastri, who headed *The Hindu* newspaper as its bureau chief for about 15 years in Bhopal, besides working with other newspapers, shares with the author two episodes of the Rajmata turning down high positions: First, to be the chief minister when it was easy for her to take it up in the SVD government of 1967 and second, when she was offered the presidentship of the Jana Sangh by Vajpayee and Advani.

Of course, the value system in politics during the Rajmata's heydays was a little better than what it is now, some two decades after her death. The rapid decline in ideology, commitment and principles is quite evident for everyone to see and no party has been able to insulate itself from the bane of the 'power-at-any-cost' syndrome. Not even the 'party with a difference'! Many instances can be cited in support of the same but suffice it to say that when diametrically opposite parties like the right-wing Shiv Sena and the NCP-Congress come together to form a government in Maharashtra in 2021 or when the BJP is seen supporting Mehbooba Mufti in Jammu and Kashmir, the design seems common for all: politics of convenience is better than the politics of principles!

Arguably, the BJP during Atal Bihari Vajpayee's time was different than the Narendra Modi-Amit Shah era. During the latters' times, the BJP gained a new shape and size which is quite unrecognizable not only to its old guard but also to the party sympathisers. The BJP is now the largest political party with a membership of 18 crore, according to the then working president of the BJP, J.P. Nadda.[3] Many independent political analysts hold a view that it is no longer a 'party with a difference.' They point out that the saffron party has now been more or less 'Congressized;' their core Hindutva agenda being perhaps the only major differentiator. In a nutshell, all the ills that the Congress had been afflicted with while at the pinnacle of its popularity and power, had gradually transferred to the new BJP in power in Delhi, for over eight years, with all its aggression on display and its overtly perceived hatred for the opposition parties. The new BJP has never given up even on a slim chance to form a government in a state despite being in minority—be it Goa and Manipur (2017) or Meghalaya (2018) or a bigger state like Karnataka. A classic example would be that of Meghalaya where it won only two seats in a 60-member house and yet formed government with the help of its ally the National People's Party (NPP).[4]

Perhaps no one can forget the day Vajpayee had lost majority by just one vote in the parliament in 1999. Could he not have managed it the way MPs and MLAs are 'managed' these days? Could he not have taken a leaf out of his friend P.V.

Narasimha Rao's book? After all, had Rao not run a minority government not long ago by managing his MPs? True, Vajpayee had made some efforts to talk to the BSP and Janata Dal (neither had decided to back him), etc., to seek their political support to sail through the no-trust motion but he had to pay a heavy price in the end for failing to manage that one single vote in support of his government.

That was a uniquely rare and intriguing case in parliamentary history and is quite relevant here. Odisha's then newly-appointed chief minister Giridhar Gamang (Gomango) (1999) from the Congress did not resign as an MP after having taken over as the chief minister and yet voted, as an MP in the parliament, making history for all the wrong reasons. This was not a voting on a bill or something of that sorts; it was a crucial trust vote the Vajpayee government was seeking with four years to go for his full term. It was the first and perhaps the last time when an appointed chief minister of a state availed his rights and powers as an MP and had actually voted. L.K. Advani had termed it as 'morally and politically fraudulent, albeit technically valid.'[5]

Gamang voted against the government and after 13 months of rule, the BJP government collapsed in April 1999, forcing mid-term elections to further burden the tax-paying people who had voted in a Vajpayee-led alliance just about a year ago. Speaker G.M.C. Balayogi did not give any speaking order and just left it to the conscience of the said member. Constitutional experts and political analysts kept debating it for a long time but a vanquished Vajpayee drove straight to the President House to submit his resignation forthwith. His former private secretary Shakti Sinha, an IAS officer of 1979 batch, wrote:

I had never seen Vajpayee more distraught than when he walked back into his room in the Parliament House after losing the vote of confidence. He was crestfallen and in tears. But the moment passed, and he was off to Rashtrapati Bhawan to submit his resignation.[6]

In today's BJP, this is more or less unimaginable.

Madhavrao was a successful union minister in the Congress party and his sister Vasundhara Raje was a union minister and chief minister of the sizeable state of Rajasthan. In that sense, she is among the most successful of Scindias if we go by the trends of contemporary politics in which what really matters is the position of power. She was an MLA, an MP and a Union minister with independent charge and remains a towering figure in Rajasthan politics, having served as the chief minister of the state for two terms. All in a period 35 years, beginning in 1985 when she became an MLA for the first time from Dholpur, where she was married.

Now their progenies are also senior politicians and have served their parties and constituencies for about two decades, in two different states.

JYOTIRADITYA SCINDIA

Jyotiraditya's entry into politics came with a big bang in 2002, though under adverse conditions. And also by chance. In September 2001, the fatal and unfortunate plane crash that took his father's life turned the Scindia family's life upside down. Only a few months before that Rajmata Scindia had passed away. The Scindia family was still recovering, although her death was considered natural at 82 years of age which came after a protracted ailment.

A chip off the old block, Rajya Sabha MP Jyotiraditya Scindia is among the tallest leaders in Madhya Pradesh. He is also among the most popular leaders of the state, a fact that was highlighted twice in about two years—in 2018 and 2020 elections to the state assembly. He led the campaigns of two different parties and pulled off victories for a large number of his supporters who contested the elections, first as Congress candidates and then as BJP flag bearers.

When the Madhya Pradesh state assembly elections took place in 2018, he was a Congress leader and the star campaigner, a face people liked to see the most. He criss-crossed the state and took a large number of public meetings and did road shows for the Congress to win in the state, though with a wafer-thin margin. Most of his supporters won their seats and strengthened the chances of the Congress forming the government. His popularity and hard work brought about a huge change in people's perceptions towards the Congress, which had been out of power for 15 years, thanks to its 'misrule' between 1993 and 2003.

Scindia was the only leader who had covered the entire state. PCC chief Kamal Nath, due to his advancing age and other preoccupations related to the elections, remained largely in Bhopal and used his stature and experience in putting the house in order. Former chief minister Digvijaya Singh was restrained from campaigning by his own party leadership because of his adverse image among voters, as he himself admitted to his party colleagues, a video of which had gone viral then.[7] He was given other tasks by the party. That left the entire burden on this 'star campaigner' who had worked miracles resulting in the party winning five more seats than the 15-year-old BJP, to form the government. Of course, the entire credit cannot be given to him for the Congress victory as Scindia was believed to be the game changer. While the Congress bagged 114 seats against the 116 seats required for a majority in a House of 230 seats, the BJP trailed by five seats at 109. Chief Minister Shivraj Singh Chouhan, a saffron stalwart, for the first time, could not get his party a majority. He chose to sit in the Opposition. For a while, that is.

It was a wafer-thin margin and the tussle was neck to neck;

an unpredictably close fight. Scindia was the hero of the 2018 elections. His Gwalior-Chambal region, consisting 34 seats, saw the Congress winning 26 seats and the BJP only seven with the BSP bagging one. The Congress had never performed so well in this belt which had been under the Scindia dynasty rule for decades. The young charismatic scion was perceived to be the chief minister and various sections of voters (young, old, women, professionals or farmers) of Madhya Pradesh had positively swung to the Congress in a big way, little realizing that the Congress, under pressure from the duo of big businessman Kamal Nath and 'anti-Scindia' Singh, would make the 75-year-old leader the chief minister and not Jyotiraditya.

A PCC office-bearer said in 2019 that he felt that Scindia, logically, was the right choice for leading the Congress. The top Congress leadership abundantly displayed their lack of ability for thinking rationally about the big picture, and handed over the destiny of 7.3 crore people to the leaders who were either 'new' to the state, or who had already ruined the state, paving way for the BJP in 2003. The 2003 defeat of the INC was so humiliating (38 seats out of 230) that Digvijaya Singh, the outgoing chief minister, had to take a kind of a political sanyas (retirement) for 10 years and had announced he won't take up any post. But that was a decision he made for himself and not for the ordinary workers who suffered a lot for 15 years being in Opposition because of the party's worst-ever performance under his leadership.

Having come into politics under trying circumstances in 2002, Scindia had always been national politics player with staunch followers in Gwalior-Chambal and large parts of Malwa, including Indore, Ujjain, Dhar, Mandsaur and Neemuch. He was deeply interested in state politics, unlike his father Madhavrao who had enjoyed Delhi more than Bhopal.

Actually, 2018 clearly belonged to Jyotiraditya but the leaders conspired with party high command to deny him what was due to him. Similar was the case, when in Rajasthan, young Sachin Pilot's claim was ignored and Ashok Gehlot was made the chief minister.

In 2001, just a few days before had Madhavrao died, he had been busy completing the unfinished tasks of several of the legal tangles related to property disputes after the death of his mother just about six months ago. Sardar Angre had already stirred up the hornet's nest. He had succeeded in creating an unpleasant situation by releasing an old and unreliable document as an authenticated will, purportedly penned by Vijaya Raje and shown to be the original one. But the national media, running after a mega juicy story of the Scindia family feud, had lapped it up and published the contents after one of the executors, Angre, had put parts of the controversial will of the Rajmata in public domain without talking to Madhavrao or perhaps to embarrass him. Newspapers carried it on the front pages.[8]

So, when Jyotiraditya suddenly decided to fight his first election, everything seemed standing tall against him, his father having suddenly gone barely five months ago. He was young and new to politics; had to shoulder all the responsibilities of the Scindia family as the 'karta' (head of household); look after his grieving mother, understand the maze of legal cases, shift his base from Mumbai, where he was working, to Guna and much more. Before he could assimilate the vast gamut of the new world that he was sucked into, completely unprepared, Jyotiraditya found himself in the electoral fray, going from door to door seeking votes. This was January–February 2002.

In his early 30s, and finding himself without his father to guide him, he had to lead a family which was in a complete disarray and in a state of severe shock. The entire Gwalior city had felt orphaned. It could only be a person of Jyotiraditya's grit who could withstand destiny's terrific blow to him and still stand up to face everything like a true Maratha warrior. One can only imagine his state of mind when he had hurriedly boarded an early evening service flight from Mumbai to Delhi, alone, to be with his mother when the two needed each other the most on 30 September 2001. That two-hour flight must have felt like an eternity to him, with a myriad thought plaguing his mind.

When Jiwajirao Scindia had passed away in Bombay in 1961, his son Madhavrao was much younger, barely 16, and was studying in school. But Jiwajirao had been ill and bedridden for a few weeks and hadn't passed away in the shocking manner in which his son did.

A graduate from the renowned Harvard University and an MBA from an equally-prestigious Stanford University, Jyotiraditya was working with a bank in Mumbai to gain work experience, when this unfortunate incident happened. As per the biographer of Madhavrao Scindia, Vir Sanghvi, Scindia had just returned home in Mumbai after enjoying lunch with his old friend Nikhil Khanna when he received the most-shocking news of his life.[9]

Unlike his father, he had studied neither at the Scindia School, Gwalior, nor at Oxford, as senior Scindia had wanted him to. Some technical issue was said to have cropped up and his St Stephen's College course credits were not given weightage by Oxford University. So, he applied to Harvard University and completed his economics degree. For schooling, his parents sent him to the Doon School, Dehradun, where he met Rahul Gandhi and they became pals, only to part ways in 2020, politically.

His maiden victory from Guna was a foregone conclusion. His first election for the parliamentary seat gave him a thumping majority and margin of about 4.5 lakh votes. Even he agrees that the overwhelming support was a tribute the voters paid to his father who had nurtured the constituency over the decades.

When Jyotiraditya joined the INC formally in 2002, Sonia Gandhi had called all the Madhya Pradesh bigwigs to her residence such as S.C. Shukla, Arjun Singh, Motilal Vora, Kamal Nath, Bhanu Pratap Singh, PCC Chief Radhakishan Malviya, Chief Minister Digivjaya Singh and Mohsina Kidwai, general secretary of the AICC. It showed how much importance she gave to the young Scindia, then.[10]

Sonia and Priyanka Vadra had both rushed to Scindia's home at 27, Safdarjung Road, New Delhi, soon after hearing the shocking news of the plane crash and even before Jyotiraditya could land from Mumbai. Both were there to be at the side of a stunned Madhavi Raje, to console her and give her moral support.

After his first election, Scindia kept on winning all his elections from Guna and then in 2009–10 became a union minister of Communication, Information Technology and Posts and later the minister of state (independent charge) for Power in Dr Manmohan Singh's ministry. He made a smooth switch from his three-piece suit to a crisp khadi kurta-payjama. A politician who loves statistics and data crunching, Scindia is a good economist and has been writing long analytical pieces in newspapers regularly about the Union budget for many years. After joining the BJP, he wrote about the agricultural reforms and praised Narendra Modi.[11]

Had the UPA government repeated itself in 2014, Scindia would have surely become a cabinet minister, given his performance. No files remained pending on his table for more than 24 hours. Just as Madhavrao had burnt the midnight oil in the railway ministry to bring it back on track, Jyotiraditya had done the same with power reforms despite being a junior minister, an official who worked with him, recalls.

As the Congress leader of some stature after his three elections victory of 2002, 2004 and 2009, his performance in the parliament was being talked about. His first speech on the budget in parliament made waves. 'I read 2000 pages in 10 days before preparing that budget speech,' he had told Nona

Walia of *The Times of India*.[12] He had then spoken about the meagre one per cent outlay on school education and had raised concern at the state of primary education. The foreign-educated politician soon mastered his Hindi and gave fiery speeches when Atal Bihari Vajpayee's government was in power. From 2004 to 2014 the UPA government was ruling the county and he became a minister towards the latter half.

Unlike Madhavrao Scindia, a keen cricketer since his school days in Gwalior and London, Jyotiraditya was not initially attracted to cricket. He liked polo and other games. Madhavrao would organize an invitation tournament (Scindia Gold Cup Cricket Tournament) in Gwalior in which a large number of top Indian players would participate and enjoy the warm personal hospitality of the 'Gwalior Maharaj.' Young Jyotiraditya Scindia would come to watch the games occasionally. Madhavrao, a senior vice-president of the BCCI, went on to become the president of the Board (1990–93) against heavy odds and won a tough election by one vote in Calcutta, the headquarters of the opposite camp, led by Jagmohan Dalmiya. He was not a minister then, just an MP sitting in the Opposition.[13]

After his father's death, members of the MPCA and office-bearers such as Dr M.K. Bhargava, former sports minister of Madhya Pradesh, Shravan Patel, Dilip Chugdar and others, managed to convince Jyotiraditya in 2006 to head the association headquartered at Indore, a city he loves and frequently visits.

He continued as president and then chairman and helped the association a great deal in every manner possible until 2017, the year when he had to step down to honour the Lodha Committee recommendations on cricket reforms. But what is important is that even as a simple member of the association, he continues to guide the new office-bearers when they reach out to him and attends the annual general body meetings. 'He does not leave his people in the lurch, a habit he has inherited from his father,' observed Dilip Chudgar, a veteran cricket administrator who has worked in the MPCA for over 30 years with both the father and the son.[14]

Jyotiraditya, taking time off from his extremely hectic political schedules—much tighter in the BJP than perhaps in Congress—is sometimes busy addressing the governing board of the Samrat Ashok Technological Institue (SATI), which was founded by the Rajmata in 1962 at Vidisha and which he heads now or addressing issues of the Scindia School or is busy looking after the several trusts he presides over, or is found in Guna or Gwalior, Indore or Ujjain attending to social, religious and political functions. Wherever the mass leader goes, he is seen surrounded by his fans and followers who are in the thousands and seldom leave him alone. On his birthday (according to the Hindu calendar) on 17 January 2021, there were more than 2000 people gathered in the evening at Rani Mahal's fairly big courtyard, who came from different districts and villages near Gwalior. All were there, uninvited, of course, with garlands or flower bouquets, and were waiting for hours to have a glimpse of their Maharaj, as witnessed by this author who had visited Gwalior to sense the mood of the people. A palace insider says there are many people who try to meet him every time he comes to Gwalior and it becomes difficult for them to manage his schedule.

'This does not seem to be a drummed-up support but looks genuine. Every time he comes to Indore I see large number of people around him which amazes me,' says Sudhir Soni, an agriculture businessman from Indore who was known to Madhavrao but is not known to Jyotiraditya at all.

For a Rajya Sabha member who is just about two years old in a new- and better-organized party than his earlier party, it is creditable that his brand image has not suffered but appears to have improved by many notches. One of the reasons is also that he believes in keeping live contact with a very large number of people across the country and abroad. People praise him for his wonderful time management skills and ability to quickly respond to unending emails and WhatsApp messages and calls from a vast range of people.

DUSHYANT SINGH

Dushyant Singh and Jyotiraditya Scindia, first cousins, are members of the BJP today and are the grandsons of Vijaya Raje. One is from Madhya Pradesh and the other from Rajasthan. Both have been MPs for almost about the same years.

While Jyotiraditya had to join politics under sudden and tragic circumstances after his father's death, Dushyant Singh's entry into the Lok Sabha seems to have been a planned one. In 2004, when Vasundhara Raje had already vacated the parliamentary constituency of Jhalawar-Baran, having entered the state assembly and having been the chief minister in late 2003, she passed on the baton to her son, a hotel management and hospitality professional by education. He had just returned to India from the US.

His father, Maharaja Rana Hemant Singh is the titular head of the Dholpur (a 15-gun salute state) princely family and stays away from politics.

Dushyant has been winning the Jhalawar constituency regularly since his first term in 2004 and has been helping his mother in the party as and when required and remains busy in his constituency and in Jaipur. His victory margins show that he has no competition in Jhalawar at all. During Parliament sessions, he is seen in Delhi but is not counted among those active and highly visible MPs who raise a number of questions or participate aggressively in debates on the floor of the House. Ruling party MPs, like him, may possibly have some compulsions that have restricted him. It would be interesting to note that once a senior BJP leader had reportedly advised party MPs against asking inconvenient questions to the ministers.

Despite being a full-time politician, Dushyant also heads a small business empire which was in the headlines in 2015 when the media began reporting about Lalit Modi's investment in his company, formed in 2005. 'Niyant Heritage Hotels Pvt Limited (NHHPL), has not done anything and has not committed any irregularity,' Singh was quoted in the business newspaper *Mint* on 18 June 2015,[15] in response to the widespread media reports about the questionable business transactions between him and Modi who was then being probed by the ED in a money laundering case. But Finance Minister Arun Jaitley, then travelling abroad, quickly came to their rescue and gave him a 'clean chit' by saying that the transactions between Modi and Singh's company were 'business transactions' and nothing else should be read into that.

Politically speaking, Dushyant Singh, in his late 40s, has generally kept a low profile and the reason could be his mother, whose profile and political stature has always been much higher. Now, after her loss in 2018 at the hustings, she, along with Dr Raman Singh and Shivraj Singh Chouhan, was made the national vice presidents of the BJP. Shivraj Singh returned as chief minister in March 2020 under dramatic conditions. Some people call the BJP's way of capturing power the 'new normal'.

꧁ꕥ꧂

10

Is the Future Nothing but History Reinvented?

9 March 2020: it was a normal day in the plush state secretariat at Bhopal. It was Monday, a day before Holi festival. Not many officers or politicians were seen in the large empty lobbies of the Shapoorji Pallonji-built swanky new secretariat building. Though COVID-19 had already struck India and initial cases were being reported across the country, it was only after American President Donald Trump and his entourage had safely returned from Gujarat that things seemed a little more serious than the normal. There were no signs of an impending political storm which people eventually witnessed later that month.

Chief minister of Madhya Pradesh, Kamal Nath, had already left Bhopal to 'celebrate' the festival of colours in Delhi on 10–11 March. Little did he realize that the colours were not to brighten up his festive mood that year, rather pale him into political insignificance sooner than later.

Kamal Nath had retained his palatial bungalow at Tughlaq Road in Lutyens Delhi which was allotted to him on account of him being a senior MP and union minister in Dr Manmohan Singh government (2004–2014) many years ago. He perhaps

wanted to 'relive' his Delhi days with friends after a gap of
several months. For a globetrotter and a rich politician, Bhopal
was a relatively small place where he had no friends of his
level and liking. One of his friends from abroad once called
him late in the night and asked him his whereabouts, to which
Kamal Nath said Bhopal. His overseas friend had reportedly
feigned ignorance and had asked where Bhopal is? The chief
minister had narrated this story, making it very juicy for the
media, present in a big number. The occasion was the launch
of a Hindi book at a Bhopal hotel, to buttress his claims that
Bhopal was not well-known to the outside world and that
he, as the chief minister, was working hard to put it on the
world map.

Only after winning the elections in December 2018 and
becoming the chief minister did Kamal Nath start staying in
Bhopal for several weeks altogether, something he had not done
before though he had got, many years ago, a very spacious
government bungalow allotted to him right opposite the chief
minister's official bungalow on the Shyamla Hills. As the PCC
chief, he did spend some more time in Bhopal in the run-up
to the polls in 2018, but not otherwise. Former Chief Minister
S.C. Shukla, who somehow never liked Nath, would dub him
'a migratory bird' because Nath was born in Kanpur, lived for
long in Calcutta and visited Chhindwara during the elections
but largely lived in Delhi after 1980. Kamal Nath had never
taken much interest in Madhya Pradesh politics and thus would
visit Bhopal very rarely.

Around 3.00 p.m. on 9 March, a few very senior bureaucrats
were seen running here and there in the secretariat and
making frenetic calls. Some were seen rushing towards the
chief minister's office on the fifth floor, while others were seen
heading to the chief secretary's office.[1] Information had been
received that a large number of MLAs, owing allegiance to
Jyotiraditya Scindia, had gone to Bengaluru and were holed

up at a sprawling resort (Palm Meadows) on the outskirts of the capital of Karnataka, a BJP-ruled state. Bureaucrats close to the chief minister quickly read the writing on the wall—the threat looming large over the future of the minority government of their boss.

It wasn't as if Kamal Nath was completely unaware of the disgruntled MLAs' restlessness and that some were in touch with the BJP since the beginning of the year. The major reason the MLAs and ministers were getting upset with him was the latter's treatment of them. 'Kamal Nath would always seem to be in a hurry, he had no time for us,' said a former MLA. A majority of the ministers and senior Congressmen were openly heard complaining that he would prefer meeting industrialists and businessmen over his own cabinet ministers. Journalists and others had nicknamed him 'Corporate Chief Minister'. The Scindia faction ministers, in particular, were aggrieved with the fact their department's key bureaucrats would not listen to them and resultantly the ministers had been rendered largely ineffective.

A small bid of revolt by a group of MLAs (Surendra Shera, Rambai, Bisahulal Singh, Kansana and Hardeep Dang) who had gone and huddled together with BJP leaders in Gurugram, near Delhi, had been successfully foiled by the Congress leaders. That group of MLAs did not belong to Scindia, though they had also gone to Bengaluru and stayed under supervision and comforts made available by BJP leader Arvind Bhadoria with the help of the Karnataka chief minister. It was the shoddy handiwork of some BJP leaders which got exposed, irking party supremo Amit Shah.[2] But then, Chief Minister Nath thought that the danger was over. Digvijaya Singh, ex-chief minister and Kamal Nath's main political advisor and crony, had already gone to the media in Delhi saying he had information that the BJP was trying to lure their MLAs and was offering huge cash as bait and that 'horse trading' had begun in Madhya Pradesh. He had also 'raided' a five-star hotel in Gurugram and with his son Jaivardhan Singh, then the Urban Development minister, and others, and had 'rescued' a few MLAs. The BJP's first plan, in which a few former ministers (Bhupendra Singh, Narottam Mishra and Vishwas Sarang) were also involved, got exposed early and failed.

But on 9 March, journalists in Bhopal were also unaware until about 2.00 p.m. when the first credible and real 'breaking news' appeared on one of the national Hindi channels, ABP, and soon all national channels began beaming their respective speculative stories that a number of ministers and MLAs of the ruling party were untraceable. No one was sure about the number but they knew that the Scindia followers who were angry with Kamal Nath had gone 'out of reach' suddenly. One of the important ministers, Govind Singh Rajput, who was in Bengaluru, told this author that 'they had checked up with their family members after having lunch at the resort if something was being shown back home on TV channels but got a negative response. So we assumed our plan was still not out.'[3]

Rajput was wrong. Kamal Nath had already got wind of it in Delhi and after speaking with Sonia Gandhi, he took Vivek Tankha, a Rajya Sabha member, and flew back to Bhopal. Kamal Nath's family has an aviation company (Span Air Private Limited) in which his son Nakul Nath, now an MP from Chhindwara, is a director, and thus Nath has had long-standing and good connect in the aviation industry. One of the ministers who flew to Bengaluru admitted to this author that 'Kamal Nath got to know from his aviation staff about our secret departure from Delhi.' But still, he could not do much on his own.

Meanwhile, as Brajesh Rajput, ABP reporter in Bhopal, told this author, he had broken the news that some MLAs had reached Bengaluru, and there was tension building up for the chief minister with a fresh wave of dissidence.

'OPERATION LOTUS' HAD BEGUN*

Puneet Nicholas Yadav, writing in *Outlook*, had then rightly predicted trouble for the minority governments in Madhya Pradesh and Rajasthan, by saying 'having succeeded in Karnataka Assembly... the BJP is bound to make strident efforts to topple Kamal Nath and Ashok Gehlot regimes.'[4]

That Jyotiraditya Scindia, the all-India general secretary of the Congress and a heavyweight in his own right would turn against his own government and raise a banner of revolt, with a large number of followers in tow who together could topple the government in Madhya Pradesh, was never ever suspected by senior party leaders in Bhopal and Delhi, mainly the out-of-touch Kamal Nath and canny Digivijaya Singh. It was also because all three important Gandhis—Sonia, Rahul and Priyanka—were close to him, especially the brother and sister duo. What the outside world did not know was that Scindia had started realizing that the trio was increasingly getting helpless, vis-à-vis Nath and Singh for reasons best known to the Gandhis. Financial support to the AICC from Madhya Pradesh was perhaps one of them. According to many media reports and intelligence inputs, large amounts of cash used to be transferred to Delhi intermittently from Bhopal during the 15 months of the Congress regime.

Intelligence agencies were in the know that the AICC was getting funds from Congress governments of the newly-elected states, including Madhya Pradesh:

> Election Commission (EC) of India has sent a critical
> Central Board of Direct Taxes (CBDT) report...to the chief

---

*'Operation Lotus' was the unofficial name of the BJP game plan to topple the Kumaraswamy-led government in Karnataka in July 2019; the same code name was used by the media, extensively, when Madhya Pradesh was destabilized using Congress dissidents.

electoral officer of the state for criminal action. The report is on the alleged illegal transfer of huge amounts of cash to the Congress's headquarters in Delhi and is said to point to aides close to former chief minister Kamal Nath.[5]

In one case, ₹20 crore had been sent to a major political party. According to news report:

> The Central Board of Direct Taxes (CBDT) said the income tax department has also detected a trail of Rs 20 crore suspect cash allegedly being moved to the headquarters of a major political party from the house of an important person who lives on Tughlaq Road, home to many VIPs.

This was a sequel to an IT raid in the capital city of Madhya Pradesh against the close aides of Madhya Pradesh Chief Minister Kamal Nath and others during which ₹281 crore of unaccounted cash was discovered.[6] But this was just the tip of the iceberg of corruption that took place through transfers and other means.

Scindia, stung by a series of insults, meanwhile, had kept his plans very close to his heart. When he had removed, from his Twitter handle, his Congress designation, and just kept it as 'public servant and cricket enthusiast' on 25 November 2019, rumour mills had begun working overtime and the media and state's intelligence officers were alarmed but just for a few days. Intelligence officers tried to inquire from people close to him. Scindia made light of the change in his status on the social media microblogging site, though media published the stories, giving a political tilt to them. Political circles and bureaucrats had, by now, got a fair idea that he was not getting on well with the chief minister. But there was nothing beyond that.

Was the Twitter status change just a normal change or was it a message laden with a solid hint to the party high command which the Gandhis failed to read properly? Many are of the opinion that Scindia's disillusionment had begun to manifest from that day. In fact, he had changed his Twitter profile in October, but most had not taken note of it until November. In the meantime, during one of his regular visits to Bhopal, he met with a large number of journalists—in groups and one by one—at the VIP guest house, Lalghati, late in the evening. He had befriended many from the fourth estate. He would give them enough time and they, in turn, exchanged lots of information with him. That particular evening, many had complained to him about the high-handedness of the chief minister and his staff, and generally expressed their unhappiness with Nath's style of functioning. Scindia heard them patiently. Much of what the political workers and ministers used to tell him often, was getting tallied with what the senior journalists of the capital had told him over the two-hour meeting that late evening—in groups and individually.

But political observers had noticed, more importantly, that Scindia had hailed the Modi government's historic step of abrogating the controversial Article 370 and had also welcomed the Ayodhya verdict of the SC in November 2019 asking people to accept the same with patience.[7] Was that another hint of him inching towards the BJP or was it just an effort to be politically correct?

His reactions appeared pregnant with political possibilities yet sounded very statesman-like. Scindia has always maintained that he loves calling spade a spade and does not believe in playing politics for the sake of politics! As a junior minister in the UPA government, he had, in close circles, praised Modi's governance in Guajarat on developmental fronts.

However, when he was not made the chief minister in 2018 nor the PCC chief in 2019, along with an assurance of a Rajya Sabha ticket from his party, he became upset and hurt. Nevertheless, as a committed Congressman he reconciled to the situation after a late-evening meeting with Rahul Gandhi and

Kamal Nath at the former's house in New Delhi and agreed to support Nath. Gandhi and Scindia had 'patched up' their differences, or so it looked on TV when the three waved in unison, before the two (Nath and Scindia) took flight to Bhopal to meet the waiting MLAs at the PCC on a chilling Thursday night of December 2018. But again, Scindia also had to struggle hard to get maximum berths (six) for his supporters in the Nath cabinet of 27 ministers. His expectation was said to be of eight to ten ministers. Scindia had tried in vain to get a berth for Rajyavardhan Singh Dattigaon too but had failed. The suave, English-speaking MLA from Badnawar in the Dhar district is now the minister of Industrial Policy and Investment Promotion in the BJP government, courtesy Scindia. His father used to be a close associate of Madhavrao Scindia. The earlier fight had been to get tickets for his supporters in the run-up to the state elections, a few months ago.

Incidentally, there was stiff opposition from the Nath-Singh lobbies to part with important portfolios but Scindia managed to snatch a few like health and transport or school education for his supporters—Silawat, Rajput and Dr P.R. Chaudhary. Home, finance, PWD/environment were kept by Nath acolytes including indegenious leader Bala Bachchan, an urbane MLA from Jabalpur, Tarun Bhanot and Sajjan Singh Verma from the Indore-Dewas region; urban development, a cash cow, was given to Digvijaya Singh's son Jaivardhan and cooperatives to veteran Govind Singh, another Digvijaya supporter and so on. But the sharp differences over the distribution of portfolios dragged on for several days, exposing the deeper chinks in the new ruling party. After utilizing him in the elections rather well, the Nath-Singh duo wanted to make Scindia weaker after power was completely theirs. That was not just public perception but the old friends of over 40 years of 'dosti' had clearly closed ranks. Scindia was absolutely in no mood to take it lying down, having already lost the race to the top.

Curiously, Scindia, keeping aside his differences with Digvijaya, who comes way below the Scindias in the princely hierarchy (Gwalior was one of the five 21-gun salute states of India), had gone to the Raghogarh Fort, residence of Jaivardhan Singh during the peak of electioneering, to send out a message of unity within the party. But such goodwill gestures were not returned with the same spirit by Digvijaya and his followers. It was after many years that a 'maharaja' was visiting a much smaller 'raja'. Raja Digvijaya Singh now, after his second marriage to a former TV anchor in 2015 at the age of 68, rarely visits his ancestral home (fort) due to a family dispute that is now an open secret. Many friends of the family had made efforts to patch them up but nothing worked.

Finally, when the cabinet team of Nath was formally constituted after a lot of bad blood, many were surprised to see its shape and size. It happened for the first time perhaps in the history of the state that all the ministers were given the cabinet rank and there was no second tier for the juniors, as has been the practice. Ministries in states have various combinations; some have deputy chief ministers (Digivjaya had two at a time but three during his 10-year rule—Subhash Yadav, Jamuna Devi and Pyarelal Kanwar), others had cabinet ministers, state ministers (with or without independent charge) and some even have had three tiers with parliamentary secretaries being the lowest tier. Digvijaya had been a deputy minister in Arjun Singh's cabinet and so was Arjun Singh under various chief ministers before getting promoted to a full-fledged minister. Normally, there is a two-tier ministry to control the burden on the exchequer.

Nath, it was said, did this under duress to accommodate junior MLAs such as Sachin Yadav (son of former deputy chief minister Subhash Yadav), Kamleshwar Patel (son of late Indrajeet Patel) and mainly Jaivardhan Singh (son of Digvijaya), all first-time ministers. This, in effect, belittled the importance of experienced ministers like Sajjan Verma, Govind Singh, Hukum

Singh Karada, Bala Bachchan, Tulsi Silawat or Dr Vijaylaxmi Sadho who were all senior MLAs. But none could complain much—it would have amounted to speaking against the all-powerful Digvijaya, the remote control of Nath's government. Digvijaya's brother Laxman Singh, who won from Chachoda assembly segment, was far more senior than his nephew, but he was not made minister. This naturally made him upset, but his grievance was conveniently ignored. He was also an MP on various occasions and should have gotten a cabinet berth, given his seniority. But Nath, like in many other matters, was helpless here too.

In May 2019, Scindia received a rude shock—an unexpected defeat from his Guna constituency in the Lok Sabha election, at the hands of a young former Congress worker K.P. Singh Yadav, not heard outside of Guna until he became the giant-killer. He was a Scindia faction worker but got upset over some alleged insult, as the story goes, and switched over to the BJP to spring the biggest surprise of the 2019 elections. He won by 125,549 votes and became a modern-day 'Raj Narain.'[8] The loss was not small despite the fact that a Modi tsunami had swept away the opposition. The BJP won 303 seats on its own, and the NDA still more—332 across India. Many stalwarts from the opposition were knocked over by the strong pro-Modi wave. A quick analysis of the Modi tsunami was done by the author for Rajya Sabha TV website the same evening as the results continued to trickle in.

Scindia had been winning the Guna seat since 2002—four times, to be precise. No Scindia had ever been defeated from Guna since 1957. He lost despite the fact that Jyotiraditya would make hectic tours of the constituency almost every month and had nurtured it well over the years. During run-up to the polls, his family members would also go out to seek votes. He had live contacts with a very large number of voters and local leaders. He would go to mourn the death in some family or attend weddings or other events, etc., every time he came down from Delhi, even when the elections were not around.

If the Congress was counting on two seats in 2019 from Madhya Pradesh, they were Guna and Chhindwara and not Bhopal from where party heavyweight Digvijaya Singh stood and suffered a massive loss from a first-timer Pragya Singh Thakur who got 866,482 votes (61.54 per cent) against Singh's 501,660 (35.63 per cent). The loss was by a staggering 364,822 votes, from a city where he had worked as the chief of state for 10 long years. From Chhindwara, Chief Minister Kamal Nath's son Nakul Nath, a first timer and a non-political person thus far, managed to win by a safe margin of 37,536 votes.[9]

Scindia lost when the Congress was in power in Madhya Pradesh—some party workers, however, affirm that he lost because the Congress was in power in Bhopal. It had been barely five months ago when the Congress had stopped the BJP in their tracks in the assembly polls. Of the eight segments of the Guna Lok Sabha constituency, five—Chanderi, Pichhor, Bamori, Ashok Nagar and Mungaoli—went the Congress's way while Shivpuri, Kolaras and Guna town were won by the BJP. Scindia's areas of influence had done exceptionally well in December 2018. There was thus no reason for Scindia to panic, though Guna proper had not been favouring him for a few years. There's another fact, supported by statistics, that, however, went against him. The Lok Sabha election of 2009 saw Scindia winning by a margin of 38.42 per cent votes, which plummeted, in five years, to 12 per cent, in 2014. A massive cause of worry, as the Modi factor was at work then also, as it was in 2019—with much more force. In 2014, the Congress had won only two of the 29 seats (Scindia and Kamal Nath) from Madhya Pradesh; five years down the line Guna also slipped out of the Congress grip. The entire picture changed from here onwards.

Of course, Scindia was cautious and had also fielded some of his non-political and trusted people in areas like Shivpuri, held for long by his aunt and the problematic Guna city, among other areas, to give him feedback in 2018–2019. He had been awfully busy in Uttar Pradesh where the party had him, along with Priyanka GandhiVadra, to help gain some foothold.

His team of private management professionals, in an earlier election, had kept him informed of all relevant data required from a constituency from their surveys. A young IITian, Pallav Pandey, who had founded Viplav Communication, a political strategy consulting company, after returning from the US in 2003, also had made multiple visits to Guna until a few years ago, if not in 2019:

> I had a new concept plan by which I wanted to increase efficiency and connect of an MP in his constituency, through a fair feedback system about local issues, their solutions and about people's perception of their leader by using technology. My ideas were liked by Scindia, so I worked with my team up to the 2014 elections of Lok Sabha in Guna.[10]

But such apolitical people, despite their professional excellence, did have their own limitations. Rural voters are often reluctant to open up to unknown people or the media. Besides them, other political outsiders were also not heartily welcomed by local Guna workers, admitted a veteran Congress leader from Guna who has been working with Jyotiraditya since his first election, thus indicating to smaller factors that added to the big and shocking outcome later. 'More importantly,' he added, 'the BJP's state government had not done much developmental works in his constituency deliberately and Scindiaji had to keep fighting with state administration, being an opposition MP, upto 2018.'[11]

What was surprising in 2019 was that none of his confidants from the field picked up courage to brief him in time about the ground level, real situation, nor did they give him any hint of a possible reversal of result. Talking to this author, Scindia recently said:

> Obviously I failed [in the Guna election], there must have been some shortcomings in me and therefore the voters punished me. There are two Gods—one up there and the other is the people and one must bow one's head before both. I shall try to improve myself and go back to people; no one is perfect. For me, the poll outcome has been a great learning.[12]

Indeed, he would not have had to leave the party, if he had won the Guna seat against heavy odds.

The political scenario would have been different then. In some quarters, however, it was being spread—through written and spoken words—that Scindia was not keen in fighting from Guna because he was completely tied down to Uttar Pradesh for canvassing, ticket finalization, fund-raising, etc., being the in charge general secretary in a state where the Congress was almost absent, at the ground level and in the Parliament. Locals say he had made elaborate arrangements with 10–15 workers earmarked on each booth in the Guna constituency. Yes, given an opportunity he would have loved to shoulder any party responsibility after the Guna elections, sources close to him aver.

But his Guna contest and eventual shock defeat, that changed the entire course of Madhya Pradesh politics forever, seem to have been preordained.

As if all this was not sufficient, Scindia had to vacate his official bungalow—27, Safdarjung Road in New Delhi—within six months of the adverse poll result. The bungalow was the one where Madhavrao Scindia had lived for many years. Jyotiraditya had grown up in that house over the years; his mother had also developed an emotional attachment to it, having lived there for decades. Chief Minister Kamal Nath had an option of including that house in the Madhya Pradesh pool from the union urban development ministry, a suggestion given to him by Rajya Sabha member Vivek Tankha.

Each state gets a small quota of a few houses in Delhi. Kamal Nath kept his own house at Tughlaq Road but showed no sympathy or large-heartedness for his party's colleague who was in need of that house. Had Nath shown a little compassion, their strained relations would have surely improved. In the Congress circles it was a hot topic in those days. Kamal Nath also made it a point not to allot him a house in Bhopal even when he was an MP, and more so when he was entitled to one. When I had broached this Delhi house topic with a minister close to Scindia, he had laughed heartily and had said 'it was good what the chief minister did or else we could not have unseated him perhaps.'

Allotting a house is entirely at the discretion of the chief minister. He used that power to allot a posh house in a government colony to his son, Nakul, a first-time MP but before he could move in the bungalow where Bhupendra Singh, now urban development minister lives, the Nath government had collapsed. Shivraj Singh then allotted Scindia a house on the capital's Shyamla Hills in January 2021 as reported in the Bhopal edition of *The Times of India* in early 2021.

Actually, there were many more reasons which kept adding fuel to the fire and began burning inside Scindia since 2019. After he had to vacate his Delhi house, he went to a private accommodation of an old family friend on Tees January Marg in New Delhi and then to a private house in Anand Lok Colony, near Gargi College, in South Delhi. It is said that about four trucks containing personal furniture, photo frames, books, family memorabilia and other domestic utility items had to be shifted to Gwalior from Delhi. After all, the Scindias had lived in that house since the late '80s.

In spite of all this, it was simply unbelievable to see Scindia leaving the Congress!

Even if he does have about 20–25 non-political friends with whom he discusses politics in Gwalior, Bhopal, Indore, Guna, Mumbai or Delhi off and on, none of them had an inkling of what he had been thinking. They all asked each other how the Maharaj had taken such a major decision. They were left wondering if he had consulted with anyone. Even most of his MLA supporters got the hint only after reaching Gurugram, though not all. In Bengaluru, things were crystal clear to them—that they were going to make history.

So, Scindia dropped the bombshell on 10 March 2020.

An irked Scindia snapped up his ties with Congress in one stroke and showed how much power he wielded as the Congress government fell within 10 days of his changing sides. He joined the BJP on 11 March and took the primary membership from party president J.P. Nadda at the party headquarters. Soon after joining the BJP, he addressed a press conference in Delhi and said, that there had been two life-changing events for him, 'one, the day I lost my father and second, yesterday when I decided to choose a new path for my life.'[13]

A day before his joining, a senior BJP leader is believed to have conveyed to him not to join the BJP but float a regional party instead, just the way his father Madhavrao had done. The leader had feared that the BJP's top leadership may not honour their commitment with Scindia once the government was formed in Bhopal. Scindia listened to each and every word of the leader but went ahead with his plan according to what he had committed to Amit Shah. Rajput told this author that all permutations and combinations had been considered over the past few months or so, including the pros and cons of floating a new regional party. He also obliquely hinted that the February 2020 exchange, unseemly and indirect though it was, between Nath and Scindia may have actually hastened the process of his quitting the Congress altogether. 'I also feel that the furutre belongs to Modi and the BJP,' he had told this author after December 2020.

'Operation Lotus' was executed so clandestinely and smoothly by Scindia in sync with the BJP leaders in the month of March 2020 that Kamal Nath, with all his power, political experience and support of official intelligence could not get the whiff of it in time to possibly prevent it and save his government. Clearly, he was not 'atma-nirbhar' but heavily dependent on his friend who had assumed the role of a 'king-maker' in 2018. It was Digvijaya Singh who had picked up the chief secretary (S.R. Mohanty, IAS 1982), and not Nath, the chief minister. Singh would often go to the secretariat to be part of meetings and individually meet bureaucrats, some of whom had worked under his regime, earlier, for his works.

Singh, it now seems, clearly let down the veteran politician from Calcutta with his overconfidence of knowing all Congressmen and their political equations. He went to Bengaluru in an effort to save the Congress government and to meet the MLAs but failed to do so. Reportedly, he had made huge offers of cash, ministerial status, etc., to many of them through some mediators. One of the ministers, very close to Scindia, told this author that 'the offer to each individual MLA was mind-boggling...in several crores.' Digvijaya is reported to have 'confidently' told as many people as possible, including the chief minister, who spoke to him during the tense power tussle many times over, that 'the government won't fall under any condition.'[14]

The former chief minister had thought that the MLAs would fall prey to various allurements, but none showed any interest. They were firmly committed to Scindia and at least three of them were very angry with Singh himself for his false promises made to them earlier to make them minister.

Scindia's supporters, 22 in all, had already reached Bengaluru in the morning that day from Delhi using three separate private jets arranged by the BJP. But before that, they had all left Bhopal or their respective constituencies for Delhi, separately. There were six cabinet ministers—Health Minister Tulsiram Silawat, Transport Minister Govind Singh Rajput, School Education Minister Dr Prabhu Ram Chaudhary, Women and Child Development Minister Imarti Devi, Labour Minister Mahendra Singh Sisodia and Food and Civil Supplies Minister Pradyuman Singh Tomar—in this group, besides senior Congress leaders like Bisahulal Singh and two-time MLA Hardeep Singh Dang. The ministers had taken precautions of leaving behind their gunmen and other staff and had started using all- new un-smart cell phones, lest they were traced before reaching the destination or were contacted by friends, relatives and party bigwigs.

Interestingly, while 17 MLAs (including six ministers) owed their strong allegiance to Scindia, others also joined the bandwagon; they were ostensibly upset with the Nath-Singh model. Dang, the only Sikh MLA in the assembly, claimed that he was neither with Nath, nor Singh nor with Scindia but was with the Congress. Yet, he was among the first to jump ship and resign his from post to join hands with the BJP which was looking for an opportunity to destabilize the Nath government for quite some time. That was the extent of frustration he had developed with the 15-month-old government. Others like the indigenous politician Bisahulal Singh, once a minister in the Congress cabinet in the late '90s, or Adal Singh Kansana, another former minister of the same vintage, had their own axe to grind against the two Congress leaders. Thus, when they got hint of the Scindia group MLAs resigning en masse, they also joined in.

All 22 MLAs were herded to the Bengaluru resort on 9 March 2020 from Delhi in what was a very confidential operation. Clearly, much spade work had been done by Scindia

before taking the plunge. People privy to the developments in
Delhi and Gurugram say once the MLAs had reached the resort,
BJP leaders Shivraj Singh, Narendra Singh Tomar, Dharmendra
Pradhan (the latter was the key man in the entire operation
from the BJP), Narottam Mishra and Arvind Bhadoria met the
MLAs. Some of them were not aware that Scindia was to join
the BJP, what they knew was that the Kamal Nath government
had to be brought down as 'their leader' was being repeatedly
wronged. Govind Singh Rajput told this author:

> The 17 MLAs had complete loyalty, love, dedication and
> confidence in Maharaj, there was no other attractions for
> them. In modern politics, such loyalty and commitment
> towards one's leader is extremely rare and difficult to
> come across.[15]

This is true in that sense that none of the leaders who left
the Congress for different reasons over the past two decades,
including Madhavrao Scindia, Arjun Singh, Sheila Dixit,
Mamata Banerjee or Sharad Pawar, could take along as many
ministers and sitting MLAs as did Jyotiraditya. After all, who
would want to give up power gained after a long wait of
15 years? Scindia loyalists proved the established traditional
political theory that ministers don't easily give up power, wrong.
They sent out a message loud and clear that if you mess up
with our leader, we will teach you a lesson. And they did.
Interestingly, most of these ministers had also closely worked
with Madhavrao Scindia.

Scindia formally resigned from the Congress party on 9
March by writing a letter to Sonia Gandhi, which he tweeted
on 10 March, after his successful meeting with Prime Minister
Narendra Modi in which Home Minister Amit Shah was also
present. Incidentally, it was the seventy-fifth birth anniversary
of his beloved father Madhavrao Scindia, the former Congress
stalwart, whom he always held as his role model.

Scindia, in his short, four-para resignation letter addressed to Sonia Gandhi said:

> Having been a primary member of the Congress Party for the last 18 years, it is now time for me to move on. I am tendering my resignation from primary membership of the Indian National Congress and as you well know, this is a path that has been drawing itself out over the last one year. While my aim and purpose remain as it has always been from the very beginning, to serve the people of my state and country, I believe I am unable to do this anymore within this party. To reflect and realise the aspirations of my people and my workers I believe it is best that I now look ahead at a fresh start.[16]

The tone and tenor of the letter indicates that had been uncomfortable in the Congress party for about a year before his resignation. In other words, since March 2019, his discomfort had begun to pinch him, yet he dragged on and kept adjusting with his senior party colleagues, as a disciplined soldier of the party. After he had lost from Guna and the Rajya Sabha seat looked increasingly difficult, he probably got more restive with no sympathy or support coming in from the expected quarters in Delhi.

Why did Scindia, a staunch Congressman for close to 20 years, think of quitting his party and join the party he had been opposing all through his political career? Had his resignation from the Congress been unavoidable? Was he afraid of a witch-hunt from Modi government? Who were his advisors? Why did he not respond to the last-minute efforts by Congress leaders Ahmed Patel, Kamal Nath/Digvijaya Singh and his friends such as Milind Deora and Sachin Pilot who were reportedly deputed by party high command to talk to him? Had the Baroda princely family (Jyotiraditya's wife Priyadarshini Raje is from the famous Gaekwad royal family of Baroda), known both to Modi and Shah, played any role in this?

There are no straight answers to any of these questions. There are, of course, many conjectures and situational and other evidence which actually help join the dots to create a politically-logical picture which may also be complete in itself. Some of them have been mentioned above, that may have led to his final decision and the way it was taken. The timing of the decision is also a significant pointer to the entire happening. The timing of the decision—approaching Rajya Sabha elections in Madhya Pradesh—is also a significant pointer to the entire happening.

One name that has been repeatedly mentioned in media reports was that of BJP leader and spokesman Syed Zafar Islam, now a Rajya Sabha member from Uttar Pradesh. He was a former investment banker and a director (senior employee) of the Deutsche Bank which he left to become a BJP spokesman. A friend of Scindia's, he is said to have been instrumental in bringing him close to Amit Shah. Though insiders claim they had not seen him with Scindia or heard of their friendship for long. In other words, he is a relatively new friend.

During that time, when a number of hectic activities were happening day and night simultaneously in Bhopal, Delhi, Bengaluru and in the state assembly and in police stations (Divijaya was detained in the Karnataka capital as he insisted on meeting the MLAs who were just not interested in allowing him entry into their temporary abode) and in the Supreme Court, etc., Zafar Islam was not only seen and heard defending Scindia on TV debates, but was also spotted travelling in a car with Scindia once or twice.

After the meetings with Amit Shah, as they say, it is history!

People from Madhya Pradesh, Delhi and other Congress states like Rajasthan, Punjab and Chhattisgarh, found it difficult to fathom this series of events. Many believe in unison that if the the Congress leadership in Delhi had managed to

224 • ABHILASH KHANDEKAR

categorically promise Scindia of sending him to the Upper House of the Parliament, perhaps they could have retained a bright young leader in the party and could have saved their own government in Bhopal—formed after 15 long years—in which Scindia had had a lion's share. Instead, the party had decided to field, yet again, Digvijaya Singh who had already served a six-year term in the Upper House. What the party's top leadership failed in doing was to tell the two self-seeking, more than 70-years-old leaders of Madhya Pradesh—Nath and Singh—that Scindia was not only equally important as were they, but he was also the party's future leader and that they needed to look after him especially after his loss from Guna. The Gandhis (Sonia and Rahul) could also have, using some intelligence, saved Madhya Pradesh from becoming 'Congress-Mukta,' a political dream that Modi has been talking about incessantly and trying to actualize in one way or another, since he grabbed power in 2014. After the shocking episode of Madhya Pradesh, the Congress clearly appeared aiding and abetting it, unwittingly.

A large number of Congress insiders who spoke to this author, on condition of anonymity, feel that because the Gandhis have been among the weakest leaders at the top since 2014, with many skeletons in their own cupboards, they could not sternly tell Kamal Nath to behave, a practice the Congress party's high command had been known to be following before with its chief ministers and other regional satraps. Punjab was another example where the chief minister did not dance to the tunes of Delhi but it was the other way round. A strong high command could have easily handled the situation in Madhya Pradesh to save the party and its government, said a Congress watcher of many years. In fact, many Congress leaders later went up and told Nath himself on his face that he had been unjust to Scindia during his chief ministership. Nath would not say anything and would listen quietly.

Curiously, Nath still holds two posts after his government was removed 20 months ago. He is the leader of the Opposition in the assembly, being the MLA and is also the State chief of the Congress party, a sign that the party has a paucity of able leaders. After all, there were only three top leaders left in the party—one young and two old. Others such as Suresh Pachori, Ajay Singh 'Rahul' and Arun Yadav among others, had lost elections badly and were almost sidelined with no public appeal left in them.

Jyotiraditya, it is also said, was terribly upset by Kamal Nath's reaction on 16 February 2020 to his statement (of 14 February in Tikamgarh), in support of contractual teachers (*athithi vidwan*), that he would hit the streets if their demands were not met by the state government; Kamal Nath reacted to it in a very cavalier manner telling the media '*toh utar jay sadko pe* (so go and do it).'[16]

Scindia took it as a gauntlet thrown down by the chief minister towards him; he did not waste time in picking it up, but quietly. Kamal Nath, much later, talking to his core group of bureaucrats, reportedly said that he had made that comment in Delhi to the media in a lighter vein and that there was nothing serious about it, or something to that effect. But it was too late to explain it and to the wrong group of people. By making such a statement, Nath burnt the last bridge between him and the Gwalior Maratha.

Nath's suicidal remark in Delhi turned out to be the flash point in the ongoing tussle and the beginning of the end of the Kamal Nath government. It is not that some efforts were made for truce between the warring groups, they were not made by Congress senior leaders but by a few top industrialists from both sides.

While being in Bengaluru, six ministers were summarily sacked by Nath in an effort to drive a wedge between the group of 22 (G-22) and to scare the others. But that did not much work. Allegations were also made against the BJP by the Congress leaders that their MLAs had been kidnapped and were being held hostage in a BJP state. But a determined group of Silawat, Bisahulal, Kansana, Rajput, Tomar, Dang, Imrati Devi, Sisodia, Dr Prabhu Ram, Dattigaon and others hit back by releazing their own videos saying they were there on their own and that there was no kidnapping. Manoj Chaudhry, an MLA from Hatpipliya (Dewas) who was generally unattached, did complain after many days of coming out of the resort that he wanted to leave the place but was 'threatened with dire consequences.' Incidentally, all those days his men were in Bengaluru, Scindia did not go there once. His long-time personal assistant Purushottam Parashar, a young man from Morena, managed the difficult show of keeping them united and following the line in letter and spirit given by Scindia in Delhi.

All of them resigned their membership of the state assembly, the government slipped into minority and eventually the chief minister failed the floor test (which actually did not end up happening), an ignominy Kamal Nath had to face, after pompously saying 'MLAs are with us,' 'majority is with us' or 'government was not in danger.'[17] Chief Minister Nath officially admitted before the media that he did not have the numbers and therefore he did not take to the floor of the assembly.

A lot of drama went on for the whole of March in 2020, simultaneously, at many places, many clues of which have yet to be traced as to who did what, where, why and when. It was an unbelievable see-saw game between the Congress and its dissidents, with the BJP playing its role, at times behind the curtain and at times openly.

Guna's loss was a lifetime shock for Jyotiraditya. Though he did not suspect the hand of the Congress leaders opposed to him, many of his supporters believed that internal sabotage by party workers may have been the result of his defeat during the strong pro-Modi wave. Some of his followers in Vidisha and other places confidently say that Congress workers had been instructed in May 2019 by a top leader not to vote for Scindia.

Those who met him immediately after the result in the last week of May 2019 in Delhi, say Scindia was seen at his lowest ebb. He was unable to know what to say or what to do. Many even told him, to assuage his hurt feelings, that many stalwarts, from Vajpayee to Indira Gandhi and Arjun Singh to Rahul Gandhi, Shivraj Singh to Digvijaya had lost one or the other election in their political journey and that it was a part of life. But Scindia reportedly told some of them that it was a 'Kali-Yuga' (among the worst periods of the Yuga cycle of time according Hindu beliefs) and that he was suffering despite doing a lot, and continuously, for the people of Guna. He was actually unable to come to terms with the new situation he found himself in. The fact that he became the first member of the Scindia family to have lost an election from the family seat of Guna was discomforting for him. His father Madhavrao had never lost an election. Rajmata Vijaya Raje too had never lost in Madhya Pradesh; she had only lost once against Indira Gandhi, who had been on her comeback trail in 1980, from Uttar Pradesh's Raebareli constituency.

However, like a diehard Maratha, he fought back the tough situation valiantly, all alone, at a time when it looked hopelessly dark all around him. He rose like a phoenix, unbothered by the trenchant criticism of his ex-party colleagues and some street-smart insignificant netas. All kinds of allegations and charges were hurled at him, particularly about his ancestral property because he had joined the BJP without letting anyone know. He was well within his own rights to secure his future, which he smartly did when he thought the Congress was not prepared to give him his due, one of his associates in Gwalior told this author. There have been a number of such examples of tall leaders who were, after losing a Lok Sabha poll, accommodated in the Upper House of the Parliament. BJP's many key Union ministers are members of the Upper House. The party used to show concern for the utility of a person and his experience which can't end with one electoral loss.

But still many questions remain unanswered.

Was his action against the Kamal Nath government, a government he reportedly considered to be corrupt, taken in a haste? Could he not have waited for another sunny day? Could the Congress have made him chief minister before the 2023 state election? Can he adjust in the BJP in the long run? Will the BJP utilize him, given his talent and energy?

In an interview with *The Times of India*, Scindia said that he 'only saw rent-seeking behaviour by Congress across the board, right from Kamal Nath, over transfers, sand mafia, and complete abdication of poll promises.' He also said that his 'career is not about a name plate, I am happy to be a BJP worker.'[18] This he had said way before he was inducted into the cabinet by Prime Minister Narendra Modi.[19]

Incidentally, in the high-stakes by-elections held in October 2020, most of his supporters from different regions such as Malwa, Nimar, Bhopal and Bundelkhand won with wide margins. The Congress used to dub him a leader of Gwalior-Chambal alone, but he toured, like he had done in 2018, the entire state. He showed that if he was popular while he was in the Congress, he was equally popular with the BJP. He was the biggest crowd puller in the by-elections in which he visited some of the constituencies such as Sawer, Sanchi, Badnawar or Surkhi three times to ensure his candidates win. Silawat won by a huge margin of over 53,000 votes, a notch below Dr Chaudhary who won by 63,000 plus votes from Sanchi, the known tourist place for a Buddha Stupa. Rajput registered a win by 41,500 votes—a sign that proved Scindia's stand against the Congress government was approved by people of

Madhya Pradesh as most of his followers won by empathic margins while representing the BJP.

A few of his supporters also lost the by-election, mainly Imarti Devi from Dabra and Munnalal Goyal from Gwalior which was a personal setback for Scindia as admitted at the time. Of course, the BJP's well-oiled election machine called the Sangahtan, worked equally hard to bring the BJP back in power in Madhya Pradesh. It was the Modi-Shah prestige which was at stake, as was Scindia's, besides own followers.

Of the 28 seats (many other seats had also fallen vacant other than the 22) that went for polls, the BJP won 19 and the Congress, only 9. The Congress's charges such as the defectors would be punished, 'corruption' by the turncoats would make life difficult for them, Scindia had ditched the Congress and so on just did not work at all. The Congress had made single-point agenda: attack Scindia! The election was between Kamal Nath-Digvijaya Singh versus Scindia.

Scindia won hands down. Well, his action was almost a repeat of what Rajmata Scindia, as a Jana Sangh MLA, had done to D.P. Mishra in 1967. The difference is only that she could manage to lure away a sizeable number of ruling Congress MLAs to her side to form the new grouping SVD. In her grandson's case, 53 years down the line, he took away his own Congress MLAs and joined the BJP. The intended outcome of both the operations was common—the removal of the Congress government and teaching a lesson to the incumbent chief minister.

That time it was D.P. Mishra, this time it was Kamal Nath. Both were veteran Congressmen; both were obstinate in their approach; both were close to Gandhi—Mishra to Indira and Nath to Sonia; both did not like Scindias. And both suffered at the hands of the Gwalior princely house, badly. Jyotiraditya Scindia, born about three years after the 1967 operation which had no code name, turned out to be a true successor of his famous grandmother Vijaya Raje Scindia.

He joined Narendra Modi's cabinet on 7 July 2021 and was entrusted with the Civil Aviation Ministry, known to be a glamorous and prestigious ministry, thought to be much smaller than Scindia's capabilities. Incidentally, his father had also 'flown' the same ministry some three decades ago.

Acknowledgments

This book, covering various aspects of history and politics and individual traits of a large number of top political figures—living and dead—would not have been possible without the help, guidance and timely corrections by many of my friends and acquaintances.

While I would like to thank all those authors—known to me and those unknown—whose books have immensely helped me, I am particularly indebted to Dr Suresh Mishra, an extraordinary historian, author and humble scholar from Bhopal. He had guided many research students during his government job as a professor of history and more so after his retirement. He was a voracious reader and a prolific writer; full of energy. He was considered an authority in Maratha history. Alas, he is not alive to read my book. He passed away during the deadly second wave of COVID-19 in April 2021, at the age of 84. However, such was his persona that even when he was in the hospital, he was working on his laptop to complete his ongoing book. Before his unfortunate demise, in a series of our meetings at his little home, made of books and not bricks, we had discussed my book project, its outline and content. He gave me valuable advice while I was attempting to write the history of the formidable Scindia dynasty. I will forever miss you, Sir!

Prashant Mehta, a former IAS officer from Madhya Pradesh cadre, who was on the staff of Madhavrao Scindia when the latter was Railways minister and then the Aviation minister, helped me by going through the chapter on Madhavrao Scindia and vetting it properly. Many thanks to you, Mehta ji.

Like Mr Mehta, his colleague Bimal Julka, former secretary in the Information and Broadcasting Ministry, New Delhi, was kind enough to share his experiences, particularly during the long disputes Madhavrao had with his mother, Vijaya Raje.

Similarly, Dr Laxmikant Markhedkar (Ganj Basoda, Vidisha), the founding president of the Madhya Pradesh Vikas Congress (MPVC) and Jayant Khanna (Rewa)—both school friends of Madhavrao Scindia—readily helped me with their inputs on how the party was formed overnight when senior Scindia left the Congress.

Hindi daily *Swadesh*'s owner-editor Rajendra Sharma—a Vishwa Hindu Parishad chief and once a close aide of the Rajmata—was very cooperative in sparing hours chatting with me on his garden swing in Bhopal and going down memory lane. He also gifted me the Special Number of his newspaper that had been brought out on the Rajmata with articles from luminaries who knew her personally. This provided me a rare insight into her personality and politics.

I am also indebted to Dhyanendra Singh of Gwalior, half-brother of Rajmata, who spent hours in Gwalior and Bhopal, along with his wife Maya Singh, discussing the life and times of Vijaya Raje with me. While a lot of material is available on the Rajmata in her own book and by others, collecting significant vignettes and personal anecdotes was much more important for me. And Dhyanendra Singh made that happen to some extent, among others.

Congress leader Mahesh Joshi, in his last days, threw much light on the politics of D.P. Mishra. Though he was much younger, he had free entry into the powerful chief minister

Mishra's residence. Joshi, a former minister in Madhya Pradesh, helped me reconstruct those times when there was a tussle between the Gwalior queen and a stubborn chief minister. He is the second source of mine who passed away before the book saw the light of the day.

A special thanks to Penguin Random House India and State University of New York Press for granting me permission to use their books *Madhavrao Scindia: A Life* by Vir Sanghvi and Namita Bhandare and *The Last Maharani of Gwalior: An Autobiography* by Vijaya Raje Scindia as references.

My book would have remained incomplete but for Vivek Shejwalkar, MP, Gwalior, and one of the simplest BJP leaders of our times. He provided me with the original membership receipt of the Jana Sangh when Madhavrao Scindia had joined the party. It proved to be an invaluable document for this book. What is laudable is the fact he had preserved that little receipt for so many years.

While I was visiting Gwalior in search of people who could shed new light on the Scindia family's internal dynamics, Abhay Raghunath Paprikar, a banker and son of the longest-serving DCC chief of Gwalior proved to be of much help. We became instant friends. I salute his memory and ability to analyse political incidents during the Congress rule in Gwalior. He is quite a well-read person. Another friend in Gwalior, Dr Keshav Pande, was equally helpful, as usual. This time in connecting me to 'Dhyanu Mama' as Mr Dhyanendra Singh is well known in political circles. His warmth and clear-headed approach are admirable.

I am also indebted to Dr M.K. Ranjitsinh, a 1961 batch IAS officer of the Madhya Pradesh cadre, who is gifted with razor-sharp memory and interests in a range of subjects from classical music and cricket to history and wildlife—the last being his first love. He is a scion of the Wakaner royal family in Gujarat and is well known among the princely families of

India. He had worked under D.P. Mishra and 'suffered' due to his relations with Scindia.

Jyotiraditya Scindia, who I have known since his marriage, was kind enough to grant an interview to me, despite his very hectic schedule. His inputs have lent immense value to this book. There were a few other members of the Scindia family whom I tried for a personal audience in Bhopal, Gwalior and Jaipur, which some of them turned down. I harbour no ill feelings for them. One of them asked me on phone why suddenly so many books on the Scindias?

I would also like to thank Dr Uday Kulkarni for having taken out time to read the book and write a glowing foreword.

Last but not the least, Yamini Chowdhury, C. Sandhya and Oorja Mishra, my worthy book editors at Rupa who, day in and day out, worked diligently to give shape to this book that is in your hand today. Reading the manuscript repeatedly, making corrections, cross-checking facts and polishing the copy: all that rigour was done without any murmur. I would love to give much of the credit for bringing out this book in time to these three friends of the literary world.

I am sincerely grateful to my wife Anjali and daughters Shreyasi and Shivani for their endurance in putting up with my gruelling schedules of writing and reading without helping them when they needed me, or so I believe!

Notes

CHAPTER 1

1. Laurd, C.E. *Gwalior State Gazetteer, Volume 1,* Superintendent Government Printing, 1908.
2. Chaware, Dilip. *Saga of a Struggle: Sushilkumar Shinde,* Chinar Publications, 2008, p. 9.
3. *Gwalior District Gazetteer,* Bhopal, Government Central Press, 1965, p. 28.
4. Maharaja of Baroda, *The Palaces of India,* Collins, 1980, p. 112.
5. Personal interview with the author in Bhopal in January 2021.
6. 'Chapter II: How Gwalior Is Ruled', *Gwalior of Today,* Government of Gwalior, 1940.
7. Kautilya, *The Arthashastra,* Penguin India, 1992, p. 186.
8. Singh, Khushwant. *India: An Introduction,* HarperCollins, 2003, pp. 63–64.
9. *Gwalior of Today,* Government of Gwalior, 1940, p. iii.
10. Menon, V.P. *Integration of the Indian States,* Orient BlackSwan, 2014, p. 339.
11. Ibid.
12. Election Commission of India, New Delhi. Data accessed in October 2021
13. Malcolm, John. *A Memoir of Central India-Including Malwa*

and Adjoining Provinces, Volume I, Irish University Press, 1832, p. 116.

14. Ibid.

15. 'Chapter II: How Gwalior Is Ruled', *Gwalior of Today,* Government of Gwalior, 1940, p. 6.

16. Malcolm, John. *A Memoir of Central India-Including Malwa and Adjoining Provinces, Volume I,* Irish University Press, 1832.

17. Roberts, P.E. *History of British India Under the Company and the Crown,* Oxford University Press, 1921, pp. 239–240.

18. Bharadwaj, S. *Vintage Gwalior,* Commissioner, Archaeology, Archives, and Museums, Government of Madhya Pradesh, 2009, p. 15.

19. Laurd, C.E. *Gwalior State Gazetteer, Volume 1,* Superintendent Government Printing, 1908, pp. 19, 111.

20. Ibid.

21. Roberts, P.E. *History of British India Under the Company and the Crown,* Oxford University Press, 1921, p. 194.

22. Agnihotri, Ajay. *Gwalior: Art, History and Culture,* Shree Natnagar Shodh Samasthan, 2015, p. 61.

23. Williams, L.F. Rushbrook. *A History of India, Part 3—The British Period,* Longmans, Green & Co. Ltd, 1926, p. 114.

24. Bharadwaj, S. *Vintage Gwalior,* Commissioner, Archaeology, Archives, and Museums, Government of Madhya Pradesh, 2009, p. 17.

25. Achal, Rakesh. 'Chalo Gwalior Ki Virasat Bachaye'.

26. *General Policy Darbar (Gwalior State),* Alijah Darbar Press, 1923–25.

27. Agnihotri, Ajay. *Gwalior: Art, History and Culture,* Shree Natnagar Shodh Samasthan, 2015.

28. Scindia, Vijaya Raje and Manohar Malgonkar. *The Last Maharani of Gwalior: An Autobiography,* State University of New York Press, 1987, p. 132.

CHAPTER 2

1. Allen, Charles and Sharada Dwivedi. *Lives of the Indian Princes/*, Century Publishing Co., 1984, p. 11.
2. Maharani Gayatri Devi, *A Princess Remembers: The Memoirs of the Maharani of Jaipur* Rupa Publications, 1995.
3. Allen, Charles and Sharada Dwivedi. *Lives of the Indian Princes/*, Century Publishing Co., 1984, p. 104.
4. Jaffrelot, Christophe. *India's Silent Revolution: The Rise of the Lower Caste in Northern India*, Ashoka University and Permanent Black, 2018, p. 78.
5. Roy, Himanshu, M.P. Singh and A.P.S. Chouhan. *State Politics in India* (Primus Books, 2017), pp. 444–446.
6. Shani, Ornit. *How India Became Democratic: Citizenship and the Making of the Universal Franchise*, Penguin Random House, 2018, p. 4.
7. Akbar, M.J. *Byline*, Roli Books, 2004), p. 203.
8. Scindia, Vijaya Raje and Manohar Malgonkar, *The Last Maharani of Gwalior: An Autobiography*, State University of New York Press,1987, p. 163.
9. Scindia, Vijaye Raje. *Rajpath Se Lokpath Par* Prabhat Prakashan, 2016.
10. Scindia, Vijaya Raje and Manohar Malgonkar, *The Last Maharani of Gwalior: An Autobiography*, State University of New York Press, 1987.
11. Ibid.
12. Scindia, Vijaye Raje. *Rajpath Se Lokpath Par* Prabhat Prakashan, 2016.
13. Menon, V.P. *The Integration of Indian States*, Orient Blackswan, 2014, p. 430.
14. Datar, Arvind P. 'The Indira We Must Not Forget', *The Indian Express*, 11 December 2017, https://indianexpress.com/article/opinion/columns/indira-gandhi-100-birth-anniversary-congress-emergency-of-1975-4976978/.
15. Zubrzycki, John. *The House of Jaipur*, Juggernaut, 2020.

16. Ghose, Sagarika. *Indira: India's Most Powerful Prime Minister* Juggernaut, 2018, p. 115.
17. Allen, Charles and Sharada Dwivedi. *Lives of The Indian Princes*, Century Publishing Co., 1984 p. 11.

CHAPTER 3

1. Scindia, Vijaya Raje and Manohar Malgonkar. *The Last Maharani of Gwalior: An Autobiography*, New York: State University of New York Press, 1987.
2. Jones, Rodney W. *Urban Politics in India*, : Vikas Publishing House, 1975, p. 296.
3. Election Commission of India.
4. Singh, L.P. *Portrait of Lal Bahadur Shastri: A* Quintessential Gandhian, Ravi Dayal Publishers, 1996, p. 162.
5. Brecher, Michael. *Succession in India,* : Oxford University Press, 1967 p. 193.
6. Ibid.
7. Mishra, Dwarka Prasad. *The Post Nehru Era–Political Memoirs*, Har-Anand Publications, 1993, p. 23.
8. Elwin, Verrier. *The Muria and Their Ghotul*, Oxford University Press, 1947, p. 92.
9. Mishra, P.L. *The Political History of Chhattisgarh*, Vishwa Bharti Prakashan, 2008, p. 7.
10. Bagchi, Suvojit. 'A King Mulls Over Two Strategies,' *The Hindu*, 25 April 2013, https://www.thehindu.com/news/national/other-states/a-king-mulls-over-two-strategies/article4651880.ece. Accessed on 22 October 2021.
11. Jagdalpuri, Lala. *Bastar Itihas Evam Sanskruti*, \ Madhya Pradesh Hindi Granth Academy, 1994, p. 59.
12. Rajan, N. *Without Fear: A Journalist's Diary*, Amarshree Printing Press, 2001, p. 16.
13. Guha, Ramachandra. *India after Gandhi: The History of the World's Largest Democracy*, Picador, 2007), p. 408.
14. Scindia, Vijaya Raje and Manohar Malgonkar. *The Last*

Maharani of Gwalior: An Autobiography, State University of New York Press, 1987, pp. 189–90.

15. Interview with the author in Bhopal.
16. Interview with the author in Gwalior.
17. Scindia, Vijaya Raje and Manohar Malgonkar. *The Last Maharani of Gwalior: An Autobiography*, State University of New York Press, 1987.

CHAPTER 4

1. Chum, B.K. *Behind Closed Doors: Politics of Punjab, Haryana and the Emergency*, Hay House, 2014.
2. Sanghvi, Vir and Namita Bhandare. *A Life: Madhavrao Scindia*, Penguin Random House, 2009, p. 66.
3. Ibid.
4. This story of how the Rajmata came closer to Jana Sangh was told to the author informally by Kushabhau Thakre many years ago in Bhopal.
5. *Swadesh,* Special Number, 2006, p. 165.
6. Scindia,Vijaya Raje and Manohar Malgonkar. *The Last Maharani of Gwalior: An Autobiography*, State University of New York Press, 1987, p. 195.
7. Vir Sanghvi and Namita Bhandare. *A Life: Madhavrao Scindia*, Penguin Random House, 2009, p. 67.
8. *Swadesh,* Special Number, 2006, p. 18.
9. *Sandarbh*, Publicity Department, Government of Madhya Pradesh, 2020, p. 426.
10. Interview with his son Ashok Singh in Bhopal.
11. Noronha, R.P. *A Tale Told by an Idiot*, Noronha Foundation, 1976, p. 135.
12. Ibid.
13. Sanghvi, Vir and Namita Bhandare. *The Last Maharani of Gwalior: An Autobiography*, State University of New York Press, 1987, p. 200.
14. Fotedar, L.P. *The Chinar Leaves: A Political Memoir*, HarperCollins, 2015.

CHAPTER 5

1. Fotedar, L.P. *The Chinar Leaves: A Political Memoir*, HarperCollins, 2015 p. 106.
2. Baru, Sanjaya, et.al. 'Introduction', *Democracy Interrupted: The Emergency, 1975–77*, (Penguin Random House, 2019.
3. Ibid. xi.
4. Scindia, Vijaya Raje and Manohar Malgonkar. *The Last Maharani of Gwalior: An Autobiography,*State University of New York Press, 1987, p. 224.
5. Sanghvi, Vir and Namita Bhandare. *A Life: Madhavrao Scindia*, Penguin, 2009), p. 104.
6. Vijaya Raje Scindia and Manohar Malgonkar. *The Last Maharani of Gwalior: An Autobiography,*State University of New York Press, 1987, p. 245.
7. Ibid.
8. Sanghvi, Vir and Namita Bhandare. *A Life: Madhavrao Scindia*, Penguin, 2009), p. 104.
9. Scindia, Vijaya Raje and Manohar Malgonkar. *The Last Maharani of Gwalior: An Autobiography*, State University of New York Press, 1987.
10. Sanghvi, Vir and Namita Bhandare. *A Life: Madhavrao Scindia*, Penguin, 2009), p. 105.
11. Ibid.
12. Naqvi, Saba. 'They Call Me Rasputin', *Outlook*, 26 February 2001, https://magazine.outlookindia.com/people/sardar-sambhajirao-angre/7947. Accessed on 17 November 2021.
13. Sanghvi, Vir and Namita Bhandare. *A Life: Madhavrao Scindia*, Penguin, 2009), p. 139.
14. Olak, Sayajiraonchi. 'Baba Bhand', *Sadhana* /2020.
15. Sanghvi, Vir and Namita Bhandare. *A Life: Madhavrao Scindia*, Penguin, 2009) p. 126.
16. Ibid.
17. Mishra, Ambreesh. 'Scindia Feud: Castle in the Heir', *India Today*, 13 November 2010, https://www.indiatoday.in/magazine/the-big-story/story/20101122-scindia-feud-castle-in-

the-heir-744753-2010-11-13. Accessed on 11 November 2021.
18. Gujral, I.K. *Matters of Discretion: An Autography*, Hay House India, 2011, p. 476.
19. *S. Gurumurthy vs H.H. Jyotiraditya M. Scindia and Others*, Suit No.1861 of 1984, in the High Court of Judicature at Bombay Ordinary Original Civil Jurisdiction, 27 January 2021. Accessed on 11 November 2021.
20. Marpakwar, Prafulla. 'Royal War: Scindias at It Again', *The Times of India*, 18 August 2005, https://timesofindia.indiatimes.com/india/Royal-War-Scindias-at-it-again/articleshow/1204829.cms. Accessed on 11 November 2021.
21. Madhavrao Scindia Memorial Lecture, 2010, Gwalior.
22. Sarin, Ritu. 'What's at Stake in the Scindia Battle? The Mother of All Fortunes', *Indian Express,* 10 February 2001.
23. Maharaja of Baroda, *The Palaces of India*, Collins, 1980, p. 112.
24. Interview of Dhyanendra Singh with author, in Bhopal.
25. Interview of Jyotiraditya Scindia with the author.

CHAPTER 6

1. Padgaonkar, Dileep. *When Bombay Burned,* UBSPD, 1993, p. 39.
2. Walter K. Andersen and Shridhar D. Damle. *The RSS: A View to the Inside*, Penguin Random House, 2018, p. 195.
3. Vidya Subrahmaniam and J. Venkatesan. 'The Winding Paths of a Temple Town', *The Hindu*, 21 September 2010, https://www.thehindu.com/opinion/lead/The-winding-paths-of-a-temple-town/article16053024.ece. Accessed on 13 October 2021.
4. Interview with author in Bhopal.
5. Kaushal, Pradeep. 'Band of Brothers', *The Indian Express*, 17 March 2002, https://web.archive.org/web/20070622031311/http:/www.expressindia.com/flair/20020317/1.html. Accessed on 11 November 2021.
6. 'Rath Yatras for Mobilising Public Opinion was a VHP-

Sadhu Brainchild', *India Today*, 28 February 1993, https://www.indiatoday.in/magazine/editor-s-note/story/19930228-rath-yatras-for-mobilising-public-opinion-was-vhp-sadhu-brainchild-810767-1993-02-28. Accessed on 29 November 2021.

7. Sharma, Hemant. *Ayodhya: A Battleground*, Rupa Publications, 2020, p. 31.
8. *Swadesh*, Special number, 2006.
9. Rao, P.V. Narasimha. *Ayodhya: 6 December 1992*, Penguin Random House, 2019, p. 77.
10. Advani, L.K. *My Country, My Life,* Rupa Publications, 2008, p. 373.
11. Elst, Koenaard. *Ayodhya and After: Issues Before Hindu Society,* Voice of India, 1991, p. 50.
12. Gandhi, Jatin and Veenu Shandhu. *Rahul*, Penguin Random House, 2019, p. 176.
13. Advani, L.K. *My Country, My Life,* Rupa Publications, 2008, p. 177.
14. Interview with author in Delhi, much before his death.

CHAPTER 7

1. Jaffrelot, Christophe. *India's Silent Revolution: The Rise of the Lower Castes in North India,* Permanent Black, 2003, p. 1.
2. Interview with author in Neemuch, once under the old Scindia state.
3. Bharti, Rajendra and Anil Mishra. *Shrimant Madhavrao Scindia—Sansamaran-Smrutiya: 1945–2001*, Vinar Media, 2005 p. 8.
4. Ibid. 156.
5. IANS. 'I Am More of a Blogger Now Than a Political Activist, Says Advani', *News 18,* 13 July 2013, https://www.news18.com/news/politics/i-am-more-of-a-blogger-now-than-a-political-activist-says-advani-623315.html. Accessed on 13 October 2021.

6. Interview with the author in Bhopal.
7. Khandekar, Abhilash. '10 More Scindias Needed', *Free Press Journal*, 1987.
8. Bharti, Rajendra and Anil Mishra. *Shrimant Madhavrao Scindia—Sansamaran-Smrutiya: 1945–2001*, Vinar Media, 2005.
9. Ibid.
10. Ibid.
11. Rasheed Kidwai and Amita Ghosh, *Sonia: A Biography*, Penguin, 2009, p. 41.
12. Hindustan Times/Shalini Singh/ 10 March 2009
13. HARDtalk India, Karan Thapar interviews Madhavrao Scindia, 2000, https://www.youtube.com/watch?v=AOzrW7Ir0k4.
14. Fotedar, L.P. *The Chinar Leaves: A Political Memoir*, HarperCollins, 2015, p. 294.
15. Personal interview with author at Vidisha.
16. Singh, N.K. 'Arjun Singh Forced To Quit As Madhya Pradesh Chief Minister', *India Today*, 15 February 1989, https://www.indiatoday.in/magazine/special-report/story/19890215-arjun-singh-forced-to-quit-as-madhya-pradesh-chief-minister-815736-1989-02-15. Accessed on 13 October 2021.
17. Sanghvi, Vir and Namita Bhandare. *A Life: Madhavrao Scindia*, Penguin, 2009) p. 267.
18. Ibid. 270.
19. Ibid. 271.
20. Advani, L.K. *My Country, My Life*, Rupa Publications, 2008, p. 468.
21. Interview with the author at Gwalior.
22. A Report in *The Hindustan Times*, New Delhi
23. Advani, L.K. *My Country, My Life*, Rupa Publications, 2008, p. 468.
24. Gujral, I.K. *Matters of Discretion: An Autography*, Hay House India, 2011,p. 398.
25. Ibid. 428.
26. Ibid. 462–464.

CHAPTER 8

1. Ram, Arun. *The Times of India*, 19 March 2021.
2. Brecher, Michael. *Succession in India,* : Oxford University Press, 1967 p. 112.
3. Nahar, Vijay. *Vasundhara Raje Aur Viksit Rajasthan*, Prabhat Prakashan, 2016, p. 43.
4. Nag, Kingshuk. *The Saffron Tide*, Rupa Publications, 2014, p. 164.
5. Interview with Tribhuvan, Senior Editor, *Dainik Bhaskar*, Jaipur.
6. 'A Royal Win for BJP in Rajasthan', *Reddif News*, 5 December 2003, https://www.rediff.com/election/2003/dec/04rajas1.htm. Accessed on 17 November 2021.
7. Interview with Author
8. Gehlot, N.S. 'Reflections on the 12th Assembly Election of Rajasthan,' *Indian Journal of Political Science*, Vol. 64, July–December 2003.
9. Phadnis, Aditi. *Political Profiles of Cabals and Kings*, B.S. Books, 2009, p. 111.
10. Deka, Kaushik. 'State of the State Conclave, Rajasthan: No Government Can Run Without the Contribution of Its Citizens, Says Vasundhara Raje', *India Today*, 24 June 2017, https://www.indiatoday.in/india/story/state-of-state-conclave-vasundhara-raje-rasjasthan-pm-modi-984582-2017-06-24. Accessed on 17 November 2017.
11. Late Dr Ashish Bose on BIMARU concept and acronym that stood for laggard states: Bihar, Madhya Pradesh, Rajasthan and Uttar Pradesh.
12. Bohra, Sanjay. 'Gehlot Attacked Raje Over Alcohol. Now, He's Under Fire Over Liquor Sale in Rajasthan,' *The Print*, 12 January 2020, https://theprint.in/india/gehlot-attacked-raje-over-alcohol-now-hes-under-fire-over-liquor-sale-in-rajasthan/348417/. Accessed on 21 October 2021.
13. Bhatt, Abhinav. 'LK Advani did not Praise Shivraj Singh Chouhan to Put Down Narendra Modi, Says BJP', NDTV,

3 June 2013, https://www.ndtv.com/india-news/lk-advani-did-not-praise-shivraj-singh-chouhan-to-put-down-narendra-modi-says-bjp-524153. Accessed on 29 November 2021.

14. Nag, Kingshuk. *The Saffron Tide*, Rupa Publications, 2014, p. 22.

15. PTI. 'Lalit Modi Gets ED Summons in Money-Laundering Case,' *India Today*, 6 June 2015, https://www.indiatoday.in/india/story/lalit-modi-gets-ed-summons-in-money-laundering-case-280984-2015-07-06. Accessed on 21 October 2021.

16. Deka, Kaushik. 'State of the State Conclave, Rajasthan: No Government Can Run Without the Contribution of Its Citizens, Says Vasundhara Raje', *India Today*, 24 June 2017, https://www.indiatoday.in/india/story/state-of-state-conclave-vasundhara-raje-rasjasthan-pm-modi-984582-2017-06-24. Accessed on 17 November 2017.

17. Himanshu Roy, M.P. Singh and A.P.S. Chouhan. *State Politics in India*, Primus Books, 2017, p. 688.

18. Parmar, Rohit. 'The Return of Raje,' *India Today*, 19 February 2021, https://www.indiatoday.in/magazine/up-front/story/20210301-the-return-of-raje-1770894-2021-02-19 Accessed on 21 October 2021.

19. Scindia, Vijaya Raje and Manohar Malgonkar. *The Last Maharani of Gwalior: An Autobiography*, State University of New York Press, 1987.

20. Sanggvi, Malavika. 'THE PRIVATE I SERIES: The Princess Diaries,' *Times of India*, 29 May 2005, https://timesofindia.indiatimes.com/THE-PRIVATE-I-SERIESThe-princess-diaries/articleshow/1125880.cms. Accessed on 21 October 2021.

21. Ibid.

22. Gupta, Suchandana. 'Princely Gift: "Shrimant" to Yashodhara', *The Times of India*, 8 November 2006, https://timesofindia.indiatimes.com/india/princely-gift-shrimant-to-yashodhara/articleshow/361078.cms?from=mdr. Accessed on 11 November 2021.

246 • ABHILASH KHANDEKAR

CHAPTER 9

1. India Today magazine's Woman Summit, Jaipur, 2018, https://www.indiatoday.in/india/photo/india-today-woman-summit-2018-rajasthan-cm-vasundhara-raje-talks-about-royalty-and-politics-1349941-2018-09-26/3. Accessed on 21 October 2021.
2. Interview with author in Gwalior.
3. PTI. 'BJP to Add 7 Crore New mMmbers: J.P. Nanda', *Times of India*, 29 August 2019, https://timesofindia.indiatimes.com/india/bjp-to-add-7-crore-new-members-j-p-nadda/articleshow/70894220.cms Accessed on 21 October 2021.
4. Gupta, Moushumi Das. 'How BJP Has Been Outplaying Congress to Form Govt in States Where it Lacked Majority', *The Print*, 13 March 2020, https://theprint.in/politics/how-bjp-has-been-outplaying-congress-to-form-govt-in-states-where-it-lacked-majority/380254/ Accessed on 21 October 2021.
5. Advani, L.K. *My Country, My Life,* Rupa Publications, 2008, p. 554.
6. Sinha, Shakti, *Vajpayee: The Years That Changed India*, Penguin Random House, 2020, p. 282.
7. 'Samarthako ke Beech Chalak Utha Digvijaya ka Dard', News Tak, https://www.youtube.com/watch?v=3ZbtmMgrO90, 16 October 2018. Accessed on 29 November 2021.
8. TNN. 'Royal Feud Out in the Open: Madhavrao Disinherited', *Times of India*, 8 February 2001, https://timesofindia.indiatimes.com/Royal-feud-out-in-the-open-Madhavrao-disinherited/articleshow/19943397.cms Accessed on 21 October 2021.
9. Sanghvi, Vir and Namita Bhandare. *A Life: Madhavrao Scindia*, Penguin, 2009, p. 331.
10. A former AICC office-bearer told this to the author.
11. Scindia, Jyotiraditya. 'India's Small Farmer Finds a Champion', *Hindustan Times*, 8 February 2021, https://www.hindustantimes.com/opinion/indias-small-farmer-finds-a-champion-101612798673556.html. Accessed on 21 October 2021.

12. Sunday Times/Nona Walia/30.3.2003
13. Sanghvi, Vir and Namita Bhandare. *A Life: Madhavrao Scindia*, Penguin, 2009, p. 196.
14. Interview with author at Indore.
15. PTI. 'Niyant Heritage Hotels Has Not Done Anything Illegal, Says Dushyant Singh', *Mint*, 18 June 2015, https://www.livemint.com/Politics/xFrIS5tMSbgbs1Db8KPtKK/Niyant-Heritage-Hotels-has-not-done-anything-illegal-says-D.html. Accessed on 17 November 2021.

CHAPTER 10

1. An eye-witness account of a top businessman from Indore who was present in the secretariat that afternoon.
2. *Patrika*, Bhopal, March 2020.
3. Interview with the author at Bhopal.
4. Yadav, Puneet Nicholas. 'Operation Lotus Finally Succeeds In Karnataka, Will Madhya Pradesh, Rajasthan Follow?' *Outlook*, 23 July 2019, https://www.outlookindia.com/website/story/india-news-operation-lotus-finally-succeeds-in-karnataka-will-madhya-pradesh-rajasthan-follow/334758. Accessed on 22 October 2021.
5. ET Bureau. 'EC Seeks Action on CBDT Report on Cash Deals in MP During Lok Sabha Polls', *Economic Times*, 17 December 2020, https://economictimes.indiatimes.com/news/politics-and-nation/ec-seeks-action-on-cbdt-report-on-cash-deals-in-mp-during-ls-polls/articleshow/79766677.cms. Accessed on 22 October 2021.
6. PTI. 'I-T Raids: EC Calls CBDT Chairman, Revenue Secretary India', *Money Control*, 8 April 2019, https://www.moneycontrol.com/news/india/it-raids-ec-calls-cbdt-chairman-revenue-secretary-3788861.html. Accessed on 22 October 2021.
7. Bhat, Misha. 'Ayodhya Case: Appropriate Security Measures in SC, Says Delhi Joint CP', *Republic World*, 9 November

2019, https://www.republicworld.com/india-news/general-news/ayodhya-case-appropriate-security-measures-in-sc-says-delhi-joint-cp.html. Accessed on 22 October 2021.

8. 'Lok Sabha 2019 Election Results: Congress' Jyotiraditya Scindia Loses in Guna Against BJP's Krishna Pal Singh,' *CNBC-TV 18*, 23 May 2019, https://www.cnbctv18.com/politics/lok-sabha-2019-election-results-jyotiraditya-scindia-of-congress-trailing-in-guna-against-dr-kp-yadav-of-bjp-by-over-41000-votes-3431061.htm,.Accessed on 22 October 2021.

9. PTI. 'Nakul Nath Wins Chhindwara LS Seat; BJP Bags Dhar, Vidisha', *Times of India*, 23 May 2019, https://timesofindia.indiatimes.com/india/nakul-nath-wins-chhindwara-ls-seat-bjp-bags-dhar-vidisha/articleshow/69468147.cms Accessed on 4 November 2021.

10. Interview with the author.

11. Informal chat with Yogendra Lumba, former DCC chief, Guna.

12. Interview with the author.

13. 'Jyotiraditya Scindia Joins BJP, Says Congress Not the Party It Used To Be', *The Print*, 11 March 2020, https://theprint.in/politics/jyotiraditya-scindia-joins-bjp-day-after-quitting-congress/378766/. Accessed on 22 October 2021.

14. Interview with the author.

15. An unnamed political friend of his with whom he spoke many times during 10–15 March 2020, shared with the author in an interview by the person in Bhopal.

16. @JM_Scindia/ 10 March 2020/11.45 a.m.

17. ANI. 'Kamal Nath Govt Will Survive, All Independent MLAs With Us, Says MLA Surendra Singh Shera', *Business Standard*, 11 March 2020, https://www.business-standard.com/article/news-ani/kamal-nath-govt-will-survive-all-independent-mlas-with-us-says-mla-surendra-singh-shera-120031100357_1.html. Accessed on 17 November 2021.

18. Rajput, Brajesh. *Woh 17 Din*, Shivna Prakashan, 2020.

19. Dua, Rohan. 'My Career Not a Nameplate, Happy to Be a BJP Worker', *Times of India* 27 October 2020.

Bibliography

Abhilash Khandekar, *Shivraj Singh and the Rise of Madhya Pradesh*, Vitasta Publishing, New Delhi, 2014.

Sagarika Ghosh, *Indira: India's Most Powerful Prime Minister*, Juggernaut Books, New Delhi, 2018.

M.L. Fotedar, *The Chinar Leaves—A Political Memoir*, HarperCollins, Noida 2015.

Shakti Sinha, *Vajpayee: The Years That Changed India*, Penguin, 2020.

Ajay Agnihotri, *Gwalior: Art, History and Culture*, Shri Natnagar Shodh Samsthan, Sitamau (MP) 2015.

Christophe Jaffrelot, *India's Silent Revolution: The Rise of the Low Castes in North Indian Politics*, Permanent Black, 2003.

Jatin Gandhi and Veenu Sandhu, *Rahul*, Penguin, 2019.

Aditi Phadnis, *Political Profiles of Cabals and Kings*, Business Standard, 2009.

BJP: Expanding Horizons—First Decade of BJP, a BJP publication, April 1990.

Koenraad Elst, *Ram Janmabhoomi vs Babri Masjid (A Case Study in Hindu Muslim Conflict)*, Voice of India, 1990.

L.P. Singh, *Portrait of Lal Bahadur Shastri—A Quintessential Gandhian*, Ravi Dayal Publisher, New Delhi, 1996.

I.K. Gujral, *Matters of Discretion—An Autobiography*, Hay House India, New Delhi 2011

M.N. Buch, *When the Harvest Moon is Blue*, Har-Anand

Publications Pvt. Ltd, New Delhi, 2008.

Rajdeep Sardesai, *2019—How Modi Won India*, HarperCollins, Noida, 2020.

Himanshu Roy, M.P. Singh and A.P.S. Chouhan, *State Politics in India*, Primus Books, New Delhi, 2017.

Walter K. Andersen and Shridhar D. Damle, *The RSS—A View to the Inside*, Penguin, Gurgaon, 2018.

Sanjaya Baru, *Democracy Interrupted—The Emergency, 1975–77*, Penguin, 2019.

Niraja Gopal Jayal and Pratap Bhanu Mehta, *The Oxford Companion to Politics in India*, Oxford University Press, New Delhi, 2014.

Uday S. Kulkarni, *The Maratha Century*, Mula Mutha Publishers, Pune, 2021.

Sir John Malcolm, *A Memoir of Central India, Including Malwa and Adjoining Provinces (Volume-I)*, Irish University Press, London, 1832.

L. F. Rushbrook Williams, *A History of India (Part 3) The British Period*, Longmans, Green & Co. Ltd, London, 1926.

P. E. Roberts, *History of British India—Under the Company and the Crown*, Oxford University Press, First edition, 1921.

C. E. Luard, *Gwalior State Gazetteer*, Calcutta, 1908.

Verrier Elwin, *The Muria and Their Ghotul*, Vanya Prakashan, 1991 (First published in 1947 by Oxford University Press).

Michael Breacher, *Succession in India: A Study in Decision Making*, Oxford University Press, London, 1966.

P.L. Mishra, *The Political History of Chhattisgarh*, Vishwa Bharti Prakashan Nagpur, 1960.

K. L. Srivastava, *The Revolt of 1857 in Central India—Malwa*, Allied Publishers Private Limited, Bombay, 1966.

Rodney W. Jones, *Urban Politics in India (Area, Power and Policy in a Penetrated System)*, Vikas Publishing House Pvt. Ltd, New Delhi, 1975. The book is exclusively about Indore city and its urban political history.

Charles Allen and and Sharda Dwivedi, *Lives of the Indian Princes*,

Century Publishing Co. Ltd, Great Britain, 1984.

N. Rajan, *Without Fear—A Journalist's Diary*, Amarshree Printing Press, Bhopal, 2001.

R.P. Noronha, *A Tale Told by an Idiot*, Noronha Foundation, Bhopal, 2015.

V.P. Menon, *Integration of the Indian States*, Orient BlackSwan, Hyderabad, 2014.

Koenraad Elst, *Ayodhya and After—Issues Before Hindu Society*, Voice of India, 1991.

P.V. Narasimha Rao, Ayodhya—*6 December 1992*, Penguin, 2006.

Hemant Sharma, *Ayodhya: A Battleground*, Rupa Publications, New Delhi, 2020.

Dileep Padgaonkar, *When Bombay Burned*, UBS Publishers Ltd, New Delhi, 1993.

L.K. Advani, *My Country, My Life*, Rupa Publications, New Delhi, 2008.

Ramachandra Guha, *India after Gandhi: History of World's Largest Democracy*, Picador India, 2007.

Dilip Chaware, *Saga of a Struggle—Sushil Kumar Shinde*, Chinar Publishers, Pune, 2008

Ornit Shani, *How India Became Democratic*, Penguin, 2018.

Khushwant Singh, *India: An Introduction*, HarperCollins, 2006.

Vir Sanghvi and Namita Bhandare, *A Life: Madhavrao Scindia*, Penguin, New Delhi, 2009.

Smita Bharadwaj, *Vintage Gwalior*, Madhya Pradesh Archaeology Department, Bhopal, 2009.

Rasheed Kidwai, *Sonia: A Biography*, Penguin, New Delhi, 2011.

Vijaya Raje Scindia and Manohar Malgaonkar, *The Last Maharani of Gwalior: An Autobiography*, State University of New York Press, 1987.

Kignshuk Nag, *The Saffron Tide: The Rise of the BJP*, Rupa Publications, 2014.

HINDI:

1. *Swadesh*, Bhopal Special number on Rajmata Scindia, October 2006.
2. *Smaran*—A booklet published by D.P. Mishra Centenary Committee, Bhopal, 2001.
3. Lala Jagdalpuri, *Bastar—Itihas Evam Sanskriti*, Madhya Pradesh Hindi Granth Academy, Bhopal, 1994.
4. Deepak Tiwari, *Rajnitinama—Madhya Pradesh, Rajnetao Ke Kisse*, Indra Publishing House, Bhopal, 2014.
5. Girijashankar, *Madhya Pradesh Me Chunavi Rajniti*, Anamika Prakashan, Bhopal, 1998.
6. Brajesh Rajput, *Woh 17 Din*, 2020.
7. Vijay Nahar, *Vasundhara Raje Aur Viksit Rajasthan*, Prabhat Prakashan, New Delhi, 2016.
8. Ram Vidrohi, *Nai Subah*, Gopalchal Prakashan, Gwalior, 2015.
9. Rajendra Bharti and Anil Mishra, *Shrimant Madhavrao Scindia—Sansamaran-Smrutiya 1945–2001*, Vinar Media, Mumbai, 2005.
10. Shiv Anurag Pateria, *Sandarbh*, Madhya Pradesh Publications Department, Bhopal, 2020.
11. Vijay Trivedi, *BJP—Kal, Aaj Aur Kal*, Eka, Chennai, 2019.
12. Mridula Sinha, *Rajpath Se Lokpath,* Prabhat Publication, New Delhi.
13. Rajendra Sharma, *Vaichariki—Collection of Editorials in Swadesh*, Bhopal, 2019.
14. Vinayak Katherdekar, *Daulatrao Shinde—Kaal aur Krutitva (1780–1827)*, Radha Publications, 2018.

Index

171, 173, 174

Bhosale, Udayanraje, 11

caste, 3, 6, 7, 131, 172, 177, 178, 186

Caste, 7, 238

Chouhan, Shivraj Singh, xiii, 5, 174, 179, 180, 183, 188, 196, 204, 218, 228, 245

Congress, x, xi, xii, xiii, xiv, 11, 34, 35, 36, 37, 38, 40, 41, 43, 44, 45, 46, 49, 51, 52, 53, 54, 55, 56, 57, 60, 64, 65, 66, 68, 69, 70, 71, 72, 73, 74, 75, 76, 77, 78, 79, 80, 81, 82, 83, 85, 86, 87, 88, 90, 92, 93, 97, 104, 105, 106, 108, 112, 119, 120, 124, 127, 128, 131– 134, 136, 138, 139, 140, 143, 144, 145, 146, 147, 149, 150, 152, 153, 154, 155, 156, 157, 158, 159, 160, 161, 162, 163, 165, 168, 169, 170, 172, 173, 174, 175, 176, 178, 179, 182, 183, 184, 186, 187, 188, 193, 194, 195, 196, 197, 200, 202, 207, 209, 210, 214, 215, 216, 217, 218, 219, 220, 221, 222, 223, 224, 225, 226, 227, 228, 229, 230, 233, 234, 247, 249

de Boigne, Benoît, 17, 18, 19, 20, 21

Desai, Morarji, 52, 57, 71, 90, 94

Dewas (Paur/ Pawar), 13

Emergency, 49, 71, 89, 91, 92, 94, 95, 98, 100, 103, 105, 187, 191, 240, 241

Fadnavis, Nana, xvi, xvii, 23

First Anglo-Maratha war, 20

First War of Independence, 26

Gandhi, Indira, 10, 34, 45, 48, 49, 50, 51, 52, 53, 56, 57, 58, 61, 63, 65, 68, 71, 72, 79, 80, 84, 85, 87, 88, 89, 90, 92, 93, 94, 100, 102, 103, 104, 105, 113, 132, 133, 138, 139, 145, 152, 164, 167, 169, 187, 228, 230, 238, 239

Gandhi, Rahul, 89, 127, 132, 183, 199, 209, 211, 225, 226, 228

Gandhi, Rajiv, 108, 138, 139, 141, 142, 145, 147, 148, 149, 151, 161, 167, 168

Gandhi, Sonia, xii, 144, 145, 146, 147, 148, 165, 199, 208, 222, 223, 225, 230

Governor General Lord